VOLUNTARY EUTHANASIA

VOLUNTARY EUTHANASIA

Experts Debate the Right to Die

EDITED BY A. B. DOWNING
AND BARBARA SMOKER

Nor dread nor hope attend
A dying animal.
A man awaits his end,
Dreading and hoping all.
W. B. YEATS

PETER OWEN · LONDON

ISBN 0 7206 0651 9

PETER OWEN PUBLISHERS
73 Kenway Road London SW5 ORE

Revised, enlarged and updated edition of *Euthanasia and the Right to Death: The Case for Voluntary Euthanasia* (1969)

First published in Great Britain in 1986

Printed in Great Britain by
Photobooks (Bristol) Ltd St Philips Bristol

Foreword

by the Right Honourable the Earl of Listowel
P.C., G.C.M.G., Ph.D.

It is almost half a century since my dear friend and mentor, Arthur Ponsonby, introduced into the House of Lords the first Bill presented to Parliament for the legalization of voluntary euthanasia. The Bill was defeated but, with the energetic support of the Euthanasia Society, it started a trend of public opinion that has been growing steadily ever since, as public opinion surveys indicate.

Sixteen years ago, in 1969, a second Bill on the subject—more practical in its prescribed safeguards than that of 1936—was introduced into the House of Lords by Lord Raglan. Though likewise debated and defeated at its second reading, it succeeded in further stimulating public discussion. The same year saw the publication of the first edition of this book; and the following year, in 1970, the subject was debated in the House of Commons. Then, in 1976, Baroness Wootton introduced into the Lords a Bill dealing with another aspect of the subject—that of passive euthanasia and the rights of incurable patients.

Though legislation has yet to be achieved, voluntary euthanasia has more adherents now in the medical and legal professions, in the religious denominations, in many different countries and among reflective people in all the walks of life, and it is much more often discussed in the press and in broadcasts than was the case in the early days of parliamentary pioneering. The legalization of suicide in the Act of 1961 is another symptom of a new attitude to the taking of life, an attitude that places more emphasis on personal responsibility than the compulsion of the law.

The importance of this change in the climate of public opinion is that, although the case for voluntary euthanasia is a moral one, it seeks to establish a legal right, and this right, which depends on legislation, cannot be established in a democracy without the tacit or explicit consent of the electorate. We can now urge that the moral right to a dignified and merciful death, from which the legal right will eventually flow, should be enshrined in the Universal Declaration of Human Rights adopted in 1949 by the General Assembly of the United Nations.

The main obstacle to the acceptance of voluntary euthanasia is not, I believe, the opposition and hostility which still arise in certain quarters, but widespread ignorance, indifference and misunderstanding of its implications. The dying leave no record of their sufferings, and the living are only, as a rule, aware of the process of dying in their own family or among their closest friends. For the young of this generation the curtain has been lifted from sex, but not from death. But the young are avid for knowledge, and seek human causes to which they can harness their ideals. Here, surely, is such a cause. For social progress can be measured by the degree of control man achieves over his environment by substituting his rational will for the blind and instinctive forces of nature. In the cycle of human life we have gone far towards mastery of the processes of reproduction. But the process of dying is still left mainly to chance and the disintegration of the body. Hence, the enormous value of this book. It will open the eyes of many to the facts of our common fate, and will oblige its readers to answer the inexorable question of how it should be faced. How few of us realize, for example, that about one in five of the annual deaths in this country is caused by cancer, or that a doctor found that 5 per cent of 220 elderly patients in the wards of a London hospital 'repeatedly expressed the wish to die'. The progress of medicine, which has brought with it many new methods of prolonging life, makes the question of whether or not to prolong a particular life more urgent than ever.

The most general misunderstanding is the confusion that often arises between voluntary and imposed, or compulsory, euthanasia. It is not proposed that euthanasia should be performed except at the express request of an adult person in a balanced frame of mind. The 'mercy-killing' of deformed or idiot children, the liquidation by the state of the senile, the incurable or the mentally defective, have not the remotest connection with what we understand by voluntary euthanasia. But it is necessary to explain this, because one so often hears the familiar argument about the 'thin end of the wedge'. Indeed, compulsion would destroy the moral case for the principle of voluntary euthanasia, because it presupposes that each of us should be free to choose between a dignified and a squalid death.

If we take the view that what is essentially human in the life that we share with the animal and vegetable kingdoms is the capacity for thought and love and aesthetic experience, and that this capacity makes us a person in the true sense of the word, we cannot wish to preserve an anonymous individual who has been stripped of personality and reduced by incessant pain or physical deterioration to the animal or vegetable level. There are many of us who would rather not outlive our usefulness, and become a burden to ourselves and others. Yet, without the medical assistance that voluntary euthanasia would authorize, but which is now a criminal offence, it is unlikely that most of us would be able to choose a dignified death. Suicide is only an option for those with the medical means, and the physical strength to use them. We must, therefore, try to enlarge the area of human freedom by winning for ourselves the right to die so far as is humanly possible in the circumstances of our choice, and for doctors the right to terminate life when they are certain that this is their patient's steadfast wish and that his condition is such that it should be carried out. Such a reform of the law would also vindicate the claim of social justice that rich and poor have an equal right to a merciful death. For it should not be forgotten that it is far easier for a doctor to follow his conscience in an affluent home, or in the private wing of a hospital, than it is in a general or geriatric ward in a working-class area, where he is exposed to the risk of blackmail or of being reported to the hospital authorities. If what matters is what the Greeks called 'the good life', we should make sure that it can be lived by everyone to the very end.

Preface

The essays in this volume concern an issue that is being brought increasingly to the attention of the public. The issue may be summarized in this question: Is it a human right for an individual to be allowed to choose for himself the merciful release of death even if he is unable to terminate his life unaided?

The range of medical control over the processes of dying is now greatly extended. Life can be prolonged and death averted in novel, revolutionary ways. But this medical progress raises many basic problems. It is accepted that human life is sacred, but does this of itself require that doctors must, in all circumstances, contrive to keep in being those—severely maimed in mind or body—whose natural will to live has already expired? Must doctors *always* extend life when they are technically able to do so, heedless of the quality of the existence they are preserving? There is a time to live, but does not human dignity demand that there is also, for all of us, a time to die?

The contributors, all eminent and respected practitioners in their field, examine the implications of such questions as these and study in depth and from different viewpoints the various, often complex, aspects brought into focus by the issue of voluntary euthanasia: humanitarian, moral, sociological, philosophical, religious, medical and legal. They hope, by their reflections and arguments, to help towards a better understanding of the options and possibilities, in the light of modern scientific application and knowledge. Euthanasia, to the majority of them, simply means an easeful death as opposed to one that occurs after acute, prolonged or needless suffering.

In presenting these essays, the publishers express their particular indebtedness to Professor Glanville Williams, Rouse Ball Professor of the Laws of England in the University of Cambridge, for much valuable guidance and for the general shape he has given to the enterprise. They wish also to thank the Reverend A. B. Downing for his careful work in the preparation of the various manuscripts.

Preface to the Revised Edition

The original edition of this book has had a steady and continuing demand through six impressions for more than fifteen years. However, it now requires to be updated, since a great deal has happened in relation to euthanasia in that period, both in Britain and overseas. New medical techniques have been introduced and there has been a gradually changing climate of opinion on the subject.

In addition to fulfilling the need for updating and revision, this new edition commemorates the Golden Jubilee of the Voluntary Euthanasia Society. The Society was founded in 1935 by distinguished members of the medical profession with the aim of persuading Parliament to legalize voluntary euthanasia, with adequate safeguards. It could be argued that the Society has little to celebrate, since that aim has yet to be achieved. However, in the fifty years of its existence, it has brought the subject before the public and made it a matter of general discussion, with increasing public support (as opinion polls have demonstrated). Moreover, it has pioneered an important international movement, with similar societies (see complete list on pp. 269–71) now active in twenty countries, pooling their experiences through the World Federation of Right-to-Die Societies, which sponsors a world conference every two years. All but one of these overseas societies have sprung up since the first edition of the present book appeared.

With one exception, all the articles in the original edition have been retained. Contributors were invited to revise and/or update their articles where necessary. New articles and additional documentary material, introduced for this edition, are indicated by an asterisk in the Contents.

Contents

*Supplementary material not included in the previous volume.

Acknowledgements

The publishers wish to acknowledge with thanks the following, for permission to quote or reprint some of the material appearing in this volume:

Dr Leslie Weatherhead and Hodder & Stoughton Ltd for quotations from *The Christian Agnostic* by Dr Weatherhead;

Professor John Hinton and Pelican Books (Penguin Books Ltd) for quotations from *Dying* by Professor John Hinton;

Dr Joseph Fletcher and the Editors of *Harper's Magazine*, New York, for reprinting the essay by Dr Fletcher which originally appeared in *Harper's Magazine*. Copyright 1960 Harper's Magazine Inc.;

Professor Yale Kamisar, Professor Glanville Williams and The Minnesota Law Review Foundation for reprinting abridged versions of the essays by Professors Kamisar and Williams which originally appeared in the *Minnesota Law Review*. Copyright 1958 The Minnesota Law Review Foundation;

The Editor of *The Times* for reprinting the article by Jonathan Glover on Arthur Koestler, which originally appeared in the newspaper in March 1983. Copyright The Times Newspaper Ltd 1983.

Dedicated in gratitude
to the memory of
C. Killick Millard, M.D., D.Sc. (1870–1952),
Founder and first Secretary of the
Voluntary Euthanasia Legislation Society, 1935–52
and to
Leonard Colebrook, F.R.S., F.R.C.O.G., F.R.C.S., D.Sc.
(1883–1967),
Chairman of the Euthanasia Society, 1960–4.

PART ONE

THE CASE FOR AND AGAINST EUTHANASIA

A. B. Downing

Euthanasia: The Human Context

Knowledge grows with a splendid, almost unimpeded, advance. We are becoming immeasurably richer in understanding as well as mere knowledge, not least about such basic concerns as birth, health and death. But it is a mark of progress to discover fresh paradoxes as well as to solve ancient problems. Childbirth, for example, is far less menacing to women than it used to be (thanks in large measure to the efforts of distinguished medical scientists such as the late Dr Leonard Colebrook, to whose memory this volume is in part dedicated); and the enlightened can now effectively control the propagation of their species. Yet the evil possibilities of a 'population explosion' pose a threatening problem which the human race has still to solve. At the other end of life, with which the accompanying essays are more especially concerned, the fact of death and the process of dying are invested with new dimensions—social and personal, collective and individual—not simply by the increase of medical knowledge but by an advance in human sensibility. Questions about death and dying are now often asked in public where they were formerly asked, if they were asked at all, in the anguish of privacy.

The possibility of birth control eventually brought a range of new options to men and women, although these options were strongly resisted and condemned by those who thought they represented an interference with the providential order of things. The present changes in death control—our enlarged powers of interference in the natural processes of dying—offer the possibility of new basic options. New options mean new duties, and involve doctors and their patients in the need to explore and clarify many basic concerns. It is such an exploration which these essays attempt, from different angles and along differing paths of experience and reflection. There are some questions about death and dying which, though compelling, are perhaps futile:

> What have we done to thee, thou monstrous Time,
> And what to thee, O Death, that we must die?

But there are others which are far from futile and which are increasingly being asked. Some of them were suggested by a distinguished medical man, Sir Theodore Fox (former editor of *The Lancet*), in his Harveian Oration to the Royal College of Physicians in 1965.[1] He remarked that 'though cures are getting commoner, so too are half-cures, in which death is averted but disability remains'. If a doctor, he said, 'goes on prolonging a life that can never again have purpose or meaning, his kindness becomes a cruelty. . . . Some of us hold life sacred, but this becomes a dreadful doctrine when it means that quantity of life is preferred to quality'. A similar indication of a new range of thinking and sensibility in these matters is provided by Dr Leslie Weatherhead, the revered former minister of the City Temple in London who is a convinced believer in the right to voluntary euthanasia. He writes:

> I sincerely believe that those who come after us will wonder why on earth we kept a human being alive against his own will, when all the dignity, beauty and meaning of life had vanished; when any gain to anyone was clearly impossible, and when we should have been punished by the State if we kept an animal alive in similar physical conditions. . . . I for one would be willing to give a patient the Holy Communion and stay with him while a doctor, whose responsibility I should thus share, allowed him to lay down his useless body and pass in dignity and peace into the next phase of being.[2]

Between life and death doctors now have a much wider range of choice. Mere biological existence can be prolonged by artificial life-supporting mechanisms. Clever apparatus and costly machines, new drugs and organ transplantation, can give a new lease of life to people who would otherwise die. All this progress, however, poses many new problems for the community and its doctors. Patients have to be

[1] The oration, entitled 'Purposes in Medicine', by Sir Theodore Fox, M.D., LL.D., F.R.C.P., is reported in full in *The Lancet* (Oct. 23, 1965), pp. 801–5.
[2] *The Christian Agnostic* (Hodder & Stoughton, 1965), p. 187.

selected, since the resources available are insufficient for all who could benefit from them. Who shall decide the selection and who shall share in making it?

It is easier to decide such questions in wartime, when there are overriding national considerations. From 1939 to 1945 penicillin and other therapeutic agents difficult to produce were reserved mainly for the armed forces. But in peacetime such questions open up a wide range of human concerns. When their implications are considered, as they were in 1967 by a body of international experts brought together by the Ciba Foundation, it is soon realized that the community is faced with some serious basic issues. For example, when an organ is urgently required for transplantation in order to save a human life, and it can only be obtained from a person who has been reduced to a mere vegetable existence maintained by artificial means, then it becomes very important to define clinical death—so that the required organ can be removed and used.

At the Ciba symposium referred to—attended by distinguished doctors and lawyers from Britain, Europe and America—the President of the Swedish Society of Surgery, Dr G. B. Giertz, asked: 'Is it in fact intended that we shall provide the medical services with resources for furnishing life-supporting measures for every individual who might qualify for it, even when the prospects of securing a recovery are negligible? Should we not accept that man shall decide what is fit for life and what is not, and direct our resources to the former?'[3] Accepting that in 'the inviolateness of human life' even the most wretched has a meaning and that our respect for human dignity, and hence for democracy, is endangered without this belief, he added:

> 'The thought that we physicians should be obliged to keep a patient alive with a respirator when there is no possibility of recovery, solely to try to prolong his life by perhaps twenty-four hours, is a terrifying one. It must be regarded as a medical axiom that one should not be obliged in every situation to use all means to prolong life. . . . We refrain from treatment because it does not serve any purpose, because it is not in the patient's interest. I cannot regard this as killing by medical means: death has already won, despite the fight we have put up, and we must accept the fact.'[4]

[3] As reported in *The Times*, London (Dec. 7, 1966).
[4] Ibid.

'Death has already won'. But this is an idea which many traditional and instinctive reactions combine in resisting, even when people believe strongly in some form of personal survival after death. Certainly 'death has already won' for many aged sufferers who wait miserably for its release in many private homes and public institutions. For them it does not come 'drifting down like a leaf', in the optimistic words of a contributor to *The Guardian*.[5] The situation is more accurately described by an articulate octogenarian, Maria Reynolds, in the same paper:

> We must be prepared for it to drift for anything up to twenty-five years and, in the course of drifting, it is liable to be caught up in tornadoes of pain and struggle, of eddies of boredom from blindness or deafness or both, or to experience the humiliation of the loss of human dignity, or confusion and sedation. . . . There is some fear—not of death, but of what one might become before death.[6]

This description brings out some of the harsh realities of dying—which are not softened or made bearable by noble attitudes to death itself.

> Death in itself is nothing: but we fear
> To be we know not what, we know not where.

The treatment of the elderly dying in hospital is a subject which leads not infrequently to expressions of concern in the national press. In April 1967, for example, a geriatric nurse asserted in a letter to *The Guardian* 'the stark truth that all patients dying of old age must now expect, as a matter of routine, to be forced through an additional period, sometimes a long period, of pain and/or acute discomfort before death finally comes'.[7] She gave two examples 'out of many' in her experience. A dying woman, aged over a hundred, was given a blood transfusion, and a very old man, senile for a long time, was kept just alive with artificial feeding and urinary apparatus well after he had become 'a thing of horror due to advanced gangrene'. If these two wretched persons were not fully conscious, it could be argued that they

[5] Aug. 15, 1967.
[6] Sept. 6, 1967.
[7] Apr. 25, 1967.

were not suffering; but is it civilized or compassionate behaviour to lengthen the course of dying in this way?

A similar example, at about the same time, was featured on the front page of the *Sunday Express*. A woman of eighty-nine was suffering from Paget's Disease—a chronic bone disease, 'incurable but not a killer' according to a doctor quoted by the newspaper. She was described by her daughter as being in a pathetic condition 'with little or no realization of life' and as having been 'saved from certain death at least twenty times by modern drugs, oxygen and intravenous injections'. The daughter, a woman of fifty-seven who was named, publicly pleaded with the doctors concerned to allow her mother to die. It seems unlikely that the daughter was mistaken in believing that her mother's case was a hopeless one.

Lest it be thought that the daily press is an unreliable guide in focusing attention on these distressing cases, let it be noted that views similar to those of the geriatric nurse and the daughter of the old lady have been publicly expressed by distinguished doctors. For example Sir George Pickering, Regius Professor of Medicine at Oxford University, has made 'a plea for the dignity of death'. In his view 'old people should be allowed to die as comfortably and in as dignified a way as possible'. He continues:

> I know of nothing more tragic than the disruption of a happy and productive family life caused by an ancient, bed-ridden, incontinent and confused parent or grandparent. What might have been a happy and respectful memory becomes a nightmare and a horror. I still recoil from the sight of old people being kept alive by a constant monitoring of their heart-beat and the team of nurses and doctors ready to pounce upon them when it stops. For my own part, when my time has come to die by natural causes, I hope I shall be allowed to do so.[8]

Similar concern was expressed, no less provocatively, by Dr Edmund Leach in his 1967 BBC Reith Lectures:

> '. . . Our ordinary morality says that we must kill our neighbour if the state orders us to do so—that is to say, as a soldier in war or as an

[8] *New Scientist* (Jan. 18, 1968).

executioner in the course of his duty—but in every other case we must try to save life. But what do we mean by that? Would a headless human trunk that was still breathing be alive? And if you think that is just a fanciful question, what about a body that has sustained irreparable brain damage but can still be kept functioning by the ingenuity of modern science? It isn't so easy'.[9]

The foregoing examples and comments relate to cases of human distress and degradation—this is not too strong a word—in the dying of persons who are senile or in varying states of unconsciousness and who therefore cannot communicate any plea for the merciful release of death. But there are many people who, as they slowly die, remain fully conscious of what is happening to them. They know that they have become an outward travesty of themselves and they are deeply sensitive to the anguish caused to those who have to watch over or nurse them in their miseries. When Dr Leonard Colebrook was Chairman of the Euthanasia Society in 1962, he wrote as follows about the sufferings, physical and mental, to which some dying persons are condemned:

> . . . In addition to pain many of the unhappy victims of cancer have to endure the mental misery associated with the presence of a foul fungating growth; of slow starvation owing to difficulty in swallowing; of painful and very frequent micturition; of obstruction of the bowels; of incontinence; and of the utter prostration that makes of each day and night a 'death in life' as the famous physician, the late Sir William Osler, described it.
>
> Diseases of the nervous system in their turn lead all too often to crippling paralysis or inability to walk; to severe headaches; to blindness; to the misery of incontinence and bedsores. Distressing mental disturbances are often added to these troubles.
>
> Bronchitis, too, with its interminable cough and progressive shortness of breath, can have its special terrors, which medical treatment in the late stages can do little to abate.
>
> All these, and many other grievous ills which may beset the road to death, are often borne with great courage and patience—even when the burden is many times heavier by reason of loneliness and/or poverty. (It should be remembered that only about half of

[9] Reported in *The Listener* (Dec. 7, 1967), p. 749.

> the dying receive skilled nursing and medical care in hospitals.) Medical progress has done much to alleviate suffering during the past century, but, in honesty, it must be admitted that the process of dying is still very often an ugly business.[10]

Statements such as these by eminent medical men and other evidence of concern about needless suffering among the dying readily prompt the idea that people, like animals, have a legal and moral right to a merciful death, or euthanasia. Such a basic right seems especially relevant now when our doctors are able to exercise an ever-increasing range of professional choices as between meaningful human life and clinical death. In making their choices doctors do not necessarily believe that they have a duty to consult the precise wishes of the persons under their care, since of course traditionally we trust our doctors to make the decisions which they think are best for us. It is obviously not easy to estimate even approximately the number of those who would clearly ask for the relief of a merciful death if they, and their doctors, knew that this was permissible under wisely framed euthanasia legislation. Taking cancer alone, which is responsible for about one-fifth of all deaths in England and Wales, Dr Colebrook suggested in his statement that it was not unreasonable to suppose that at least one in every hundred fatal cases would choose to hasten the end rather than endure a lingering death. On that assumption the legalization of voluntary euthanasia would bring relief to about one thousand cancer cases a year—perhaps considerably more. With the sufferers from other diseases, he added, the total might well add up to about four thousand, and increase with time.[11]

The idea of legalizing the right to a merciful death for human beings raises many important moral, social, legal and medical questions. Until 1966 supporters of the principle of voluntary euthanasia, in statements published by the Euthanasia Society, sought to alter the law in such a way that an adult person of sound mind, whose life was already ending with much suffering, would have the legal right to choose between an easy death and a hard one and to obtain medical aid in the fulfilment of his clear request to this effect. The Society's proposals therefore left out of account the sufferings of those with clouded minds or damaged brains unable to make their wishes

[10] 'A Plan for Voluntary Euthanasia' (Euthanasia Society pamphlet, 1962), pp. 5-6.
[11] Ibid., p. 9.

explicitly and firmly known. Since 1967 it has been suggested that merciful relief could be made possible for sufferers in this tragic category, as well as for dying persons able to communicate their wishes clearly, by enabling adult persons to sign an advance declaration having legal force and suitably filed, to the effect that they would wish to have euthanasia in certain medical situations. In the proposals now put forward by the Society (which are given in Appendix 1), the various possible options and medical circumstances are carefully defined so as to provide proper safeguards.

The possibility of advance declarations already exists, and is increasingly favoured, in respect of certain medical matters such as signifying willingness to donate one's body for research or to surrender anatomical parts and organs for purposes of transplantation. The important advantage of the suggested advance declaration concerning euthanasia is that, if the declarant were to become unconscious beyond recovery or mentally impaired through some fatal accident or disease, both his doctors and relatives would have clear information as to what his wishes would be in such a condition. The doctors would still retain their freedom of decision, but their judgment would be more informed in an important respect, namely their patient's own wishes.

What, now, are the general proportions of this very human problem of suffering in death? It is possible to answer this question in broad terms and to provide other indications of contemporary attitudes to death, dying and suicide.

In the United Kingdom well over half a million people die every year; the figure for 1965 was 628,000 and for 1966 643,600. Of these deaths more than one-fifth are caused by cancer and nearly one-third by degenerative heart diseases and similar conditions, and these proportions are tending to increase. These figures indicate an amount of individual suffering beyond computation. Some deaths are almost certainly hastened by compassionate doctors with or without the consent, tacit or otherwise, of the sufferers. Just as certainly others are kept alive until the last gasp can no longer be averted. In yet many other cases people die under conditions of home or institutional care which are deficient, sometimes seriously so. There are not only a larger number of deaths each year in a larger population and one having a greater proportion of persons over sixty-five, but also a significant number of people who bring about their own deaths. The suicide rate was 11.3 per 100,000 of the population in England and Wales in 1961 (giving a total of 5,216); the number of people attempting suicide is usually six to eight times as many. It has been estimated that at least one thousand people commit suicide every day throughout the world. In addition, in most countries, wide publicity is often given to the tragic cases of mercy-killing which occur from time to time and which not uncommonly spark off controversy about the rightness or otherwise of putting an end to the lives of loved ones whose sufferings have become unendurable and apparently meaningless. Increasingly, in many public and private ways, the problems concerning death are ventilated.

In Europe the problems connected with euthanasia are not infrequently discussed in public both through the popular media and in professional journals. Dr Paul Juret, a French medical scientist, writing in an international penal law review,[12] observed that scarcely a year passes without a 'dramatic' case concerning euthanasia stirring public opinion and he lists nine examples between the years 1950 and 1966. Six of the cases occurred in France and five different European nationalities were involved. Although firmly opposed himself to any liberalization of the law on the subject, he recognizes that doctors can be confronted by what he calls an 'inhuman dilemma' precisely because they possess moral sensibilities.[13]

Of the nine sample cases cited by Dr Juret four concern infants given a merciful death by anguished parents. In 1962 almost world-wide attention was given to the trial, in Liège, of a Belgian mother and her family doctor, who were arraigned for bringing about the death of an infant born grossly defective as a result of thalidomide. Both were acquitted, in the glare of unparalleled publicity and to popular rejoicing. On the first day of the trial the mother created a deep impression by her rejoinder to the presiding judge when he observed that her child could have been cared for in an institution: 'That was a solution for my problem, but not for my child's.' The case caused widespread debate, the argument being concerned not only with the mercy-killing of children but with the principle of voluntary euthanasia as one of the options open to doctors and their patients.

At about the time of the Liège trial two well-known French

[12] *Revue Internationale de droit pénal*, 38 (1967), 415.
[13] Ibid., 431.

journalists, Igor Barrère and Etienne Lalou, planned a programme on euthanasia for French television. For this purpose they assembled a large amount of evidence, in a large 'file of human cases'. They were in fact astonished by the heavy response to their request for material, more than ten thousand 'letters and confessions' being received from patients, relatives and doctors. The broadcast was advertised but was, in the end, cancelled when the producers received a letter from a woman who had had an operation for cancer. She wrote that she was suffering and knew that she was going to die. She was also in favour of euthanasia. But she earnestly begged the producers of the programme to cancel what she believed was 'a monstrous crime of useless and voluntary cruelty against people who are incurable as well as against their relatives', for human suffering was not something to be investigated in public but behind closed doors and then only by doctors who understood the bodies and spirits of their patients.[14] It was a dramatic end to a brave enterprise.

Five years later, in 1967, the BBC broadcast a 'live' television debate on 'mercy-killing', with witnesses, between Professor Glanville Williams and Mr Leo Abse, M.P. Here the debate suffered because the two sides based their arguments on conflicting premises, Professor Williams confining himself to 'the right to die' and Mr Abse exposing the dangers of 'the right to kill'.

Although the French broadcast did not take place, the material for it was fortunately not wasted. Barrère and Lalou edited the vast amount of material they had collected and published it in book form.[15] They confessed, at the end of their inquiry, that they found themselves even less capable of coming to a final judgment on the problem of euthanasia than they had been before. Certainly their book puts the problem of euthanasia in its most human context. It may be added that in their opinion Switzerland is the one country which has examined the legal problem of euthanasia 'with the most humanity and breadth of view'. There it is not regarded as murder if the motive is to grant a compassionate release from incurable suffering, much being left to the discretion of those dealing with the case.

The chief argument for legalizing voluntary euthanasia is that it would allow some individuals to escape from useless suffering by a

[14] *Le Dossier Confidentiel de l'Euthanasie* (Paris: Editions Stock, 1962), p. 28.
[15] See n. 14 above.

merciful death at their own request. The argument is based on the demands of compassion. We shall probably never be able to eliminate totally from human experience the suffering which is both hard to bear and hard to behold. Life for human beings would indeed take on a different character if all suffering were eliminated and such a prospect cannot in practice be envisaged. What the supporters of voluntary euthanasia have in mind is the *reduction* of human suffering when the victim desires it and its termination is under our control. In the words of the former Dean of St Paul's, the Very Reverend W. R. Matthews: 'It seems to be an incontrovertible proposition that, when we are confronted with suffering which is wholly destructive in its consequences and, so far as we can see, could have no beneficial result, there is a prima facie duty to bring it to an end' (see p. 68). It would seem to be this moral situation which Professor John Hinton had in mind when he wrote as follows:

> Whenever this problem is considered there always lingers in the mind the thought that euthanasia should so rarely be necessary. The suffering during fatal illness ought to be better relieved. But while the dying do sometimes experience anguish, even if in theory it could have been alleviated, the fact that euthanasia could have curtailed much distress for some people cannot be entirely dismissed. As long as one can truly say that for the patient merciful death has been too long in coming, there is some justification for euthanasia. It seems a terrible indictment that the main argument for euthanasia is that many suffer unduly because there is lack of preparation and provision for the total care of the dying.[16]

This cautious statement by Professor Hinton presents some of the issues very clearly. Their practical implications are indicated in a further passage:

> According to one large survey of the care of patients dying at home with cancer, the general practitioners found the local facilities to be deficient in more than half the areas, rural, urban or industrial. When there are such deficiencies, it explains in part why it has been found that about 15 per cent of people dying at home have a

[16] *Dying* (Pelican, 1967), p. 146.

considerable period of suffering. They needed more help than they got.[17]

These issues and human considerations will seem far from theoretical to those with friends or relatives doomed to useless suffering in a protracted death. Those who support the legalization of voluntary euthanasia believe that these sufferers have a right to die sooner rather than later, if they themselves wish it. They believe that it ought to be legally possible for doctors to hasten death, by a few hours or days or months or even years, if this is what the sufferer himself steadily wishes and clearly requests and if the doctors themselves are satisfied that death offers the only merciful release. This possibility may disturb and shock those who have had no experience of the ugliness or degradations of incurable suffering. By the bed of an actual sufferer the proportions of the problem are seen quite differently. It becomes no longer a question of the sanctity of 'life' and the need to prolong a suffering existence just as long as it is technically possible, but a case in which the compelling demands of compassion and dignity combine to impose a quick and merciful death as the only *natural* solution.

Death is both a friend and an enemy. The aim of this volume is to suggest that we have a basic human right, in certain circumstances, to decide for ourselves when it is one more than the other. When we are confronted with this fateful choice our society and our doctors must in the end allow us, suffering in life or triumphant in dying, to 'hold fast to our own discriminations'.

[17] Ibid., p. 151.

Eliot Slater

Death: The Biological Aspect

A little while ago a friend of mine suffered a bereavement. He had living in his home his mother-in-law, an old lady of seventy-six who enjoyed only very feeble health, owing to chronic kidney and arterial disease, and had been in hospital a number of times in recent years. One day this lady was suddenly taken ill with a stroke. She called to her family from the bathroom and when they arrived they found that she was paralyzed down the right side and was unable to speak. There seems to have been some panic in the home. One might have thought that the lady could have been put quietly to bed to wait for the doctor. Instead of that, when the attention of a doctor could not be obtained immediately, first the hospital and then the ambulance service was contacted. The old lady was put in the ambulance and, sinking fast, was driven to one of our most famous London teaching hospitals. By the time she was wheeled into the casualty ward, she had apparently breathed her last. The young and efficient casualty officer was, however, far from being dismayed. All the resuscitation services that the hospital could provide were mobilized, with doctors, nurses and technicians, and for eighteen hours the patient's heart was kept beating and the elaborate and beautiful apparatus for artificial respiration did her breathing for her.

Mercifully enough, this determined battle was fought in vain. When at a later time my friend asked the doctor what had been the point of it all, he received a very significant reply. The casualty officer admitted that, even if it had been possible to preserve the patient's life, only the shell of a human being—speechless, paralyzed and demented—would have remained. Yet, he maintained, it was not within his discretion to think of what the ultimate issue would be. He had one duty, and one duty only, to do all that lay within his powers to ward off death.

This is not quite the teaching which I enjoyed when I was a medical student. I was then taught, 'Thou shalt not kill, but needst not strive officiously to keep alive'. The effort made by the hospital doctor in my friend's case seems to me to have been officious in the extreme. Nevertheless, the point of view expressed by the young doctor is one which in this age is probably beginning to gain ground; and if this is so, then we shall need to examine again the basic principles on which we face these primary issues of life and death.

A friend of mine, who was brought up in a Catholic school, warmly supported the doctor's view in argument with me. Anything less than that, he felt, would be liable to grave abuse. Who is the doctor to assume the responsibility of letting a patient die? Even if the most energetic treatment is only likely to secure a few more days of life, it should not be spared. Now, of course, there is no logical limit to this line of argument. If the duty of the medical man is to be assessed in this way, then he must disturb the dying man to provide him with a few more hours, indeed a few more minutes or even moments; and the last injection of coramine will take precedence over the wish of the wife to say farewell. On the other hand, if the process is not pushed to its last absurd limits, then, wherever else the line is drawn, the doctor cannot evade the responsibility of saying that now the time has come when we must let death take its course. This, surely, is one of the natural and inescapable responsibilities which the doctor has to take as part of his duty.

I have discussed the same story with another acquaintance, a doctor engaged in busy general practice. He took a rather different view to my jesuitical friend. He thought that an older and more experienced man would have probably refrained from doing all that the casualty officer did; but he thought that what was right for the older man was not necessarily right for the younger. Until one had learned the limits of one's craft, one should seek to push it to its limits. Unless one fought for every patient with all the power at one's command, one would be only too liable to take on a defeatist attitude, to the point even of failing in one's obvious duty. Time and again, the apparently useless life one had saved had subsequently shown itself full of value and meaning.

This attitude is less dogmatic and more reasonable. But if we are to bring a rational approach to the problem, we must abandon the absolute imperative for such considerations as a balance of probabilities. If there is a chance, however small, of saving not only life but health, that must be placed on a higher scale of values than the mere prolongation of the automatic action of heart, lungs and bowels. A few more hours of mental lucidity and capacity to communicate are in a different dimension from months of coma, dementia or idiocy. Death performs for us the inestimable office of clearing up a mess too big to mend; if we are going to intervene, then we must have at least some hope of doing this ourselves.

Reflecting about the way we think of these things, the psychiatrist inclines to the view that, for many of us, our attitude to death is neurotic. Not only are we moved by emotional and non-rational motivations, but we do not face the issue squarely. We push uncomfortable ideas out of our minds. It has been said that, just as people's minds were in a bad way on the subject of sex at the beginning of this century, until Freud let some light into a dark cupboard, so now we have the same kind of attitude towards death. It would hardly be in better taste today to inquire of an elderly man whether he was afraid of dying and how he felt about his approaching end, than, in the days of Queen Victoria, to have opened a conversation with a young lady on the subject of the physical relations of the sexes. Indeed, the possibility of a fatal outcome is hardly ever discussed between doctor and patient, even when illness has set the plainest signpost. Most doctors feel it is kindest to refrain from telling the patient of the facts and the probabilities, and sometimes tell lies about them.

It may be that they are justified; though they should surely regard themselves in honour bound to give a plain and honest answer to a straight question, if it is ever put. In this, however, the patient himself very frequently fails. Even the greatest are affected by the weakness. When Johannes Brahms, the composer and a man of great energy of personality, was an old man he developed a cancer of the jaw. For a time he interested himself in the progress of medical investigations; but when these failed to reach any satisfactory conclusion, his curiosity grew less. Finally, he gave explicit instructions that in no circumstances was he to be given any news about his health which might be unpleasant. And in fact he was able to conceal from himself, to the last, that he was a dying man.

Medical men themselves are not immune. When I was a young man, I had a colleague of my own age who had suffered a number of attacks of rheumatic disease of the heart. As a result, the valves of the heart had become scarred. One of the unpleasant possibilities which may arise in such a state is that a germ settles down on the diseased valve where, because of the scarring and the inadequate blood supply, it is beyond the reach of the normal defence processes of the body. Ulceration of the valve may then cause a chronic state of blood-poisoning or septicæmia. My colleague once confessed to me that it was his one great fear that he might develop bacterial endocarditis, as this disease is called, small though the chance might be. With this fear he had to live every day of his life. It would assail him if ever he had a sore throat. At his last attack of rheumatism he had been in a state of panic until his temperature settled down. Yet with all this he lived an active and ostensibly happy life.

The time came when he had yet another attack of rheumatism, and was admitted to one of the London teaching hospitals, where he could get the most skilled help. Once or twice a week his friends would go to see him. At first he eagerly discussed his illness and the progress of investigation. But his temperature refused to settle and gradually took on the ominous swinging curve from morning to evening. The temperature-chart was removed from his room. Investigations ceased and were replaced by a uniform nursing régime. His comments on his own state ceased too. His mental horizon came nearer, so that he seemed to look at no future beyond the next few days. After about three months of illness he died, so far as I know without ever making any reference to the possibility of his death. Certainly he never spoke of it to any of us and, I was told, not to any of his doctors.

A neurotic attitude to death is no fault exclusively of our present age, and has been stronger than it is now. So sensible a man as Francis Bacon was convinced that death was wholly horrible, though it was he who suggested a rational approach to the fears it engendered:

> . . . Nay further, I esteeme it the office of a Physitian not onely to restore health, but to mitigate pains and dolors, and not onely when such mitigation may conduce to recovery, but when it may serve to make a faire and easy passage: for it is no small felicitie which *Augustus Caesar* was wont to wish to himselfe, that same *Euthanasia* . . . in my judgment they ought both to enquire the skill, and to give the attendances for the facilitating and asswaging of the pains and agonies of death.[1]

[1] *New Atlantis* (1626), written 1614/18.

Looking back from our present viewpoint, we see generation after generation of the Dark Ages sunk in a state of miserable mental enslavement. Passing the centuries under review, we see the black shadow lift only slowly. If the fears of Hell receded, those of death with its funereal pomp retained their place. The physical aspects of bodily decay kept their morbid grip on the imagination. It needed a robust spirit to overthrow them:

> The Knell, the shroud, the mattock and the grave;
> The deep damp vault, the darkness and the worm;
> These are the bugbears of a winter's eve,
> The terrors of the living, not the dead.[2]

The fears described in these lines have become old-fashioned. One wonders how much the practice of cremation has done to strip death of one of its more unsightly trappings.

One may observe how the preacher and the poet, in order to bring out the horror of dying, draw a picture in which the assault of death is made on the vigorous and intact personality. This is in fact most unusual, though it may occur. When the young man in all his vigour and love of life sees the close approach of death, it is not surprising that he recoils with a cry of dismay, even panic. This was the case with James Elroy Flecker, who died of tuberculosis while still in his prime:

> I am afraid to think about my death;
> When it shall be, and whether in great pain
> I shall rise up and fight the air for breath,
> Or calmly wait the bursting of my brain.[3]

And the concluding lines:

> I know dead men are deaf, and cannot hear
> The singing of a thousand nightingales.
> I know dead men are blind, and cannot see
> The friend that shuts in horror their great eyes.
> And they are witless. Oh, I'd rather be
> A living mouse than dead as a man dies.[4]

[2] Edward Young (1683–1765), *Night Thoughts*: 'Night' iv, l.10.
[3] 'No Coward's Son'.
[4] Ibid.

It is, perhaps, one particular type of temperament that is more than normally susceptible to the fear of death, presenting itself simply as an inevitable end. These are the ruminative obsessionals, of whom a great example was Dr Johnson. They are the people who suffer under a sense of external compulsion; they know the irrationality of the ideas which afflict them, but are still unable to resist them. Many of them are weighed down by the oppressive sense of the ineluctable passage of time. The ticking of the clock reminds them that an end is approaching them in measured, unvarying steps. Death hovers over them, casting a shadow that is felt even in youth, and deepens always as time advances. Everything that is ephemeral is a reminder, and spring is more painful to bear, with its promises doomed to extinction, than are autumn and winter. Only the great enduring things—the mountains, the sea, the stars, perhaps the thought of God—can console.

These people are exceptional; and though most of us have feelings like this at some time, the moments of oppression are usually short and infrequent. It is not easy to say how far the average man has faced the issue and adjusted to it, or how far he has merely succeeded in pushing it out of his mind. As a rule, I think, he refuses to give any thought at all to his ultimate end. He accepts it, but turns his back on it as something wholly unpleasant, inevitable but requiring no mental preparation. It is only those whose lives have become ones of active suffering who can come to think of death as a blessing and a release. The greater the comfort and the pleasantness of our days, the sharper and more distressing the contrast between the time now and the time to come. With what terrifying speed, as one grows older, do the years slip by! How intolerable to think that one day our prized identities must cease to be, that the sun will rise on a world which knows us no more!

These thoughts are natural enough; but how often do we look at the opposite side of the picture? Do we ever consider the appalling alternative, if, like the struldbrug, we were condemned to live for ever? Would the thoughtful man really welcome the elimination of all possibility of ever ceasing to be, even if he were endowed with perpetual youth? One steps back from the thought as from the abyss, and the mind reels as it does when called to contemplate a universe without beginning and without end.

On such lines will run the thoughts of the average man, who is not endowed with a religious faith which professes to provide the answer to this dilemma, who is unread in the stoic philosophers, and who has little idea of the part that death plays in nature's economy. On this last aspect, the biologist has something significant to contribute. P. B. Medawar, for example, has considered what the consequences would be if we had a race whose individuals were indeed potentially immortal, but subject to the normal accidents of existence, such as being afflicted with disease or being devoured by predators. He shows that on genetical grounds, although such a race might begin its existence with all individuals, of whatever age, showing an equal vigour and fecundity, the mere continuance of racial existence would cause a change by which vigour became concentrated in the young, while disease and relative incapacity was postponed to later ages. The phenomenon of senescence would enter the picture; and the natural conclusion of senescence is so-called natural death.

It is, now, generally agreed among biologists that growth and reproduction on the one side and ageing on the other are intimately bound up together. With many races, deterioration in vigour commences as soon as actual growth ceases. In our own species the running down of all the tissues of the body is well in hand, even before reproductive capacity has come to an end. If we consider merely the capacity for growth, this is greatest at the moment of conception and diminishes rapidly thereafter. By the age of ten, hearing capacity, especially for the higher tones, has reached its peak, and subsequently declines. By the age of twenty, the adaptive capacity of the eyes is growing less. By thirty, muscular strength and neuromuscular speed and accuracy of co-ordination are showing a deficit which spells the end of many athletic careers. At forty, the heart and blood-vessels are no longer those of a young man; and many of the chronic killing diseases have taken a hold on the less fortunate members of the population. By fifty, psychologists are measuring intellectual impairment, especially learning ability, in quantitative measurements on standardized tests. Emotional reactions are becoming slack and conventionalized, the imagination is weakening, and the capacity for fresh creative thinking, at least, has gone. By the age of sixty, senility, in greater or lesser degree, has arrived. H. S. Simms has noted that from about ten onwards there is a logarithmic increase in the mortality due to various types of disease process. The mortality from most infections, for instance, rises by about 5 per cent with every year of age. If mortality could be maintained at the figure for the age of ten, man would have a life expectancy of eight hundred years.

One may ask, is anything known of the basic causes of what we call senescence, or, when it appears as a mental disease, senile dementia? The cells of the body are potentially immortal. They can be removed from the body and maintained in tissue culture almost indefinitely. The changes of senescence are largely in the state of balance between the tissues, in the chemistry of the body and the composition of the tissue fluids. There are glandular changes, perhaps particularly involving the suprarenal glands. There is a lower rate of living, and a reduced capacity of adaptation to environmental changes. Reserve capacities have to be called on sooner.

On the psychological side, the old man can still cope with what he is habitually accustomed to, but loses his power of adapting to the new. While his memory store, his vocabulary or store of words, his arithmetical ability, and his power to use stored knowledge, are largely maintained, his ingenuity and his capacity for abstract reasoning drop. The rate of decline in the power to perceive new relations, starting about the age of twenty-five, is such that by the age of eighty he has no more ability of this kind than a child of eight. With the intellectual changes there are changes in temperament. Increasing insecurity and incapacity to tolerate anxiety are compensated for by increasing tenacity and over-caution. Emotions of all kinds are less easily controlled, and he becomes more irritable. The general level of mood alters too, so that any upset is likely to be accompanied by depression. Above all energy fails, and initiative is replaced by inertia and early fatigue.

The physical changes which take place in the brain are seen mainly in the dying off and dropping out of nerve cells. The dead cells disappear and their place is taken by gap-fillers, the cells of connective tissue. Indeed, the whole brain may shrink.

There is no evidence that the process is caused by any specific disease; it is a manifestation of molecular death, of dying, not by inches, nor by millimetres, but by microns. Nevertheless, no clear line can be drawn between physiological and pathological processes in this connection.

The time at which such changes become clinically detectable and the speed with which they proceed vary very greatly from one individual to another. Some part at least must be played by genetical factors, by the hereditary constitution. The tendency to long-living has frequently been shown to run in families. In his studies of uniovular twins who lived into old age Kallmann has shown that there is a close resemblance between the members of a twin pair in their degree of preservation at a late age, even when they have lived very different lives. This is most easily explained by the fact that such twins have the same hereditary endowment.

It seems, then, to the biologist that the idea of the medical man that death is the chief enemy is misplaced. The light drains from the sky long before the sun sets. It is at an earlier stage that we should seek out our opponent, before his inroads have gone too far. This is indeed a difficult matter. Senescence is a part of our essential constitution, and is not easily defeated. The processes of natural selection, which over other spans of life tend constantly to keep a species vigorous by eliminating the feeble and the diseased from the reproductive cycle, are here of no assistance. The hereditary constitution, which predisposes to a deterioration that occurs only after the end of reproductive life, is at no disadvantage while reproduction is still occurring, and will have its full representation in the next generation. Genes which cause such a constitution are immune to natural selection, and may accumulate indefinitely.

The race itself is potentially eternal; and *sub specie aeternitatis* the senescence of the individual is no disadvantage. Death itself becomes then a boon to the individual and a benefit to the race, by eliminating the worn out and those whose part has already been played. In human communities, if the aged and the sick did not die within no long span after they had ceased to be self-supporting, the burden on society would become disastrous.

The death and the removal from the community of those of an earlier generation have another essential part to play in maintaining the adaptability of the species as a whole. Environments are constantly changing—for the animal world in the changes wrought by climate and by man, for man by the pressure of his own social development. To cope with these changes, the species has to throw up constantly a new team. Even if they retained all their youthful vigour, and kept the advantage of a rich experience, the old would prove defective by being bound by the habits of reaction, the habits of thinking of the past. Furthermore, new types of individual, new in point of genetical constitution, will be needed. Time and again species have died out on this earth and have become extinct because they became genetically stereotyped, and could not produce a sufficient range of variability.

Just as in the mechanical world, advances occur most rapidly where new models are being constantly produced, with consequent rapid obsolescence of the old, so too it is in the world of nature. If we wish the human race to thrive, then we must accept the subordination of individual to racial values; we must acquiesce in the need for one generation to give place to the next.

This does not mean that we should consider that we already have the best of all possible worlds. There are many reasons for thinking that it would be advantageous to man if the rate of exchange of generations were a little slower, and if the mature individual could continue, with the wisdom of accumulated experience and with the vigour that precedes middle age, for a longer time than the lustrum or so which we enjoy at present. We are demanding of our youth longer and longer training periods; so that fully active and responsible life is becoming shorter at that end. There would be a great saving of human values if we could extend it at the other. To indulge in a daydream, how many men and women would enjoy the prospect, if the life expectation and the vigour were granted them, to change over in their fifties or sixties, go back to university and train in some slightly or radically different field for another, a different, career. Human society, it seems to me, would lose little if, with a higher proportion of mature individuals, it became a little more conservative, a little more insulated from the clamour of the hungry generations pressing on them from the rear.

Such a prospect is likely to remain a daydream, for the reasons given, for a very long time. It is impossible to predict what advances in human pathology and physiology will bring us, but from the genetical side the only way I can see towards the extension of man's expectancy of maturity with vigour would be by a gradual rise in the mean age of mothers at the birth of their children. If we were to marry later, and finish having our families at a later age, then man would be harnessing the forces of natural selection on his side.

To return, now, to the main theme. The position of the biologist when he is asked to contemplate the death of the individual is that this is an end which is devoutly to be wished. Death plays a wholly favourable, indeed an essential, part in human economy. Without natural death, human societies and the human race itself would certainly be unable to thrive.

This seems to me to put a definite onus on the philosopher, the psychologist and the educationist. We should train the individual to be able to regard his eventual death with open eyes and equanimity. Death at a ripe age should be no occasion for regret or mourning. Illness and accident, not to speak of war, remain the enemies of mankind; but death is not. No life story is complete without its end as well as its beginning; and we should hope to face the turning of the last pages with as much interest as any of the intermediate ones. Just what is it, of which death deprives us? We have already said good-bye to yesterday; when we come to die, it is not the past but the future of which we take our leave.

He who regards his own extinction as a personal catastrophe has, I believe, a perverted sense of values, one that is based on an excessive egocentricity. Such an extreme valuation of the self may, perhaps, be regarded as a decay product of Christian beliefs. Christianity first taught man the value of the individual human personality, and taught him also to believe in the immortality of the individual human spirit. When belief in personal immortality decays, then the temporal self takes a place in a man's loyalties which it is unable to bear. Something less temporary and less trumpery is needed. What that shall be is for each one of us to choose for himself; but something we must have for which, for each of us, his own self is wholly expendable. I suppose that the way of thinking of the biologist would lead him to regard himself as an infinitesimal unit in a fantastically complex and beautiful web of life, stretching millions of years into the past and on for an illimitable time into the future—growing, changing and advancing, but constantly under threat. In this progression each generation occupies the world only on a short-lived lease; but while that lease endures it has a total responsibility. It is a trustee and a guardian, whose greatest crime would be to sacrifice the future to the present. In such a vista, personal death is seen in proper proportion.

Antony Flew

The Principle of Euthanasia

I

My particular concern here is to deploy a general moral case for the establishment of a legal right to voluntary euthanasia. The first point to emphasize is that the argument is about *voluntary* euthanasia. Neither I nor any other contributor to the present volume advocates the euthanasia of either the incurably sick or the miserably senile except in so far as this is the strong, constant, and unequivocally expressed wish of the afflicted candidates themselves. Anyone, therefore, who dismisses what is in fact being contended on the gratuitously irrelevant grounds that he could not tolerate compulsory euthanasia, may very reasonably be construed as thereby tacitly admitting inability to meet and to overcome the case actually presented.

Second, my argument is an argument for the establishment of a legal right. What I am urging is that any patient whose condition is hopeless and painful, who secures that it is duly and professionally certified as such, and who himself clearly and continuously desires to die should be enabled to do so: and that he should be enabled to do so without his incurring, or his family incurring, or those who provide or administer the means of death incurring, any legal penalty or stigma whatsoever. To advocate the establishment of such a legal right is not thereby to be committed even to saying that it would always be morally justifiable, much less that it would always be morally obligatory, for any patient to exercise this right if he found himself in a position so to do. For a legal right is not as such necessarily and always a moral right; and hence, *a fortiori*, it is not necessarily and always a moral duty to exercise whatever legal rights you may happen to possess.

This is a vital point. It was—to refer first to an issue now at last happily resolved—crucial to the question of the relegalization in Great Britain of homosexual relations between consenting male adults. Only when it was at last widely grasped, and grasped in its relation to this particular question, could we find the large majorities in both Houses of Parliament by which a liberalizing bill was passed into law. For presumably most members of those majorities not only found the idea of homosexual relations repugnant—as most of us do—but also believed such relations to be morally wrong—as I for one do not. Yet they brought themselves to recognize that neither the repugnance generally felt towards some practice, nor even its actual wrongness if it actually is wrong, by itself constitutes sufficient reason for making or keeping that practice illegal. By the same token it can in the present instance be entirely consistent to urge, both that there ought to be a legal right to voluntary euthanasia, and that it would sometimes or always be morally wrong to exercise that legal right.

Third, the case presented here is offered as a moral one. In developing and defending such a case I shall, of course, have to consider certain peculiarly religious claims. Such claims, however, become relevant here only in so far as they either constitute, or may be thought to constitute, or in so far as they warrant, or may be thought to warrant, conclusions incompatible with those which it is my primary and positive purpose to urge.

Fourth, and finally, this essay is concerned primarily with general principles, not with particular practicalities. I shall not here discuss or—except perhaps quite incidentally—touch upon any questions of comparative detail: questions, for instance, of how a Euthanasia Act ought to be drafted;[1] of what safeguards would need to be incorporated to prevent abuse of the new legal possibilities by those with disreputable reasons for wanting someone else dead; of exactly what and how much should be taken as constituting an unequivocal expression of a clear and constant wish; of the circumstances, if any, in which we ought to take earlier calculated expressions of a patient's desires as constituting still adequate grounds for action when at some later time the patient has become himself unable any longer to provide sufficiently sober, balanced, constant and unequivocal expressions of his wishes; and so on.

I propose here as a matter of policy largely to ignore such particular and practical questions. This is not because I foolishly regard them as unimportant, or irresponsibly dismiss them as dull. Obviously they

[1] See Appendix 1.

could become of the most urgent interest. Nor yet is it because I believe that my philosophical cloth disqualifies me from contributing helpfully to any down-to-earth discussions. On the contrary, I happen to be one of those numerous academics who are convinced, some of them correctly, that they are practical and businesslike men! The decisive reason for neglecting these vital questions of detail here in, and in favour of, a consideration of the general principle of the legalization of voluntary euthanasia is that they are all secondary to that primary issue. For no such subordinate question can properly arise as relevantly practical until and unless the general principle is conceded. Some of these practical considerations are in any event dealt with by other contributors to this volume.

2

So what can be said in favour of the principle? There are two main, and to my mind decisive, moral reasons. But before deploying these it is worth pausing for a moment to indicate why the onus of proof does not properly rest upon us. It may seem as if it does, because we are proposing a change in the present order of things; and it is up to the man who wants a change to produce the reasons for making whatever change he is proposing. This most rational principle of conservatism is in general sound. But here it comes into conflict with the overriding and fundamental liberal principle. It is up to any person and any institution wanting to prevent anyone from doing anything he wishes to do, or to compel anyone to do anything he does not wish to do, to provide positive good reason to justify interference. The question should therefore be: *not* 'Why should people be given this new legal right?'; *but* 'Why should people in this matter be restrained by law from doing what they want?'

Yet even if this liberal perspective is accepted, as it too often is not, and even if we are able to dispose of any reasons offered in defence of the present legal prohibitions, still the question would arise, whether the present state of the law represents a merely tiresome departure from sound liberal principles of legislation, or whether it constitutes a really substantial evil. It is here that we have to offer our two main positive arguments:

(a) First, there are, and for the foreseeable future will be, people afflicted with incurable and painful diseases who urgently and fixedly want to die quickly. The first argument is that a law which tries to prevent such sufferers from achieving this quick death, and usually thereby forces other people who care for them to watch their pointless pain helplessly, is a very cruel law. It is because of this legal cruelty that advocates of euthanasia sometimes speak of euthanasia as 'mercy-killing'. In such cases the sufferer may be reduced to an obscene parody of a human being, a lump of suffering flesh eased only by intervals of drugged stupor. This, as things now stand, must persist until at last every device of medical skill fails to prolong the horror.

(b) Second, a law which insists that there must be no end to this process—terminated only by the overdue relief of 'death by natural causes'—is a very degrading law. In the present context the full force of this second reason may not be appreciated immediately, if at all. We are so used to meeting appeals to 'the absolute value of human personality', offered as the would-be knock-down objection to any proposal to legalize voluntary euthanasia, that it has become hard to realize that, in so far as we can attach some tolerably precise meaning to the key phrase, this consideration would seem to bear in the direction precisely opposite to that in which it is usually mistaken to point. For the agonies of prolonged terminal illness can be so terrible and so demoralizing that the person is blotted out in ungovernable nerve reactions. In such cases as this, to meet the patient's longing for death is a means of showing for human personality that respect which cannot tolerate any ghastly travesty of it. So our second main positive argument, attacking the present state of the law as degrading, derives from a respect for the wishes of the individual person, a concern for human dignity, an unwillingness to let the animal pain disintegrate the man.

Our first main positive argument opposes the present state of the law, and of the public opinion which tolerates it, as cruel. Often and appositely this argument is supported by contrasting the tenderness which rightly insists that on occasion dogs and horses must be put out of their misery, with the stubborn refusal in any circumstances to permit one person to assist another in cutting short his suffering. The cry is raised, 'But people are not animals!' Indeed they are not. Yet this is precisely not a ground for treating people worse than brute animals.

Animals are like people, in that they too can suffer. It is for this reason that both can have a claim on our pity and our mercy.[2]

But people are also more than brute animals. They can talk and think and wish and plan. It is this that makes it possible to insist, as we do, that there must be no euthanasia unless it is the firm considered wish of the person concerned. People also can, and should, have dignity as human beings. That is precisely why we are urging that they should be helped and not hindered when they wish to avoid or cut short the often degrading miseries of incurable disease or, I would myself add, of advanced senile decay.

3

In the first section I explained the scope and limitations of the present chapter. In the second I offered—although only after suggesting that the onus of proof in this case does not really rest on the proposition—my two main positive reasons in favour of euthanasia. It is time now to begin to face, and to try to dispose of, objections. This is the most important phase in the whole exercise. For to anyone with any width of experience and any capacity for compassion the positive reasons must be both perfectly obvious and strongly felt. The crucial issue is whether or not there are decisive, overriding objections to these most pressing reasons of the heart.

(a) Many of the objections commonly advanced, which are often mistaken to be fundamental, are really objections only to a possible specific manner of implementing the principle of voluntary euthanasia. Thus it is suggested that if the law permitted doctors on occasion to provide their patients with means of death, or where necessary to do the actual killing, and they did so, then the doctors who did either of these things would be violating the Hippocratic Oath, and the prestige of and public confidence in the medical profession would be undermined.

As to the Hippocratic Oath, this makes two demands which in the special circumstances we have in mind may become mutually

[2] Thus Jeremy Bentham, urging that the legislator must not neglect animal sufferings, insists that the 'question is not "Can they *reason*?" nor "Can they *talk*?" but "Can they *suffer*?"' (*Principles of Morals and Legislation*, Chap. XVII, *n.*)

contradictory. They then cannot both be met at the same time. The relevant section reads: 'I will use treatments to help the sick according to my ability and judgment, but never with a view to injury and wrong-doing. I will not give anyone a lethal dose if asked to do so, nor will I suggest such a course.'[3] The fundamental undertaking 'to help the sick according to my ability and judgment' may flatly conflict with the further promise not to 'give anyone a lethal dose if asked to do so'. To observe the basic undertaking a doctor may have to break the further promise. The moral would, therefore, appear to be: not that the Hippocratic Oath categorically and unambiguously demands that doctors must have no dealings with voluntary euthanasia; but rather that the possible incompatibility in such cases of the different directives generated by two of its logically independent clauses constitutes a reason for revising that Oath.

As to the supposed threat to the prestige of and to our confidence in the medical profession, I am myself inclined to think that the fears expressed are—in more than one dimension—disproportionate to the realities. But whatever the truth about this the whole objection would bear only against proposals which permitted or required doctors to do, or directly to assist in, the actual killing. This is not something which is essential to the whole idea of voluntary euthanasia, and the British Euthanasia Society's present draft bill is so formulated as altogether to avoid this objection. It is precisely such inessential objections as this which I have undertaken to eschew in this essay, in order to consider simply the general principle.

(b) The first two objections which do really bear on this form a pair. One consists in the contention that there is no need to be concerned about the issue, since in fact there are not any, or not many, patients who when it comes to the point want to die quickly. The other bases the same complacent conclusion on the claim that in fact, in the appropriate cases, doctors already mercifully take the law into their own hands. These two comfortable doctrines are, like many other similarly reassuring bromides, both entirely wrong and rather shabby.

To the first the full reply would probably have to be made by a doctor, for a medical layman can scarcely be in a position to make an

[3] The Greek text is most easily found in *Hippocrates and the Fragments of Heracleitus*, ed. W. H. S. Jones and E. T. Withington for the Loeb series (Harvard Univ. Pr. and Heinemann), Vol. 1, p. 298. The translation in the present essay is mine.

estimate of the number of patients who would apply and could qualify for euthanasia.[4] But it is quite sufficient for our immediate purposes to say two things. First, there can be few who have reached middle life, and who have not chosen to shield their sensibilities with some impenetrable carapace of dogma, who cannot recall at least one case of an eager candidate for euthanasia from their own experience—even from their own peacetime experience only. If this statement is correct, as my own inquiries suggest that it is, then the total number of such eager candidates must be substantial. Second, though the need for enabling legalization becomes progressively more urgent the greater the numbers of people personally concerned, I wish for myself to insist that it still matters very much indeed if but one person who would have decided for a quick death is forced to undergo a protracted one.

To the second objection, which admits that there are many cases where euthanasia is indicated, but is content to leave it to the doctors to defy the law, the answer is equally simple. First, it is manifestly not true that all doctors are willing on the appropriate occasions either to provide the means of death or to do the killing. Many, as they are Roman Catholics, are on religious grounds absolutely opposed to doing so. Many others are similarly opposed for other reasons, or by force of training and habit. And there is no reason to believe that among the rest the proportion of potential martyrs is greater than it is in any other secular occupational group. Second, it is entirely wrong to expect the members of one profession as a regular matter of course to jeopardize their whole careers by breaking the criminal law in order to save the rest of us the labour and embarrassment of changing that law.

Here I repeat two points made to me more than once by doctor friends. First, if a doctor were convinced he ought to provide euthanasia in spite of the law, it would often be far harder for him to do so undetected than many laymen think, especially in our hospitals. Second, the present attitude of the medical establishment is such that if a doctor did take the chance, was caught and brought to trial, and even if the jury, as they well might, refused to convict, still he must expect to face complete professional disaster.

(c) The next two objections, which in effect bear on the principle, again form a pair. The first pair had in common the claim that the facts

[4] See Downing, pp. 24–5; also pp. 27–8 for his reference to Professor Hinton's work, *Dying* (Pelican, 1967).

were such that the question of legislative action need not arise. The second pair are alike in that whereas both might appear to be making contentions of fact, in reality we may have in each a piece of exhortation or of metaphysics masquerading as an empirical proposition.

Of this second relevant pair the first suggests that there is no such thing as an incurable disease. This implausible thesis becomes more intelligible, though no more true, when we recall how medical ideologues sometimes make proclamations: 'Modern medicine cannot recognize any such thing as a disease which is incurable'; and the like. Such pronouncements may sound like reports on the present state of the art. It is from this resemblance that they derive their peculiar idiomatic point. But the advance of medicine has not reached a stage where all diseases are curable. And no one seriously thinks that it has. At most this continuing advance has suggested that we need never despair of finding cures *some day*. But this is not at all the same thing as saying, what is simply not true, that *even now* there is no condition which is at any stage incurable. This medical ideologue's slogan has to be construed as a piece of exhortation disguised for greater effect as a paradoxical statement of purported fact. It may as such be instructively compared with certain favourite educationalists' paradoxes: 'We do not teach subjects, we teach children!'; or 'There are no bad children, only bad teachers!'

The second objection of this pair is that no one can ever be certain that the condition of any particular patient is indeed hopeless. This is more tricky. For an objection of this form might be given two radically different sorts of content. Yet it would be easy and is common to slide from one interpretation to the other, and back again, entirely unwittingly.

Simply and straightforwardly, such an objection might be made by someone whose point was that judgments of incurability are, as a matter of purely contingent fact, so unreliable that no one has any business to be certain, or to claim to know, that anyone is suffering from an incurable affliction. This contention would relevantly be backed by appealing to the alleged fact that judgments that 'this case is hopeless, *period*' are far more frequently proven to have been mistaken than judgments that, for instance, 'this patient will recover fully, *provided that* he undergoes the appropriate operation'. This naïve objector's point could be made out, or decisively refuted, only by reference to quantitative studies of the actual relative reliabilities and unreliabilities of different sorts of medical judgments. So unless and until such quantitative empirical studies are actually made, and unless and until their results are shown to bear upon the question of euthanasia in the way suggested, there is no grounded and categorical objection here to be met.

But besides this first and straightforwardly empirical interpretation there is a second interpretation of another quite different sort. Suppose someone points to an instance, as they certainly could and well might, where some patient whom all the doctors had pronounced to be beyond hope nevertheless recovers, either as the result of the application of new treatment derived from some swift and unforeseen advance in medical science, or just through nature taking its unexpected course. This happy but chastening outcome would certainly demonstrate that the doctors concerned had on this occasion been mistaken; and hence that, though they had sincerely claimed to know the patient's condition to have been incurable, they had not really known this. The temptation is to mistake it that such errors show that no one ever really knows. It is this perfectly general contention, applied to the particular present case of judgments of incurability, which constitutes the second objection in its second interpretation. The objector seizes upon the point that even the best medical opinion turns out sometimes to have been wrong (as here). He then urges, simply because doctors thus prove occasionally to have been mistaken (as here) and because it is always—theoretically if not practically—possible that they may be mistaken again the next time, that therefore none of them ever really knows (at least in such cases). Hence, he concludes, there is after all no purchase for the idea of voluntary euthanasia. For this notion presupposes that there are patients recognizably suffering from conditions known to be incurable.

The crux to grasp about this contention is that, notwithstanding that it may be presented and pressed as if it were somehow especially relevant to one particular class of judgments, in truth it applies—if it applies at all—absolutely generally. The issue is thus revealed as not medical but metaphysical. If it follows that if someone is ever mistaken then he never really knows, and still more if it follows that if it is even logically possible that he may be mistaken then he never really knows, then, surely, the consequence must be that none of us ever does know—not *really*. (When a metaphysician says that something is never really such and such, what he really means is that it very often is, *really*.) For it is of the very essence of our cognitive predicament that we do all sometimes make mistakes; while always it is at least theoretically possible that we may. Hence the argument, if it holds at all, must show that knowledge, *real* knowledge, is for all us mortal men for ever unattainable.

What makes the second of the present pair of objections tricky to handle is that it is so easy to pass unwittingly from an empirical to a metaphysical interpretation. We may fail to notice, or noticing may fail convincingly to explain, how an empirical thesis has degenerated into metaphysics, or how metaphysical misconceptions have corrupted the medical judgment. Yet, once these utterly different interpretations have been adequately distinguished, two summary comments should be sufficient.

First, in so far as the objection is purely metaphysical, to the idea that *real* knowledge is possible, it applies absolutely generally; or not at all. It is arbitrary and irrational to restrict it to the examination of the principle of voluntary euthanasia. If doctors never really know, we presumably have no business to rely much upon any of their judgments. And if, for the same metaphysical reasons, there is no knowledge to be had anywhere, then we are all of us in the same case about everything. This may be as it may be, but it is nothing in particular to the practical business in hand.

Second, when the objection takes the form of a pretended refusal to take any decision in matters of life and death on the basis of a judgment which theoretically might turn out to have been mistaken, it is equally unrealistic and arbitrary. It is one thing to claim that judgments of incurability are peculiarly fallible: if that suggestion were to be proved to be correct. It is quite another to claim that it is improper to take vital decisions on the basis of sorts of judgment which either are in principle fallible, or even prove occasionally in fact to have been wrong. It is an inescapable feature of the human condition that no one is infallible about anything, and there is no sphere of life in which mistakes do not occur. Nevertheless we cannot as agents avoid, even in matters of life and death and more than life and death, making decisions to act or to abstain. It is only necessary and it is only possible to insist on ordinarily strict standards of warranted assertability, and on ordinarily exacting rather than obsessional criteria of what is beyond reasonable doubt.

Of course this means that mistakes will sometimes be made. This is in practice a corollary of the uncontested fact that infallibility is not an option. To try to ignore our fallibility is unrealistic, while to insist on remembering it only in the context of the question of voluntary euthanasia is arbitrary. Nor is it either realistic or honourable to attempt to offload the inescapable burdens of practical responsibility, by first claiming that we never really *know*, and then pretending that a decision not to act is somehow a decision which relieves us of all proper responsibility for the outcome.

(d) The two pairs of relevant objections so far considered have both been attempts in different ways to show that the issue does not, or at any rate need not, arise as a practical question. The next concedes that the question does arise and is important, but attempts to dispose of it with the argument that what we propose amounts to the legalization, in certain circumstances, of murder, or suicide, or both; and that this cannot be right because murder and suicide are both gravely wrong always. Now even if we were to concede all the rest it would still not follow, because something is gravely wrong in morals, that there ought to be a law against it; and that we are wrong to try to change the law as it now subsists. We have already urged that the onus of proof must always rest on the defenders of any restriction.

In fact the rest will not do. In the first place, if the law were to be changed as we want, the present legal definition of 'murder' would at the same time have to be so changed that it no longer covered the provision of euthanasia for a patient who had established that it was his legal right. 'Does this mean,' someone may indignantly protest, 'that right and wrong are created by Acts of Parliament?' Emphatically, yes: and equally emphatically, no. Yes indeed, if what is intended is *legal* right and *legal* offence. What is meant by the qualification 'legal' if it is not that these rights are the rights established and sanctioned by the law? Certainly not, if what is intended is *moral* right and *moral* wrong. Some moral rights happen to be at the same time legal rights, and some moral wrongs similarly also constitute offences against the law. But, notoriously, legislatures may persist in denying moral rights; while, as I insisted earlier, not every moral wrong either is or ought to be forbidden and penalized by law.

Well then, if the legal definition of 'murder' can be changed by Act of Parliament, would euthanasia nevertheless be murder, morally speaking? This amounts to asking whether administering euthanasia legally to someone who is incurably ill, and who has continually wanted it, is in all relevant respects similar to, so to speak, a standard case of murder; and whether therefore it is to be regarded morally as murder. Once the structure of the question is in this way clearly displayed it becomes obvious that the cases are different in at least three important respects. First, whereas the murder victim is (typically) killed against his will, a patient would be given or assisted in obtaining euthanasia only if he steadily and strongly desired to die. Second, whereas the murderer kills his victim, treating him usually as a mere object for disposal, in euthanasia the object of the exercise would be to save someone, at his own request, from needless suffering, to prevent the degradation of a human person. Third, whereas the murderer by his action defies the law, the man performing euthanasia would be acting according to law, helping another man to secure what the law allowed him.

It may sound as if that third clause goes back on the earlier repudiation of the idea that moral right and wrong are created by Act of Parliament. That is not so. For we are not saying that this action would now be justifiable, or at least not murder morally, simply because it was now permitted by the law; but rather that the change in the law would remove one of the possible reasons for moral objection. The point is this: that although the fact that something is enjoined, permitted, or forbidden by law does not necessarily make it right, justifiable, or wrong morally, nevertheless the fact that something is enjoined or forbidden by a law laid down by established authority does constitute one moral reason for obedience. So a doctor who is convinced that the objects of the Euthanasia Society are absolutely right should at least hesitate to take the law into his own hands, not only for prudential but also for moral reasons. For to defy the law is, as it were, to cast your vote against constitutional procedures and the rule of law, and these are the foundations and framework of any tolerable civilized society. (Consider here the injunction posted by some enlightened municipal authorities upon their public litter bins: 'Cast your vote here for a tidy New York!'—or wherever it may be.)

Returning to the main point, the three differences which we have just noticed are surely sufficient to require us to refuse to assimilate legalized voluntary euthanasia to the immoral category of murder. But to insist on making a distinction between legalized voluntary euthanasia and murder is not the same thing as, nor does it by itself warrant, a refusal to accept that both are equally immoral. What an appreciation of these three differences, but crucially of the first, should do is to suggest that we ought to think of such euthanasia as a special case not of murder but of suicide. Let us therefore examine the second member of our third pair of relevant objections.

This objection was that to legalize voluntary euthanasia would be to legalize, in certain conditions, the act of assisting suicide. The question therefore arises: 'Is suicide always morally wrong?'

The purely secular considerations usually advanced and accepted are not very impressive. First, it is still sometimes urged that suicide is unnatural, in conflict with instinct, a breach of the putative law of self-preservation. All arguments of this sort, which attempt directly to deduce conclusions about what *ought* to be from premises stating, or mis-stating, only what *is* are—surely—unsound: they involve what philosophers label, appropriately, the 'Naturalistic Fallacy'. There is also a peculiar viciousness about appealing to what is supposed to be a descriptive law of nature to provide some justification for the prescription to obey that supposed law. For if the law really obtained as a description of what always and unavoidably happens, then there would be no point in prescribing that it should; whereas if the descriptive law does not in fact hold, then the basis of the supposed justification does not exist.[5] Furthermore, even if an argument of this first sort could show that suicide is always immoral, it could scarcely provide a reason for insisting that it ought also to be illegal.

Second, it is urged that the suicide by his act deprives other people of the services which he might have rendered them had he lived longer. This can be a strong argument, especially where the suicide has a clear, positive family or public obligation. It is also an argument which, even in a liberal perspective, can provide a basis for legislation. But it is irrelevant to the circumstances which advocates of the legalization of voluntary euthanasia have in mind. In such circumstances as these, there is no longer any chance of being any use to anyone, and if there is any family or social obligation it must be all the other way—to end your life when it has become a hopeless burden both to yourself and to others.

[5] I have argued this kind of point more fully in *Evolutionary Ethics* (London: Macmillan, 1967). See Chap. IV, 'From *Is* to *Ought*'.

Third, it is still sometimes mentioned that suicide is in effect murder—'self-murder'. To this, offered in a purely secular context, the appropriate and apparently decisive reply would seem to be that by parity of reasoning marriage is really adultery—'own-wife-adultery'. For, surely, the gravamen of both distinctions lies in the differences which such paradoxical assimilations override. It is precisely because suicide is the destruction of oneself (by one's own choice), while murder is the destruction of somebody else (against his wishes), that the former can be, and is, distinguished from the latter.

Yet there is a counter to this own-wife-adultery move. It begins by insisting, rightly, that sexual relations—which are what is common to both marriage and adultery—are not in themselves wrong: the crucial question is, 'Who with?' It then proceeds to claim that what is common to both murder and suicide is the killing of a human being; and here the questions of 'Which one?' or 'By whom?' are not, morally, similarly decisive. Finally appeal may be made, if the spokesman is a little old-fashioned, to the Sixth Commandment, or if he is in the contemporary swim, to the Principle of the Absolute Sanctity of Human Life.

The fundamental difficulty which confronts anyone making this counter move is that of finding a formulation for his chosen principle about the wrongness of all killing, which is both sufficiently general not to appear merely question-begging in its application to the cases in dispute, and which yet carries no consequences that the spokesman himself is not prepared to accept. Thus, suppose he tries to read the Sixth Commandment as constituting a veto on any killing of human beings. Let us waive here the immediate scholarly objections: that such a reading involves accepting the mistranslation 'Thou shalt not kill' rather than the more faithful 'Thou shalt do no murder'; and that neither the children of Israel nor even their religious leaders construed this as a law forbidding all war and all capital punishment.[6] The question remains whether our spokesman himself is really prepared to say that all killing, without any exception, is morally wrong.

It is a question which has to be pressed, and which can only be answered by each man for himself. Since I cannot give your answer, I can only say that I know few if any people who would sincerely say 'Yes'. But as soon as any exceptions or qualifications are admitted, it

[6] See, f.i., Joseph Fletcher, *Morals and Medicine* (1954; Gollancz, 1955), pp. 195–6. I recommend this excellent treatment by a liberal Protestant of a range of questions in moral theology too often left to far from liberal Roman Catholics.

becomes excessively difficult to find any presentable principle upon which these can be admitted while still excluding suicide and assistance to suicide in a case of euthanasia. This is not just because, generally, once any exceptions or qualifications have been admitted to any rule it becomes hard or impossible not to allow others. It is because, particularly, the case for excluding suicide and assisting suicide from the scope of any embargo on killing people is so strong that only some absolutely universal rule admitting no exceptions of any sort whatever could have the force convincingly to override it.

Much the same applies to the appeal to the Principle of the Absolute Sanctity of Human Life. Such appeals were continually made by conservatives—many of them politically not Conservative but Socialist—in opposition to the recent efforts to liberalize the British abortion laws. Such conservatives should be, and repeatedly were, asked whether they are also opponents of all capital punishment and whether they think that it is always wrong to kill in a 'just war'. (In fact none of those in Parliament could honestly have answered 'Yes' to both questions.) In the case of abortion their position could still be saved by inserting the qualification 'innocent', a qualification traditionally made by cautious moralists who intend to rest on this sort of principle. But any such qualification, however necessary, must make it almost impossible to employ the principle thus duly qualified to proscribe all suicide. It would be extraordinarily awkward and far-fetched to condemn suicide or assisting suicide as 'taking an innocent life'.

Earlier in the present subsection I described the three arguments I have been examining as secular. This was perhaps misleading. For all three are regularly used by religious people: indeed versions of all three are to be found in St Thomas Aquinas's *Summa Theologica*, the third being there explicitly linked with St Augustine's laboured interpretation of the Sixth Commandment to cover suicide.[7] And perhaps the incongruity of trying to make the amended Principle of the Absolute Sanctity of Innocent Human Life yield a ban on suicide is partly to be understood as a result of attempting to derive from secularized premises conclusions which really depend upon a religious foundation. But the next two arguments are frankly and distinctively religious.

[7] Part II: Q. 64, A5. The Augustine reference is to *The City of God*, 1, 20. It is worth comparing, for ancient Judaic attitudes, E. Westermarck's *Origin and Development of the Moral Ideas*, Vol. 1, pp. 246–7.

The first insists that human beings are God's property: 'It is our duty to take care of God's property entrusted to our charge—our souls and bodies. They belong not to us but to God';[8] 'Whoever takes his own life sins against God, even as he who kills another's slave sins against that slave's master';[9] and 'Suicide is the destruction of the temple of God and a violation of the property rights of Jesus Christ.'[10]

About this I restrict myself to three comments here. First, as it stands, unsupplemented by appeal to some other principle or principles, it must apply, if it applies at all, equally to *all* artificial and intentional shortening *or* lengthening of any human life, one's own *or* that of anyone else. Alone and unsupplemented it would commit one to complete quietism in all matters of life and death; for all interference would be interference with someone else's property. Otherwise one must find further particular moral revelations by which to justify capital punishment, war, medicine, and many other such at first flush impious practices. Second, it seems to presuppose that a correct model of the relation between man and God is that of slave and slave-master, and that respect for God's property ought to be the fundamental principle of morals. It is perhaps significant that it is to this image that St Thomas and the pagan Plato, in attacking suicide, both appeal. This attempt to derive not only theological but all obligations from the putative theological fact of Creation is a commonplace of at least one tradition of moral theology. In this derivation the implicit moral premise is usually that unconditional obedience to a Creator, often considered as a very special sort of owner, is the primary elemental obligation.[11] Once this is made explicit it does not appear to be self-evidently true; nor is it easy to see how a creature in absolute ontological dependence could be the genuinely responsible subject of obligations to his infinite Creator.[12] Third, this objection calls to mind one of the sounder sayings of the sinister Tiberius: 'If the gods are insulted let them see to it themselves.' This remark is obviously

[8] See the Rev. G. J. MacGillivray, 'Suicide and Euthanasia', p. 10; a widely distributed Catholic Truth Society pamphlet.
[9] Aquinas, loc. cit.
[10] Koch-Preuss, *Handbook of Moral Theology*, Vol. II, p. 76. This quotation has been taken from Fletcher, op. cit., p. 192.
[11] Cf., for convenience, MacGillivray, loc. cit.; and for a Protestant analogue the Bishop of Exeter quoted by P. Nowell-Smith in *Ethics* (Penguin, 1954), pp. 37–8 *n.*
[12] I have developed this contention in *God and Philosophy* (Hutchinson, 1966; reissued 1984 by Open Court of La Salle, Ill., as *God, a Philosophical Critique*), §§ 2.34 ff.

relevant only to the question of legalization, not to that of the morality or the prudence of the action itself.

The second distinctively religious argument springs from the conviction that God does indeed see to it Himself, with a penalty of infinite severity. If you help someone to secure euthanasia, 'You are sending him from the temporary and comparatively light suffering of this world to the eternal suffering of hell.' Now if this appalling suggestion could be shown to be true it would provide the most powerful moral reason against helping euthanasia in any way, and for using any legislative means which might save people from suffering a penalty so inconceivably cruel. It would also be the strongest possible prudential reason against 'suiciding onself'.[13] (Though surely anyone who knowingly incurred such a penalty would by that very action prove himself to be genuinely of unsound mind; and hence not *justly* punishable at all. Not that a Being contemplating such unspeakable horrors could be expected to be concerned with justice!)

About this second, peculiarly religious, argument there is, it would seem, little to be done except: either simply to concede that for anyone holding this belief it indeed is reasonable to oppose euthanasia, and to leave it at that; or, still surely conceding this, to attempt to mount a general offensive against the whole system of which it forms a part.

(e) The final objection is one raised, with appropriate modifications, by the opponents of every reform everywhere. It is that even granting that the principle of the reform is excellent it would, if adopted, lead inevitably to something worse; and so we had much better not make any change at all. Thus G. K. Chesterton pronounced that the proponents of euthanasia now seek only the death of those who are a nuisance to themselves, but soon it will be broadened to include those who are a nuisance to others.[14] Such cosy arguments depend on two

[13] This rather affected-sounding gallicism is adopted deliberately: if you believe, as I do, that suicide is not always and as such wrong, it is inappropriate to speak of 'committing suicide'; just as correspondingly if you believe, as I do not, that (private) profit is wrong, it becomes apt to talk of those who 'commit a profit'.

[14] I take this quotation, too, from Fletcher, op. cit., p. 201: it originally appeared in *The Digest* (Dec. 23, 1937). Another, much more recent specimen of this sort of obscurantist flim-flam may be found in Lord Longford's speech to the House of Lords against Mr David Steel's Abortion Bill as originally passed by the Commons. Lord Longford (formerly Pakenham) urged that if that bill were passed, we might see the day when senile members of their lordships' House were put down willy-nilly.

assumptions: that the supposedly inevitable consequences are indeed evil and substantially worse than the evils the reform would remove; and that the supposedly inevitable consequences really are inevitable consequences.

In the present case we certainly can grant the first assumption, if the consequence supposed is taken to be large-scale legalized homicide in the Nazi manner. But whatever reason is there for saying that this would, much less inevitably must, follow? For there are the best of reasons for insisting that there is a world of difference between legalized voluntary euthanasia and such legalized mass-murder. Only if public opinion comes to appreciate their force will there be any chance of getting the reform we want. Then we should have no difficulty, in alliance doubtless with all our present opponents, in blocking any move to legalize murder which might conceivably arise from a misunderstanding of the case for voluntary euthanasia. Furthermore, it is to the point to remind such objectors that the Nazi atrocities they probably have in mind were in fact not the result of any such reform, but were the work of people who consciously repudiated the whole approach to ethics represented in the argument of the present essay. For this approach is at once human and humanitarian. It is concerned above all with the reduction of suffering; but concerned at the same time with other values too, such as human dignity and respect for the wishes of the individual person. And always it is insistent that morality should not be 'left in the dominion of vague feeling or inexplicable internal conviction, but should be . . . made a matter of reason and calculation'.[15]

[15] J. S. Mill's essay on Bentham quoted in F. R. Leavis, *Mill on Bentham and Coleridge* (Chatto & Windus, 1950), p. 92.

Joseph Fletcher

The Patient's Right to Die

On his way to the hospital a minister stops at a house near his church to say a word of personal sympathy to a couple sitting on the porch with their family doctor. Upstairs the man's mother is in bed, the victim of a series of small cerebral haemorrhages over the last eleven years. Her voice went two years ago and there is now no sign that she hears anything. Communication has ended. Says the son, with a complex question-asking glance at his wife, 'My mother is already dead.'

Listening to those tell-tale words, the doctor shakes his head sympathetically and helplessly. To the minister, that involuntary gesture seems almost a ritual. Earlier that day another doctor did exactly the same thing when the minister told him about his talk with a family whose twenty-year-old son has been lying in the 'living death' of complete coma for four years. A motor-car crash hopelessly shattered his cerebral cortex. Since then only the brain stem has sustained life. All thought and feeling have been erased, and he has not moved a single muscle of his body since the accident. But he is in 'excellent health', although he feels no stimulus of any kind, from within or without. Once an angular blond youth of sixteen, he is now a baby-faced 'brunette' seemingly ten years old. He is fed through an in-dwelling nasal tube. He suffers no pain, only reacts by reflex to a needle jab. His mother says, 'My son is dead.'

Later, at the hospital, the minister visits a woman in her early seventies. He had last seen her at her fiftieth wedding-anniversary party two months earlier. She has now been in the hospital for a week with what was tentatively thought to be 'degenerative arthritis'. But the diagnosis is bone cancer. Both legs were already fractured when she arrived at the hospital and little bits of her bones are splintering all the time; she has agonizing shaking attacks that break them off. She turns away from her clerical caller and looks at her husband: 'I ought to die.

Why can't I die?' It is the living who fear death, not the dying.

The minister leaves, somehow feeling guilty, and goes upstairs to Surgical. An intern and a young resident in surgery grab his arms and say, 'Come on, join our council of war.' They go into an empty room where two staff physicians and the chaplain are waiting. In the next room a man is dying, slowly, in spite of their ingenious attempt to save him from pneumonic suffocation by means of a 'tracheotomy', a hole cut in his throat through which an artificial respirator is used. The question is: should they take away the oxygen tank, let the patient go? The chaplain is pulled two ways. One of the doctors is against it, the other joins the resident in favour. The intern says he doesn't 'like' it. The visiting clergyman says, 'I would'. They do. The oxygen is removed, the light turned off, the door closed behind them. Then they send the chaplain to comfort the widow out in the alcove at the end of the hall, saying, 'We are doing everything we can.'

This heartbreaking struggle over mercy-death has become a standard drama in hospital novels. Physicians and clergymen struggle constantly in the most vital, intimate and highly personal centres of human existence. The 'primary events' of birth, procreation and death are their daily fare. Ultimate as well as immediate concerns tax their capacity for creative and loving decisions. Squarely and continually confronting them is death, the prospect of non-being which lurks out of sight though never wholly out of mind for most of us. Because most people cannot look it in the eye they cling to irrational, phobic and sentimental attitudes about voluntary death and the medical control of dying. They cannot see death as experienced doctors and ministers do—in perspective, a familiar adversary. This is the case even among psychologists. For example, many aspects were discussed in a symposium in recent years, 'The Meaning of Death', at a convention of the American Psychological Association. But nothing whatever was said about the growing problem of dying in dignity. Bad words such as 'euthanasia' were not mentioned.

We are, however, becoming somewhat less irrational than our forbears on this subject. At the level of sheer logic, one of the most curious features of the 'theological era' of the past is that most people feared and sought to avoid death at any and every cost, except sometimes for honour's sake. Even though they professed to have faith in personal survival after death, it was their Worst Enemy. Nowadays, when faith is waning not only in the prospect of hell but even of heaven, there is a trend towards accepting death as a part of reality, just as 'natural' as life. Churchmen, even clergymen, are dropping the traditional faith in personal survival after death, just as many unbelievers do. Curiously, it is the sceptics about immortality who appear to face death more calmly. They seem somehow less inclined to hang on desperately to life at the cost of indescribable and uncreative suffering for themselves and others.

But a painful conflict persists. For instance, not long ago a man came to me deeply depressed about his role, or lack of one, in his mother's death. She had been an invalid for years, requiring his constant care and attention. At last her illness reached a 'terminal' stage and she had to be taken to hospital. One Saturday after work when he arrived in her semi-private room the other patient greeted him by crying out, 'I think your mother has just passed away. See. Quick!' His immediate reaction was relief that her suffering, and his, were now ended; so he hesitated to act on the other patient's plea to breathe into his mother's mouth in an effort to resuscitate her. Ever since, he had been troubled by a profound sense of guilt. His 'conscience' accused him. This conflict is a 'lay' version of what many doctors, if not most, feel when they forgo some device that might sustain a patient's life a little longer. Some are comforted when their action, or inaction, is interpreted to them as a refusal to prolong the patient's *death*.

Vegetable or Human?

In truth, the whole problem of letting people 'go' in a merciful release is a relatively new one. It is largely the result of our fabulous success in medical science and technology. Not long ago, when the point of death was reached, there was usually nothing that could be done about it. Now, due to the marvels of medicine, all kinds of things can keep people 'alive' long after what used to be the final crisis. For example, there is the cardiac 'pacemaker', a machine that can restart a heart that has stopped beating. Turn off the machine, the heart stops. Is the patient alive? Is he murdered if it is taken away? Does he commit suicide if he throws it out of the window? Artificial respirators and kidneys, vital organ transplants, antibiotics, intravenous feeding—these and many other devices have the double effect of prolonging life and prolonging dying. The right to die in dignity is a problem raised more often by medicine's successes than by its failures. Consequently, there is a new dimension in the debate about 'euthanasia'. The old-fashioned question was simply this: 'May we morally do anything to put people mercifully out of hopeless misery?' But the issue now takes a more troubling twist: 'May we morally omit to do any of the ingenious things we *could* do to prolong people's suffering?'

For doctors, this dilemma challenges the Hippocratic Oath which commits them to increasingly incompatible duties—to preserve life and to relieve suffering. This conflict of conscience is steadily magnified by the swelling numbers of elderly people. Medical genius and sanitation has resulted in greater longevity for most of our population. In consequence, the predominant forms of illness are now degenerative—the maladies of age and physical failure—not the infectious diseases. Disorders in the metabolic group, renal problems, malignancy, cardio-vascular ills, are chronic rather than acute. Adults in middle life and beyond fill the beds of our hospitals, and the sixty-five-and-over class grows fastest of all. In these circumstances, many people fear the prospect of senility far more than they fear death.

Unless we face up to the facts with moral sturdiness our hospitals and homes will become mausoleums where the inmates exist in a living death. In this day of 'existential' outlook, in its religious and non-religious versions, we might think twice on Nietzsche's observation, 'In certain cases it is indecent to go on living'. Perhaps it is a supreme lack of faith and self-respect to continue, as he put it, 'to vegetate in a state of cowardly dependence upon doctors and special treatments, once the meaning of life, the right to life, has been lost'.

Consider an actual case, in a top-flight hospital. After a history of rheumatic heart disease a man was admitted with both mitral and aortic stenosis—a blockage of the heart valves by something like a calcium deposit. The arts and mechanics of medicine at once went into play. First open-heart surgery opened the mitral valve; then—the patient's heart still sluggish—the operation was repeated. But the failure of blood-pressure brought on kidney failure. While the doctors weighed a choice between a kidney transplant and an artificial kidney machine, staphylococcal pneumonia set in. Next, antibiotics were tried and failed to bring relief, driving them to try a tracheotomy. Meanwhile the heart action flagged so much that breathing failed even through the surgical throat opening. The doctors then tried oxygen through nasal tubes, and failed; next, they hooked him into an artificial respirator. For a long time, techically speaking, the machine did his breathing. Then, in spite of all their brilliant efforts, he died.

Should they have 'let him go' sooner into the Christian heaven or Lucretius's 'long good night'? If so, at what point? Would it have been 'playing God' to stop before the second operation? Before the tracheotomy? Before the respirator? Only the ignorant imagine that these are easy decisions. In practice they are complex even for those who favour merciful deaths in principle. Doctors as responsible ministers of medicine carry an awesome responsibility. Indeed, by their very use of surgical, chemical and mechanical devices they are, in a fashion, playing God. In this case from the beginning some of the doctors had little hope, but they felt obliged to do what they could. A few insisted that they had to do everything possible *even if they felt sure they would fail.* Where can we draw the line between prolonging a patient's life and prolonging his dying?

The ugly truth is that sometimes patients *in extremis* try to outwit the doctors and escape from medicine's ministrations. They swallow Kleenex to suffocate themselves, or jerk tubes out of their noses or veins, in a cat-and-mouse game of life and death which is neither merciful nor meaningful. Medical innovation makes it ever easier to drag people back to 'life' in merely physiological terms. Yet when these patients succeed in outwitting their medical ministrants, can we say that they have committed suicide in any real sense of the word? Who is actually alive in these contrivances and contraptions? In such a puppetlike state most patients are, of course, too weakened and drugged to take any truly human initiative.

The classical deathbed scene, with its loving partings and solemn last words, is practically a thing of the past. In its stead is a sedated, comatose, betubed object, manipulated and subconscious, if not subhuman. This is why, for example, one desperate woman is trying to guarantee herself a fatal heart attack to avoid anything resembling her mother's imbecile last years. It is an unnerving experience to any sensitive person to hear an intern in the terminal ward of a hospital say with defensive gallows-humour that he has to 'go water the vegetables' in their beds.

Families—and their emotional and economic resources—deserve some reckoning too. And finally, all of us are potential patients. Surely we need to give these questions a fresh look, even though the obligation lies heaviest on the leaders in medicine and allied fields.

Medical Morals and Civil Law

It is an oversimplification to think of the issue any longer as 'euthanasia' and decide for or against it. Euthanasia, meaning a merciful or good death, may be achieved by direct or indirect methods. If it is direct, a deliberate action or 'mercy-killing' to shorten or end life, it is definitely murder as the law now stands. But indirect euthanasia is another matter, the more complicated and by far the more frequent form of the problem. There are three forms it can take: (1) administering a death-dealing pain-killer, (2) ceasing treatments that prolong the patient's life—or death, if you prefer, and (3) withholding treatment altogether.

An example of the first form is the administration of morphine in doses which are pyramided to toxic, fatal proportions. The doctor has been forced to choose between doing nothing further to alleviate suffering, or giving a merciful dose which kills both the pain and the patient. Usually he chooses the latter course. An example of the second form is the hospital scene described earlier when two doctors, a resident, an intern, a chaplain and a visiting minister agreed to 'pull the plug' and disconnect the bubbling life-prolonging oxygen tank.

To illustrate the third form of indirect euthanasia we might look at this particular problem. A poliomyelitis patient, a young woman, is struck down by an extensive paralysis of the respiratory muscles. Lacking oxygen, her brain suffers irreparable damage from suffocation. She *could* be kept 'alive' for months—maybe longer—by artificial respiration through a tracheotomy. However, is there anything in moral law, either the law of nature, the law of Scripture, or the law of love, that obliges us to use such extraordinary means, such gimmicks? If we forgo their use, and let the patient die of natural asphyxiation, we have 'euthanased' in the third, indirect form. Both Protestant and Catholic teachers have favoured such a course. Or, to take another case, if a patient with incurable cancer gets pneumonia, may we morally withhold antibiotics that would cure the pneumonia and let the patient 'go', thus escaping a protracted and pain-ridden death? Roman Catholics are not so sure about this one, but most others are agreed that the best and most loving course would be to withhold the antibiotics.

Some of those who have tried to face these issues—the Euthanasia Societies in America and England, for example—have wanted to restrict both direct and indirect euthanasia to *voluntary* situations where the patient has consented. Such a concept is applicable to people, of whom there are many, who have private understandings with doctor friends and with their families in anticipation of the end. But what of the patient who has never stated his wishes and is past making a mentally competent choice? Under this code, mercy would have to be denied no matter how hideous and hopeless his suffering. Yet in modern medical practice most terminal patients are in precisely this submoral condition. Therefore, many moralists are prepared to approve even involuntary forms of indirect euthanasia. Pope Pius XII, for example, said that in deciding whether to use reanimation techniques, if life is ebbing hopelessly, doctors may cease and desist, 'to permit the patient, already virtually dead, to pass on in peace'.* This decision could be made by the family and doctor *for* the patient. In the same vein, a former Archbishop of Canterbury (Lord Lang) agreed that 'cases arise in which some means of shortening life may be justified'. Both of these Church leaders of the recent past preferred to leave the decision as to *when* in the physician's hands.

This is probably the wisest policy, provided the doctors do not take a rigid or idolatrous view of their role as 'life' savers. Medicine's achievements have created some tragic and tricky questions. Margaret Mead, the anthropologist, in a lecture on medical ethics at Harvard Medical School, called for an end to the present policy of pushing the responsibility off on physicians. It is certainly unfair to saddle the doctors with all the initiative and responsibility, to create such a 'role image' for them, when pastors and relatives might take it. There is some wisdom, nevertheless, in Pope Pius XII's injunction to the family of the dying to be guided by the doctors' advice as to *when* 'vital functions' have ceased and only minimal organic functioning continues.

The *direct* ending of a life, with or without the patient's consent, is euthanasia in its simple, unsophisticated and ethically candid form. This is opposed by many teachers, Roman Catholics and others. They claim to see a moral difference between deciding to end a life by deliberately doing something and deciding to end a life by deliberately *not* doing something. To many others this seems a very cloudy

* This pronouncement by the Pope is also cited in the essay by Professor Glanville Williams, p. 146 *n.* 10.

distinction. What, morally, is the difference between doing nothing to keep the patient alive and giving a fatal dose of a pain-killing or other lethal drug? The intention is the same, either way. A decision *not* to keep a patient alive is as morally deliberate as a decision to *end* a life. As Kant said, if we will the end we will the means. Although differences persist in its application, the *principle* of mercy-death is today definitely accepted, even in religious circles where the pressures of death-fear have been strongest. Disagreements concern only the 'operational' or practical question: who does what under which circumstances?

Doctors and laymen have asked lawmakers to legalize *direct* euthanasia, thus far unsuccessfully. While this writer's decision is in favour of the direct method, it may be necessary to settle temporarily for an intermediate step in the law. One distinguished jurist, Glanville Williams, has suggested that since there is little immediate hope of having the direct-method proposal adopted, it might be more practical to try for a law to safeguard the doctors in the *indirect* forms of mercy-death which *they are now practising anyway*, and which leading moralists of all persuasions could endorse. Such a measure would provide that a medical practitioner is not guilty of any offence if he has sought to speed or ease the death of a patient suffering a painful and fatal disease. Doctors would then have protection under the law, freedom to follow their consciences. To bring this matter into the open practice of medicine would harmonize the civil law with medical morals, which must be concerned with the quality of life, not merely its quantity.

The Vitalist Fallacy

The biggest obstacle to a compassionate and honest understanding of this problem is a superstitious concept of 'nature' inherited from an earlier, pre-scientific culture. People often feel that death should be 'natural'—that is, humanly uncontrolled and uncontrived. Sometimes they say that God works through nature; therefore any 'interference' with nature by controlling what happens *to* people in the way of illness and death interferes with God's activity. This argument has a specious aura of religious force. For example, one doctor with an eighty-three-year-old patient, paralyzed by a stroke and a half-dozen other ailments, tells the compassionate family that he will do nothing, 'leave it to God'. But God does not co-operate; their mother goes on gasping. Maybe the doctor needs a better and more creative theology.

For the fact is that medicine itself is an interference with nature. It freely co-operates with or counteracts and foils nature to fulfil humanly chosen ends. As Thomas Sydenham said three hundred years ago, medicine is 'the support of enfeebled and the coercion of outrageous nature'. Blind, brute nature imposing an agonized and prolonged death is outrageous to the limit, and to bow to it, to 'leave things in God's hands', is the last word in determinism and fatalism. It is the very opposite of a morality that prizes human freedom and loving kindness.

The right of spiritual beings to use intelligent control over physical nature rather than submit beastlike to its blind workings, is at the heart of many crucial questions. Birth control, artificial insemination, sterilization and abortion are all medically discovered ways of fulfilling and protecting human values and hopes in spite of nature's failures or foolishnesses. Death control, like birth control, is a matter of human dignity. Without it persons become puppets. To perceive this is to grasp the error lurking in the notion—widespread in medical circles—that life as such is the highest good. This kind of vitalism seduces its victims into being more loyal to the physical spark of mere biological life than to the personality values of self-possession and human integrity. The beauty and spiritual depths of human stature are what should be preserved and conserved in our value system, with the flesh as the means rather than the end. The vitalist fallacy is to view life at any old level as the highest good. This betrays us into keeping 'vegetables' going and dragging the dying back to brute 'life' just because we have the medical know-how to do it.

Medicine, however, has a duty to relieve suffering equal to preserving life. Furthermore, it needs to re-examine its understanding of 'life' as a moral and spiritual good, not merely physical. The morality of vitalism is being challenged by the morality of human freedom and dignity. Natural or physical determinism must give way to the morality of love. Doctors who will not respirate monsters at birth—the start of life—will not much longer have any part in turning people into monsters at the end of life.

W. R. Matthews

Voluntary Euthanasia: A Christian View

The proposal to legalize, under stringent conditions, voluntary euthanasia, has called forth much criticism from Christians. We ought not to be surprised at this, because the sacredness of human life and personality is a fundamental tenet of the Christian faith. Some of its earliest battles against paganism were fought against customs which presupposed that human lives could rightly be disposed of according to the convenience or pleasure of the State, or of some other human institution, such as the family. From the first the Church stood against the exposure of unwanted babies and against gladiatorial shows, in which human lives were sacrificed for the amusement of the populace. The racial theories and practices of the Nazis remind us that this emphasis on the sacredness of human personality is needed today, and I should like to make it quite clear that I have no sympathy whatever with any design either to breed or to destroy human beings for some purpose of the State. I hold firmly the doctrine of the sacredness of human personality.

When a Christian first hears of the proposal to legalize voluntary euthanasia he naturally thinks that it is a dangerous one, because it may weaken, or even seem to contradict, the principle of the sacredness of human personality. That was my own primary reaction and, therefore, I wish to treat opponents of voluntary euthanasia with respect and to recognize that they have a case. I have come, however, to believe that they are mistaken, and I will try to state briefly the reasons which have caused me to change my mind.

It seems plain to me that the principle of the sacredness of human personality cannot be stretched to cover the case of those whom the proposed legislation has in mind. We have to present to ourselves the condition of a man who is incurably ill and destined to a period of agonized suffering, relieved only by the administration of narcotic drugs. The situation here, in many instances, is that a disintegration of the personality occurs. Nothing could be more distressing than to observe the gradual degeneration of a fine and firm character into something which we hardly recognize as our friend, as the result of physical causes and of the means adopted to assuage intolerable pain. It is contended that the endurance of suffering may be a means of grace and no Christian would deny this, but I would urge that, in the case of a man whose existence is a continuous drugged dream, this cannot be alleged.

Though we must readily agree that endurance of suffering in the right spirit may be a means of grace for the deepening of the spiritual life, we are bound to hold that, in itself, suffering is evil. If it were not so, how could it be a duty to relieve it as far as we are able? We should all revolt against a person who complacently regarded the suffering of someone else as 'a blessing in disguise' and refused to do anything about it on those grounds. It seems to be an incontrovertible proposition that, when we are confronted with suffering which is wholly destructive in its consequences and, so far as we can see, could have no beneficial result, there is a prima facie duty to bring it to an end.

We sometimes hear it said that voluntary euthanasia is an attempt to interfere with the providential order of the world and to cut short the allotted span of life. It seems to be assumed by those who argue in this way that God has assigned to each one a definite number of days—'the term of his natural life'—and that to take any measure to reduce this number must in all circumstances be wrong. But we must observe that this argument would cut both ways and would equally condemn any attempt to lengthen the term. All medical treatment, which after all is an interference with the natural processes, would on this assumption be wrong, and many of us who are alive now because doctors have saved our lives have in effect no right to continue to exist in this world. Surely this view of the providential order is not the true one. Worked out to its logical conclusion it would lead to intolerable absurdities and even to the doctrine that every human effort to lengthen life or improve its condition is to be reprobated as contrary to the will of God.

No one is really prepared to act on this assumption. I suggest that a truer view of the providential order would be as follows: The Creator has given man reason, freedom and conscience and has left him with the possibility of ordering his own life within limits. He is to do the best he can with the material presented to him, and that means that it is the will of God that we should use our reason and conscience and our power to choose when we are faced with evils that have a remedy. My view of Providence then leads me to suppose that we are required by our belief in God to give the most earnest consideration to the proposal to legalize voluntary euthanasia. We are not at liberty to dismiss it on some preconceived prejudice.

The less reflective critics of voluntary euthanasia allege that it would be legalized murder, or suicide, or both. But surely before we fling these ugly words about we should be careful to inquire what we mean by them.

Legally, since the Suicide Act of 1961 (passed without any opposition), it is no longer a criminal offence for any person to commit suicide or to attempt to do so, although it remains an offence, punishable by heavy penalties, to assist a suicide. Morally the act of the suicide may be wrong because he takes his own life solely on his own judgment. It may be that he does so in a mood of despair or remorse and thus evades the responsibility of doing what he can to repair the wrong or improve the situation. He may fling away his life when there is still the possibility of service and when there are still duties to be done. The proposals for voluntary euthanasia, as advocated by the contributors to this volume, have nothing in common with this kind of suicide. The choice of the individual concerned—a person faced with hopeless and useless suffering—is submitted to the objective judgment of doctors and his decision can only be carried out with their assistance.

Murder consists in the taking of the life of another person with deliberate intention, 'with malice aforethought'. Very few people are prepared to take the command 'Thou shalt not kill' as universally applicable and admitting no exceptions. If we did so, we should all have to be vegetarians. But supposing the command to apply only to human life, we can all imagine circumstances in which it would be a duty to kill. For example, if an innocent person is being murderously assaulted and there is no other way of defending him, we ought to try to kill the assailant. The suggestion that voluntary euthanasia—under the conditions considered by the contributors to this volume—is murder, seems to me absurd. The life which is abbreviated is one which the patient ardently wishes to resign; there is no malice in the hearts of those who co-operate, but rather love and compassion; the community is not deprived of any valuable service. None of the conditions which constitute the sin of murder are present in voluntary euthanasia as envisaged in this volume.

Something must be said in reply to those who deprecate the raising of these questions and would prefer to leave things as they are. 'Why not leave it to the doctor?' they cry, imagining—I do not know with what justification—that doctors often take measures to shorten the suffering of the hopelessly ill.

This attitude appears to me to be really immoral, because it is an excuse for shuffling off responsibility. By what right do we place this terrible burden on the individual doctor? We have to remember that, as the law stands at present, if he does not do all he can to preserve the tortured life up to the last possible gasp, he renders himself liable to grave penalties—even perhaps to the charge of murder. Is this a position in which one's conscience can be easy? The answer must be, no. There is no honourable way of dealing with the question except by making up our minds whether or not voluntary euthanasia under proper safeguards is ethically justifiable and, if we decide that it is, embodying that conclusion in the law. Moreover, if the legitimacy of properly safeguarded euthanasia at the request of a patient is accepted, every sufferer *in extremis* and in severe pain has a right to be able to choose it. It is unjust that he should have to depend upon the views of the individual doctor who happens to attend him.

I have met the argument that we can never be certain that any illness is incurable; that 'while there is life there is hope'. It is of course true that we hear of remarkable recoveries which confound the prognosis of the physician. I do not disregard the potentialities of 'spiritual healing', nor would I exclude even the possibility of miracle, but I do not see how anyone who has had any experience of visiting the sick can question the proposition that there are cases where nothing but a miracle could restore the patient or stave off his dissolution within a brief period, and where nothing but useless agony can be anticipated. We cannot regulate our conduct at all unless we assume that it must be guided by the knowledge that we have. We take for granted that known causes will be followed by known effects in the overwhelming majority of cases. Any other assumption would strike at the roots of sanity.

The advance of medical science has changed the conditions of human life. It is true that the ultimate principles of Christian morals do not change. The root of all Christian morality is the injunction to love

God and our neighbour; as St Paul says, 'love is the fulfilling of the law'. But though the fundamental principles do not change, their application may differ as the needs of the time require. Rules which were once valid and useful may become obsolete and even an obstacle to the true 'fulfilling of the law'. We must beware lest, in holding fast to 'the letter', we betray 'the spirit'. In my belief it is the vocation of the Christian to be alert to see where the law of love points to 'new duties'.

The great master-principle of love and its child, compassion, should impel us to support measures which would make voluntary euthanasia lawful and which, as stated by the Euthanasia Society, 'would permit an adult person of sound mind, whose life is ending with much suffering, to choose between an easy death and a hard one, and to obtain medical aid in implementing that choice'.

Luke Gormally

A Non-Utilitarian Case against Voluntary Euthanasia[1]*

In the debate about voluntary euthanasia there have been a number of impressive contributions in recent years arguing that it is in all circumstances wrong and that it ought not to be legalized.[2] Usually these contributions have presented their conclusions as particular applications of a more general understanding of the nature of morality and moral reasoning.[3] A fully adequate discussion of the issues arising in this debate would involve pursuing a range of questions of a more general kind. Though desirable in itself, such a discussion would distract attention from the case against voluntary euthanasia. So this essay does not aim to be comprehensive. Rather, as a contribution to public debate, it seeks to focus on the most fundamental issue which divides adversaries in the debate: the nature of human life and dignity.

Readers seeking a comprehensive treatment of the topic can consult the fuller discussions referred to. In regard to the specific debate about legalization they will also wish to read the contribution by Professor Yale Kamisar in the present collection. Professor Kamisar offers weighty reasons, which he himself describes as utilitarian in character, for thinking that voluntary euthanasia ought not to be legalized. The present essay may be thought of as complementing Professor Kamisar's. It concentrates primarily on the morality of voluntary euthanasia, and offers reasons of a non-utilitarian kind (i.e. reasons which refer not to the consequences of engaging in euthanasia but to the kind of act it is) for an adverse judgment both on the morality of euthanasia and on the proposal to legalize it.

It should be noted that the main argument advanced in this essay against the morality and lawfulness of voluntary euthanasia is one which does not rely on specifically religious premises. The writer does

* The notes for this article will be found on pp. 90–5.

hold that revealed truths about the nature of man offer powerful reasons for thinking voluntary euthanasia in all circumstances impermissible. But in the present essay he seeks to address those who do not accept that there is such a thing as a body of revealed truth. Many advocates of voluntary euthanasia are secular humanists. Frequently, it seems, they erroneously assume that a case against voluntary euthanasia can be made out only within a framework of religious belief.

The essay falls into four main sections. The first (1 a–k) outlines an argument, which is essentially simple in structure, showing that voluntary euthanasia is never morally acceptable. The second section (2 a–b) identifies two principle assumptions which advocates of voluntary euthanasia make in arguing that it is sometimes morally acceptable and that it ought to be treated as legally permissible. Each of these assumptions is shown to be unsatisfactory. In the third section a contrast is drawn between the conception of the value of human life (and therefore dignity) presented in the first section of the essay and the conception of the value of human life (and dignity) which proponents of voluntary euthanasia characteristically invoke. The contrast has implications for many other debates about particular questions of morality and public policy. Finally, in the fourth section, brief consideration is given to the proposal that voluntary euthanasia should be legalized.

1. An Argument to Show that Voluntary Euthanasia Cannot Be Reasonable

(a) Voluntary euthanasia is not simply suicide and it is a mistake to think that the view one takes of the ethics of voluntary euthanasia can be settled by the view one takes of the ethics of suicide. Much writing on the subject assumes that if one can show that suicide might be reasonable, it is sufficient to add to this demonstration no more than a reference to the idea of autonomy in order to show that voluntary euthanasia might be reasonable. If it can be right for people to kill themselves, it is claimed, we should recognize that those who are incapable of carrying out the deadly deed are entitled, in virtue of their right to self-determination, to have others do it for them.

Voluntary euthanasia is not a mere extension of the self-determination which is exercised in suicide. If Dr Jones kills Mrs Smith at Mrs

Smith's request it is necessary that Dr Jones should have a good reason for doing so. Dr Jones is not a mere instrument of Mrs Smith's will; he is a responsible agent answerable for what he does. Voluntary euthanasia is precisely not an exercise of self-determination on the part of the one who dies.

(b) It is agreed on both sides of the debate that the mere fact of a request from Mrs Smith for euthanasia does not supply Dr Jones with a good reason to carry out the deed. The request may be prompted by false beliefs and unfounded fears. Whether voluntary euthanasia is or is not morally acceptable depends on whether Dr Jones can have in principle a good reason for killing Mrs Smith when Mrs Smith asks to be killed.

(c) Advocates of voluntary euthanasia claim that good reason can be supplied by the wretched condition of Mrs Smith and the view she takes of it. It is open to a patient to take one of a number of quite different views of her condition when, typically, that condition is degenerative, involves intensifying (and possibly intractable) pain, and increasing dependence on others. The patient's responses may include the following:

> (i) the decision to endure suffering, prompted by the thought that her situation calls for courage and by the belief that the human spirit can grow even in circumstances of extreme deprivation;
>
> (ii) the decision to refuse anything but palliative treatment and ordinary nursing care in the belief that she has no duty to strive to prolong her life, accompanied by the hope that she can endure what she has to endure, since she does not think it right to aim to shorten her sufferings by terminating her life;
>
> (iii) the decision to seek to have her life terminated, since she believes her life no longer possesses value; there is nothing to live for, since she is conscious of nothing but pain, thinks of dependence as indignity, and believes that in these respects her situation can only worsen.

Response (iii) is a euthanasiast response. The patient's outlook on life is such that pain, dependency and deprivation are experienced as rendering that life without value and possibly without meaning.

Whatever the range of considerations that influence the decision to seek an end of one's life, they will be thought of as lending support to the conclusion 'I no longer have a worthwhile life'; for it is *this* conclusion which purports to make the decision for euthanasia reasonable. Whether the conclusion is expressed or not, considerations which are taken to amount to that conclusion are relied on in any decision for euthanasia which claims to be reasonable. For it would not be thought reasonable to seek to have one's life ended if one thought it worthwhile.

(d) The purpose of section 1 of this essay is to inquire not into the reasonableness of the practical conclusions of the one seeking to die but rather into the reasonableness of the decision taken by the one who carries out the killing. Now the one who is to execute euthanasia will need, as someone thinking in a euthanasiast framework, to assure himself that the person seeking to die no longer has a worthwhile life. It is some such thought which purports to make euthanasia reasonable. For an advocate of euthanasia would think it unreasonable to accede to a request for euthanasia if he thought the person making the request had a worthwhile life.

So we must ask ourselves whether human lives can be truly evaluated in this way—that is, whether assessments in terms of 'worthwhileness' give an adequate and true account of the value of a human life.

What kind of judgment is being made when a human life is assessed as worthwhile or not worthwhile? The account of what is involved differs in detail from one thinker to another. Some think that all that goes into making such a judgment is a calculation of the balance between pleasure and pain in a human life; a surplus of pleasure over pain means that life has positive utility, it is 'worthwhile'. Conversely, a surplus of pain over pleasure means that life has negative utility, that it is not 'worthwhile'. This is the mode of assessing a life advocated by classical (or Benthamite) utilitarians. Other kinds of utilitarians wish to take account of more than pleasure and pain in assessing the value of human activity and human lives: a variety of types of achievement may be held to confer value on a life. But whatever variety of factors are allowed to count in assessing the value of a life, in one crucial respect that assessment always has the same character. It presumes to offer a total summation of the present 'worthwhileness' of a life (in this sense it may be spoken of as a 'global assessment')[4] and in undertaking to do so it is involved in a calculation and balancing of values and disvalues present or realizable in a human life.[5] But the idea that one can carry out some such calculation and balancing itself assumes that all values are reducible to a common measure, and that one can be traded off against another. What is false is the belief that the value of a human life can be adequately expressed as the outcome of a calculation.[6]

(e) Anyone who recognizes the dimension of spirit[7] characteristic of human life should realize the inadequacy of putative global assessments of the value of a particular human life. We can come to recognize this inadequacy by reflecting on the manifestations of spirit. Such manifestations are many; as material for reflection here I choose a central manifestation which itself bears directly on our theme: the acknowledgement of certain absolute[8] claims on human allegiance and human living. The claims of truth and justice are recognized as binding in ways which do not make sense on any utilitarian conception of what it is to be reasonable. Respect for truth and the requirements of justice do not enter into our thinking about what to do as considerations on a par with a whole range of other considerations, all being measured on some common scale with a view to calculating the balance of utility or disutility, worthwhileness or lack of worthwhileness. The example of Socrates in refusing to be party to the murder of Leon of Salamis brings out the point:

> The Thirty Commissioners summoned me and four others to the Round Chamber and ordered us to go and fetch Leon of Salamis from his home for liquidation . . . their object being to implicate as many people as possible in their evil. . . . When we came out of the Round Chamber the other four went off to Salamis and arrested Leon, and I went home.[9]

Socrates' refusal to collaborate exemplifies the belief that it is better to suffer evil than to do evil (for it was likely that his refusal would lead to his own unjust killing). What underlies this belief is a certain understanding of the nature of human responsibility: the intentional doing of wrong to another is not merely the bringing about of one undesirable state of affairs in the world; it is both the doing of injustice and the corruption of oneself. A utilitarian framework of thought obscures these truths, for, as part of the scheme for reducing values to a common measure, the utilitarian locates value exclusively in states of affairs (and so characteristically assesses human action by reference to the states of affairs which are the consequences of action).[10] Faced with Socrates' choice, a utilitarian might think that since the foreseeable outcome of a refusal to collaborate with the Thirty Commissioners will be two deaths (Leon's death and his own death), whereas the likely outcome of collaboration will be one death (that of Leon), it would in the circumstances be reasonable to collaborate. Now clearly for Socrates such a proposal was not to be entertained. It was not to be entertained because it would have amounted to gross injustice to Leon (treated as disposable for Socrates' advantage), and would have corrupted and dishonoured Socrates' own humanity.[11] (Note that it is not essential to the argument here to show that all utilitarians must embrace the practical conclusion of the collaborator. What is crucial to the argument is the claim that the collaborator cannot be shown to be wrong on the basis of utilitarian considerations.)

Socrates' example brings out a fundamental truth about human responsibility and thereby a fundamental truth about the way human beings are to be valued. His example shows that when a man is thinking about doing something proposed to him, the thought of what he will make of himself by so acting does not enter into his deliberation simply as the thought of one more desirable or undesirable state of affairs which he might bring about in the world. What a person makes of himself in and through what he does is an ineliminable part of his responsibility: that part which concerns the very character of his humanity. So the claims that truth and justice make upon us are claims in which the character of our humanity is at stake. To refuse those claims is to dishonour our humanity. That is why the value we recognize in truth and justice shows the way in which human beings are to be valued.[12]

(f) Regard for justice exhibits what has been referred to as the dimension of spirit in man and thereby shows itself to rest on the recognition of that dimension. For it is characteristic of the just man to refuse to treat a human being as though the value of that person could be expresssed by reference to some calculation of utility. In particular, human beings may not be killed simply for some advantage to be gained thereby. Only if in some sense a man *deserves* death do we say it is just to kill him intentionally. Implicit in the idea of desert is a recognition of man as spirit; for, unlike the other animals, he is answerable for what he does, since he can know the difference between good and evil and it is up to him which he chooses. Justice rests on this high conception of human dignity.

It will be remembered that what we are discussing here is not justice in its own right but rather what human regard for justice shows about the character of human life: that dimension of it which has been named 'spirit'. Since regard for justice exhibits that valuation of human life which is associated with the recognition of spirit. Human life is not something that can enter into our calculations of utility or advantage, as if it were reducible to a common scale of value. If you judge that it is reasonable to kill someone on the grounds that he has not got a worthwhile life, you will not only be making that judgment on grounds that fail to respect human dignity; you will be at least implicitly denying that in human life which constitutes our dignity.

To learn about human dignity is like learning the meaning of a word: you show you know the meaning of a word by using it correctly. Similarly you show you know about human dignity by treating human beings justly.[13]

(g) Humans can be touched by exemplary witnesses to the true character of human dignity, and touched in ways which help them to respect that dignity in their own persons. There is a chain of such witnesses through human history, people who have recognized the costly demands of justice and truth, and in particular have recognized that it is better to suffer evil than to do evil. In our own day, when Václav Benda was released after serving a four-year term in a Czech prison for refusing to collaborate with the political police by condemning a civil rights manifesto which he had not seen, he simply said: 'There is this commandment "Thou shalt not bear false witness".'[14] Benda's attitude is no more explicable in utilitarian terms than Socrates' attitude. Their refusals to collaborate were not based on any calculation of how to maximize pleasure, advantage, satisfaction of preferences, or any other utility. What makes sense of each of their uncompromising stances is the belief that there are values which can make absolute claims on human beings, claims which we must meet if we are to hold in honour our dignity as persons—that is, our dignity as beings who can become good through choosing to honour truth and justice. And the root of that goodness lies in the purity with which we love those goods which make us good.

Purity of heart is a kind of nonsense for a utilitarian. Killing which is unjust, and lies, may be thought required and justifiable in pursuit of those objectives he sets himself.[15]

Defences of euthanasia find their ultimate rationale in the claim that the person to be killed does not have a worthwhile life, and that claim in turn rests on the belief that an adequate account of the value of a human life can be arrived at by some calculation of the ingredient factors thought relevant. Whatever range of factors may be taken account of in the calculation, the reality of spirit is not among them, since it is not something which is reducible to the terms in which the calculation is necessarily made.

So a judgment that someone does not have a worthwhile life is neither an adequate nor a true judgment on the value of a human life. That is why killing which rests for its justification on such a judgment is not reasonable and is unjust.

(h) Propaganda for euthanasia is of course directed towards denying the reality of spirit: for that reason it has the character, in D. H. Lawrence's phrase, of doing dirt on life. It presses upon us an impoverished and reduced understanding of human life and human possibilities. In so far as the propaganda succeeds, it blinds people to the nature of their humanity (they come to think their value is entirely a matter of what they can bring about which might count as evidence of 'worthwhileness'), or at least it discourages them from respecting their humanity.

(i) A euthanasiast might claim to concede some recognition of the reality of spirit, but hold one or other of two positions about the spiritual. He might hold that if the spiritual is anything it is merely one among the pleasures or the satisfactions which is to be counted in our reckoning of utilities: it is one of the things which may convey utility to a life. According to this view, it remains that the value of a life is to be understood entirely by reference to the calculation of utilities. But it belongs to the very nature of spirit to reject what Wordsworth called 'the lore of nicely calculated less or more' when it comes to principles of conduct. That is what the examples of Socrates and Václav Benda show.

(j) The second position which a euthanasiast might conceivably hold is that the spiritual is, indeed, the truly valuable thing about man and that man, in consequence, is to be valued only when he is able to manifest the spiritual; the spiritual exists only in those in full command of their mental faculties. It is true, of course, that the references which have been made to Socrates and Václav Benda are to persons in mature possession of their powers, and the manifestations of the spirit are manifestations of an active power. But what makes a human being liable to have such powers is a (second-order) capacity to develop them,[16] a capacity characteristic of human nature, just as characteristic as the human powers we see exercised. Since the manifestations of spirit consist in the exercise of active powers, and these powers have their roots, so to speak, in a radical capacity characteristic of human nature, then the dimension of spirit is essential to the human species. A human being belongs to this (essentially spiritual) species at every stage of his development and deterioration, as a frog belongs to its (essentially vertebrate) species at every stage of its development.[17] The alternative to a unitary view of man which would also seek to accommodate the reality of 'spirit' is some form of dualism. (On dualistic assumptions about the nature of human life in arguments for euthanasia, see 2a below.)

If human beings are essentially spiritual as well as essentially fleshly, each human life presents us with a mystery which, if recognized, will not allow us to think that a utilitarian judgment on the worthwhileness of a life exhaustively states the value of that life. For the value inherent in that life is not reducible to the terms of utilitarian reckoning. If you decide to kill someone because you think his life is not worthwhile, you show yourself blind to the nature of human dignity.

(k) Because the crucial judgment required to rationalize euthanasia is a judgment that the person to die does not have a worthwhile life—because it is this judgment which bears the onus of justifying the killing—there is a logical connection between voluntary euthanasia on the one hand and non-voluntary and involuntary euthanasia on the other.[18] If this judgment is justificatory in voluntary euthanasia, why should it cease to have justificatory force when the killing of the incompetent and unwilling sick is contemplated? For, as has been noted already (1c above), even in voluntary euthanasia the mere fact that Mrs Smith asked Dr Jones to kill her is not considered to provide reason for Dr Jones to comply with the request. Reason for killing is thought to derive rather from the consideration that Dr Jones (along with Mrs Smith) thinks Mrs Smith no longer has a worthwhile life.

Historically, there is a very close connection between the voluntary euthanasia movement and the objective of legalizing non-voluntary euthanasia. It is clear that many members of the movement have seen and continue to see the legalizing of voluntary euthanasia as a strategic move towards the longer term goal of legalizing non-voluntary euthanasia.[19] Chesterton's observation about the aspirations of propagandists for voluntary euthanasia is still accurate: 'Some are proposing what is called euthanasia; at present only a proposal for killing those who are a nuisance to themselves; but soon to be applied to those who are a nuisance to other people.'[20]

The point being made in this essay about the connection between voluntary and non-voluntary euthanasia needs to be distinguished both from the point about the historical connection between advocacy of voluntary and of non-voluntary euthanasia, and from a second point: the claim that if voluntary euthanasia is legalized, non-voluntary euthanasia will be legalized thereafter. That claim is a prediction which, though highly plausible in the view of the present writer, just might be falsified.

The fundamental connection, to which attention is being drawn here, is between the pattern of thought which seeks to justify voluntary euthanasia and the pattern of thought which seeks to justify non-voluntary euthanasia. In voluntary euthanasia the real onus of justification is borne by this judgment: X (Mrs Smith) does not have a worthwhile life. But if it is possible to make such a judgment, and if such a judgment justifies the killing of a human being, what *logically* is to stop the claim that non-voluntary euthanasia is justifiable? If the value of a human life can truly be assessed in terms of function and utility, why should we not kill those whom we judge to be useless? This question ought to make advocates of voluntary euthanasia pause. The first part of the present essay is intended to suggest to them that, consciously or not, they have embraced a false valuation of human life which alone makes voluntary euthanasia seem reasonable. The logic of that false valuation reaches well beyond voluntary euthanasia.

2. *Two Doubtful Assumptions of Euthanasiast Argument*

(a) Advocates of voluntary euthanasia are apt to see human dignity as something that waxes and wanes, and this view is often tied to a dualistic conception of man in the sense that the person is thought of as something other than the human body.[21] Dignity is said to attach to 'personality', but personality is distinguished from 'mere biological life'.[22] 'Biological life' is understood as no more than a precondition of personal life, which itself is understood to be a function of the exercise of conscious abilities. What is valuable in human life is entirely a matter of conscious satisfactions (to the securing of which utilitarian calculation is directed).

Sometimes the ravages of sickness are spoken of as destroying the person, so that it is appropriate to characterize the continuing life of the human being as that of a subhuman animal or even a vegetable. A very clear expression of this view is to be found in the Foreword to the present volume (p. 7):

> If we take the view that what is essentially human in the life that we share with the animal and vegetable kingdoms is the capacity for thought and love and aesthetic experience, and that this capacity makes us a person in the true sense of the word, we cannot wish to preserve an anonymous individual who has been stripped of personality and reduced by incessant pain or physical deterioration to the animal or vegetable level.

Maybe some such conception informs the view one often hears expressed that if we 'put down' animals when they are in intractable pain we should kill human beings when they too suffer intractable pain.

Dualism is also transparent in the way euthanasiasts refer to the body as 'property'. Human beings are said to 'own' their bodies, and because they own them they are entitled to dispose of them. This sort of dualism seems to be a deeply embedded assumption in much advocacy of euthanasia. It is hardly possible to debate the merits of dualism within the confines of this essay. It is, however, worth noting that some of the most widely admired work in philosophy over the past fifty years has been associated with the overthrow of dualism in modern philosophical anthropology and philosophical psychology. Perhaps continuing advocacy of euthanasia in part reflects what little effect the revolution in this sector of philosophy has had on secularist ethics.

A defensible alternative to dualism understands the life of a human being as the life of a substantial organic unity. There are many *kinds* of organism; 'human' names one kind. The life of an individual human being is a unified life, it belongs to it in its totality. When we speak of an organism as existing, we mean it is alive. Life, like existence, is not one among a number of characteristics of living beings. The life of a living thing belongs to it in its totality. There is a unified life, the nature of which differs with each kind of organism. In the course of individual growth and development this life will be more or less fully manifested in and through the development of characteristic capacities. The life of a human being, and so the life of a human person, is manifested both in thought and in heartbeat, in choice and in respiration. To be a human person is to be a live human body.

Given this background understanding of human life, it is a gross error to speak of 'mere biological life'. Life is not a generic property common to all organisms. The life of individual organisms differs in kind according to the species to which the organisms belong. However underdeveloped or reduced the life of an individual human being may be, that life is human, and therefore personal. That life cannot be the life of another kind of animal or the life of some kind of vegetable.

Since life belongs to the totality of an organism, and since the life characteristic of a human organism is personal life, the body is not a 'subpersonal' condition of 'personhood', nor is bodily life to be thought of as merely instrumental for the development of other abilities which are supposed to be distinctively personal, so that life could be disposed of when those abilities wane and fail.

Finally, our bodies are not property. If our bodies were property, what account would have to be given of the 'self' which owns that property? Our selves are bodily. The view that human bodily life is not truly personal life runs deep through propaganda for euthanasia. It makes for the profoundest difference between the traditional conception of human dignity and the conception of dignity invoked by euthanasiasts (see section 3 below).

(b) Advocacy of voluntary euthanasia and its legalization typically relies on a second set of assumptions. Jurisprudents like Professor

Glanville Williams, who are classical liberals in the tradition of J. S. Mill, rest a large part of their case for the legalization of voluntary euthanasia on the claim that a man should be at liberty to pursue whichever of his desires causes no harm to his fellow human beings. Such liberty is said to be the precondition of respect for autonomy and self-determination.[23]

We need to take a critical look, however briefly, at the notions of autonomy and self-determination. Is it the case that the true precondition of autonomy and self-determination is a liberty which is to be constrained only by considerations of harm to one's fellow human beings? We can set aside the difficulties associated with giving content to the idea of 'harm', since deeper difficulties must arise for the liberal from consideration of what is involved in autonomy.

It could hardly be argued that political freedom or liberty is to be prized if it simply means the freedom to fulfil whatever desires people *happen* to have. Our sense of the value of freedom must derive from our sense of the value of that development in human lives in virtue of which human beings come to be able to distinguish between intrinsically worthwhile and worthless desires. Satisfaction of some desires makes for human fulfilment, satisfaction of others for human misery. In so far as human beings are able to identify with intrinsically worthwhile desires and to engage in stable commitments and projects in pursuit of the realization of those desires, they show themselves to be human beings who have achieved autonomy or a state of genuine self-determination. Political freedom is valuable in providing opportunity for the exercise of autonomy in this sense.

But this ideal development could not have been achieved without the existence of institutions (such as the family, the school, the university) which impose constraints conducive to the formation of genuinely autonomous persons. So the existence of autonomous agents *presupposes* constraints. You will not get the development of autonomous agents in a political arrangement in which the only acceptable ground for constraints is the avoidance of non-consensual harm to others (i.e. harm to persons to which those persons have not consented).

Now, clearly, one of the institutions whose constraints are conducive to the formation of the autonomous individual is the criminal law. Knowledge that one lives in a society governed by canons of justice provides a sense of elementary security, without which there cannot be that sense of belonging to a community which is so conducive to nurturing autonomy. It would be radically destructive of this arrangement if it became lawful to kill a person because 'he did not have a worthwhile life' (on this see further section 4 below). So a true sense of the requirements for autonomy ought to lead us to reject the legalization of voluntary euthanasia.

3. *Competing Conceptions of Human Life and Human Dignity*

If the argument in section 1 is correct, at the heart of the euthanasia debate is a deep difference of belief about the valuation to be placed on human life. If it is true that there is a dimension of spirit in human life, a dimension manifested in the respect human beings can show for the absolute claims certain basic values make upon them (claims unintelligible in terms merely of utility), we are faced with a kind of life whose value is not reducible to any capacity to achieve utilitarian satisfactions. How can we fail to register the distinctive dignity of a being capable of a martyr's testimony to the claims of truth (a testimony given, perhaps, in the midst of prolonged suffering)?[24] This is a manifestation of the *kind* of life of which human beings are capable, a kind of life which transcends utilitarian categories of value.

To be human is to share a particular kind of life, the capacities for entering into which we develop in the course of growth. It is only human beings, however, who become developed human beings. The kind of individual who becomes a developed human being, with the abilities that we think of as most distinctively personal, would not have been capable of that development unless it was all along in his nature so to develop. This radical developmental capacity must be one in nature with the developed personal abilities which fully exhibit its nature. In other words there is no such thing as an individual human being whose life is not personal in character.

Because this unitary view of man underlies the traditional ethic of respect for life, and because that life is of a kind which transcends utilitarian categories of value, then that life in none of its phases is to be intentionally destroyed on the basis of a utilitarian valuation ('unlikely to yield a balance of pleasure over pain, or satisfaction over dissatisfaction'; 'no further use'; 'grossly diminished function').

On a unitary view of man, the most fundamental value of our lives is *given* in and with the bodily reality of each of us. This is a value which exists in advance of any particular achievement. To cherish and care for a human life in the most fragile phases of its existence is to recognize this fundamental value. The respect to be accorded to this value is shown in the nurturing given by good parents to young children in the vulnerable beginnings of their lives, and in turn is shown in the *pietas* which informs the care given by grown children to parents in their years of fragile decline.

The valuation of human life here defended belongs with acceptance of the vulnerabilities and fragilities of the human condition. Because the body is intrinsic to our personal lives (and not a merely instrumental condition of those lives), our profound dependence as bodies both on other persons (first of all our biological parents) and on the natural environment is intrinsic to our personal existence. Dependency, fragility, vulnerability are not subversive of the dignity of human beings. For to live with dignity is to live in accordance with a true estimate of the nature of the human condition. Isolated individualism and the refusal of dependence betray a false valuation of human life—one which locates value exclusively in personal achievements, and fails to see the more fundamental value which belongs to each of us and which is a gift to those who acknowledge it.

The euthanasiast, whose outlook is governed by utilitarian values and a dualistic understanding of man, fails to understand the value which inheres in and is given with human bodily existence. For the typical advocate of euthanasia, such value as attaches to human life is a matter of individual achievement. A life which may be thought to have little prospect of achieving a surplus of pleasure over pain, or of otherwise satisfactory conscious experience over unsatisfactory conscious experience, will be judged to be a life lacking in value. Nothing is recognized as standing in the way of a decision intentionally to terminate a life judged to be not worth living. It is this judgment, as we have seen, which carries the burden of justifying euthanasia, whether voluntary, non-voluntary or involuntary.

The euthanasiast's conception of human dignity is shallow and no guarantee of justice (see section 4 below). Since many human beings are reckoned to lack a worth which should be honoured in them, they may be exploited and disposed of. The intellectual defence of euthanasia is of a piece with many forms of exploitation of the weak by the powerful, which characteristically rely on defining the weak as in some way lacking the dignity and claims to respect owing to the powerful. Opposition to such exploitation tends to rely on a doctrine of human equality, but this doctrine makes sense only if we see value in the one respect in which human beings are indeed equal—that they are all living members of the human race. If humanity itself—mere humanity—has no value, to say that all men are equal is empty rhetoric. But there is a real point in saying that all men are equal: we do not choose whom to treat justly and whom not to treat justly, but we apply questions of right and desert to all without exception. And if we can forget questions of desert when thinking about killing someone, we can put people outside considerations of justice altogether.[25]

The profound affinity that the intellectual defence of euthanasia has with the defence of exploitation must surely, once recognized, be a source of unease to those who have joined the movement for euthanasia out of what they think to be mercy and compassion. But mercy—true mercy—cannot find expression in destruction. Mercy recognizes the claims of the other on our care.

4. *The Proposed Legalization of Voluntary Euthanasia*

It has been said about views which stand opposed to euthanasia that: 'Since the laws of a country apply impartially to all its citizens, it is morally wrong for any law to reflect a contentious sectarian viewpoint.'[26]

The challenge that is being thrown down here is one which touches the moral basis of our homicide laws. Two points should be noted about the circumstances in which it has been considered justifiable intentionally to kill[27] another human being. First, traditional defences of killing in capital punishment and warfare are defences of killing authorized by civil authority, not of private killing (as in euthanasia). Euthanasia could never be truly authorized by civil authority, since what legitimizes the use of the sword by civil authority is the citizen's need of protection against *unjust* attack. If civil authority itself kills the innocent or purports to legitimize killing of the innocent, it removes the basis of its authority to use the sword.[28]

Second, truly lawful killing, when it exists, proceeds on a conception of justice: the one who is killed is thought of as *deserving* death. Implicit in this idea of desert is a recognition of man as spirit: that, unlike the other animals, he is answerable for what he does, since he can know the difference between good and evil and it is up to him which he chooses. So to kill a man because he deserves it is to act on a high conception of human dignity.

As we have seen, it is just this conception of human dignity which the euthanasiast requires to repudiate in order to make euthanasia seem justifiable. But what he thereby repudiates is the foundation of the canons governing the just treatment of human beings and not some merely 'contentious sectarian viewpoint'.

The laws of our country with regard to homicide (with the exception of abortion legislation) do respect the conception of human life and human dignity defended in this essay. Intentional killing is lawful only if it is authorized by civil authority and only if the person to be killed can be said to have deserved death.

Killing which seeks justification in the judgment that someone does not have a worthwhile life is killing which is proposed on a false valuation of human life. To make such killing legal would be to legalize killing, the rationale for which is that it is advantageous even though it is not just. As such it would represent a radical departure from those canons of justice which have governed the law of homicide and thereby protected human beings.

In his scholarly article of 1958, 'Some Non-Religious Views against Proposed "Mercy-Killing" Legislation', Professor Yale Kamisar foresaw among 'the possible radiations from the proposed legislation' that ought to give us 'cause to pause', 'the emergence of the legal precedent that there are lives "not worth living"'.[29] If there is truth in the contentions of the present essay, that would be a necessary rather than a possible consequence of legalizing voluntary euthanasia. And a consequence which, the evidence suggests, militant advocates of legislation would welcome.

It is not always the case that what is morally undesirable should be legally prohibited. If, however, what it is proposed to permit would subvert the most elementary canons of justice required for the protection of human life, we have every reason vigorously to oppose that proposal.

Conclusion

In section 1 of this essay the writer argued that acceding to a request for euthanasia (and so killing another person) could be made to seem reasonable only if the judgment that the person to die did not have a worthwhile life provided a sound basis for killing a human being. A judgment of that kind, or considerations amounting to such a judgment, are required to make euthanasia seem reasonable, in the sense that not even advocates of euthanasia would deem it reasonable to kill a person whom they judged to have a worthwhile life.

Against this cornerstone of the euthanasiast's position, it was argued that a judgment about the worthwhileness of another person's life could not in principle be a reasonable basis for killing that person. For such a judgment expresses a calculation of another's value (whether as productive of pleasure, or satisfaction of preferences, or of some other utility) which ignores the dimension of spirit characteristic of human life. The nature of that dimension is shown centrally by the way human beings can recognize and respond to certain absolute claims upon them, in particular those of justice. The nature and absoluteness of the requirements of justice are a manifestation of the honour due to our humanity and thus of the dignity of all humanity. The examples of a Socrates or a Václav Benda show that a man would dishonour *his own* humanity if he treated human beings in accordance with any other view of *their* humanity than that implied in the requirements of justice. On these requirements human life is not such that it may be terminated according to some utilitarian calculation of advantage. The only reason for killing a man which is consistent with recognizing the true dignity of human beings is that the man deserves death. There is room for debate about the circumstances in which it may be reasonable to say that a man deserves death; there can be no doubt that human pain, misery and dependence are not among them.

ACKNOWLEDGEMENTS

My thinking was first set in the direction taken in section 1 of this essay by Professor Elizabeth Anscombe's contributions to the Linacre Centre Working Party which produced the Report *Euthanasia and Clinical Practice*. However, what I have written does not reflect the complexity, depth and refinement of her thinking on the topic of killing.

I should also like to acknowledge a general debt to the writings of John Finnis, as well as to his encouragement and support.

More immediate debts in the writing and revision of the paper have been incurred. I am grateful to Peter Corbishley and John Finnis, and to my colleagues Fred Fitzpatrick and Teresa Iglesias, for their detailed comments on a first draft. My greatest debt is to Mary Geach, who commented on the first draft and gave me the benefit of detailed suggestions and generous help in revising it. Any defects in the final version reflect only on the writer.

NOTES

These Notes should of course be read in conjunction with the Rejoinder by Barbara Smoker on pp. 96–109.

[1] The opportunity was taken in writing the final draft of this essay to expand some notes and add others in order to meet points made in Barbara Smoker's Rejoinder. It should be noted that in accepting the invitation to contribute to the present volume I did not undertake to make a distinctively Roman Catholic contribution, since such an undertaking seemed likely to be unprofitable. I had hoped that an essay which did not rest its arguments on any revealed truths might lead to a fruitful exchange. I do not think Barbara Smoker's Rejoinder demonstrates that my argument rests on assumptions in principle inaccessible to the humanist. In the latter part of the Rejoinder she takes as her target official statements of the Roman Catholic Church. Her criticisms do not seem to me well taken, since she overlooks the central importance of the idea of intention (and of what a person 'intentionally' brings about) both in the Catholic moral tradition and in the tradition of common morality (see *n.* 27 below). I have discussed the topics of killing and letting die and of ordinary and extraordinary means elsewhere, in *Is There a Morally Significant Difference between Killing and Letting Die?* (Linacre Centre Paper 2, London, Linacre Centre, 1978) and *Ordinary and Extraordinary Means of Prolonging Life* (Linacre Centre Paper 3, London, Linacre Centre, 1979).

[2] See, among others, Germain Grisez and Joseph M. Boyle, Jr., *Life and Death with Liberty and Justice: A Contribution to the Euthanasia Debate* (Notre Dame, Ind., and London: University of Notre Dame Press, 1979); Philip E. Devine, *The Ethics of Homicide* (Ithaca, N.Y., and London: Cornell University Press, 1978).

[3] Barbara Smoker is mistaken in thinking that the Catholic moral tradition characteristically regards 'moral norms' as self-evident. Aquinas, who can be taken to be a classical exponent of that tradition, did indeed hold that the first principles (i.e. the starting-points) of moral reasoning were in some sense self-evident. However, these 'self-evident' first principles are not moral principles but basic goods: those intrinsically valuable goods which give point to our activities and striving and which are constitutive of human flourishing. That these goods are basic is obvious to a person with some experience of pursuing what is valuable for its own sake. Relative to these goods, moral norms or principles are derivative: they state the general requirements which, in so far as

they inform choice, lead to participation in the basic goods of a kind which makes for flourishing. (On these points see John Finnis, *Natural Law and Natural Rights*, Oxford: Clarendon Press, 1980, chaps 3–5.)

[4] Barbara Smoker claims that the justification for killing in the case of voluntary euthanasia does not rest, as I state, on a 'global assessment' of the value of a particular human life, but on 'searching assessments both of the subjective rationality of the person who wishes to die and of the objective reasonableness of that wish'. But what are the criteria of reasonableness? Ms Smoker gets round to saying that they do concern 'the worthwhileness' of a life, but not, she claims, in the sense I use the term. However, the judgment that a life is 'not worthwhile' on her own analysis rests on a calculation that a person has 'irremediable negative experiences that far outweigh the positive ones at the present time and in the likely future'. Such a calculation looks like an attempt at a 'global assessment'. How does Ms Smoker think she can carry out the calculation, given the fundamental problem posed for all such attempts by the incommensurability of values (see *n.* 6 below)? Barbara Smoker's proposed calculation also assumes that there is nothing to the value of a life other than 'valuable' ('positive') experiences. My own essay proposes a radically different view of the value of human lives, lacking which we also lack a conception of justice (see *n.* 15 below for Ms Smoker's views on 'just killing').

[5] The possibility of some such calculation seems to be assumed in the following statement by Barbara Smoker in 'The Moral Case for Voluntary Euthanasia' (radio script for a BBC World Service programme broadcast in January 1984): 'The principle of utilitarianism, which advocates the maximization of happiness, also advocates the minimization of suffering. To those of us who accept this principle of moral philosophy, life's value depends on the experiences that it brings, and the states of mind at the receiving end. Clearly, then, the experiences of those suffering from incurable conditions that they themselves find consistently intolerable must constitute adequate grounds on utilitarian principles for terminating their lives.'

[6] On the impossibility of such calculation because of the incommensurability of the basic values constitutive of human flourishing, see Germain Grisez, 'Against Consequentialism', *American Journal of Jurisprudence*, 23 (1978), 21–62. Any form of consequentialism, whether Benthamite utilitarianism or not, assumes that the values which are at stake in human life, and which may be realized in human choice, are commensurable (i.e. measurable on a common scale); otherwise the calculations of optimal outcomes of action cannot be made. This common assumption of all forms of consequentialism is indefensible. It is not just the Benthamite utilitarian who is vulnerable to what I say in criticism of consequentialism. I know of no plausible solution to the problem of incommensurability, without which the utilitarian enterprise cannot get off the ground.

[7] In section 1e the term 'spirit' is used principally to refer to the human capacity to recognize certain absolute claims of justice, a capacity which when exercised shows the way in which human beings are to be valued (see in particular the final paragraph of the above section). But in response to the objection that a man is to be valued in this way only when he is able to exercise this spiritual capacity (see 1j), claims are advanced about some metaphysical implications of the manifestation of the spiritual. It is maintained that spiritual capacities or powers do not come to be exercisable powers in a human life except in virtue of a process of development which implies a radical capacity in human nature of a spiritual kind, a capacity to develop such powers. This means that human beings are essentially spiritual. In this essay I have not sought, however, to undertake an extended metaphysical analysis of the character of spirit. In particular, I have not tried to demonstrate from the intentional nature of human rational activity that such activity is not explicable as the activity of a physical organ since it can have no spatial location. An argument to this conclusion is not required to advance the case put forward in section 1.

[8] On absolute claims Barbara Smoker writes: 'In humanist thinking there is no such thing as an absolute principle: various principles compete for pre-eminence according to their relevance to the particular circumstances of the case and to individual priorities.' What distinguishes this assertion from a declaration in favour of arbitrariness?
[9] Plato *Apology* 32c–e.
[10] For this feature of utilitarianism, see Anselm Mueller, 'Radical Subjectivity: Morality versus Utilitarianism', *Ratio*, 19 (1977), 115-32.
[11] Socrates' stance is not to be understood (as Ms Smoker would understand it) in terms of what Socrates found compatible with his 'self-image'. People can be rational or irrational about their 'self-images'. Was Socrates rational in refusing to be party to murder in circumstances in which his refusal would not save the prospective victim and was also likely to lead to his own death? My answer is 'Yes', since murder involves both grave injustice to the victim and the dishonouring and corruption of one's own humanity. On this view, Socrates had no other defensible option but to refuse collaboration in murder, since injustice and the corruption of one's own humanity are contrary to the norms of what is reasonable in the conduct of one's life. The utilitarian can provide no such justification for the rationality of Socrates' behaviour, since defences of collaboration in murder are perfectly compatible with utilitarian conceptions of what it is to be rational in the conduct of one's life. A utilitarian defence of Socrates (as in Barbara Smoker) trivializes Socrates' stance by reducing it to a matter of 'self-image'. On this view, since it just happened to be the case that Socrates could not live with the thought of being party to murder, it was rational *for him* not to collaborate. But for anyone who could live with that thought (and corruption effects just such moral callousness) it might well be rational to collaborate. This brings out the resourcefulness of utilitarianism: its capacity for *rationalizing* almost any preference.
[12] For an extended analysis of the implications of Socrates' example see John Finnis, *Fundamentals of Ethics* (Oxford: Clarendon Press, 1983), pp. 112–20.
[13] I owe this way of putting the point to Mary Geach.
[14] Quoted in Erazim Kohák, *The Embers and the Stars: A Philosophical Inquiry into the Moral Sense of Nature* (Chicago, Ill.: University of Chicago Press, 1984), p. 102.
[15] Barbara Smoker thinks that killing is unjust, in circumstances in which the victim wishes to live, only when it is unnecessary. This view simply removes any ground for a distinction between just and unjust killing. What people think 'necessary' is dictated by what they want to achieve. Millions of human beings have been murdered (as I would say) because others have thought it 'necessary' to eliminate them. The defence of euthanasia must seem unproblematic to anyone who shares Ms Smoker's views on 'just' killing.
[16] Compare this with Anthony Kenny's definition of mind as 'a capacity for capacities' of an intellectual kind. 'Knowledge of a language such as English is itself a capacity or ability: an ability whose exercise is the speaking, understanding, reading of English. To have a mind is to have a capacity at a further remove from actualization: to have the capacity to acquire such abilities as a knowledge of English.' As Kenny notes, one implication of this view of mind is that 'it is possible to say that babies have minds even though they do not yet display intellectual activities of the appropriate kind' (A.J.P. Kenny, 'Fourth Lecture: The Origin of the Soul', in A.J.P. Kenny, H.C. Loguet-Higgins, J.R. Lucas and C.H. Waddington *The Development of Mind: The Gifford Lectures 1972–73*, Edinburgh: Edinburgh University Press, 1973 p. 46). What Kenny says about mental abilities I am saying about spiritual powers: their development depends upon a second-order capacity in the nature of human beings.
[17] Barbara Smoker describes the view that someone is a human being from conception to death as 'manifest nonsense', by which I suppose she means 'manifestly untrue'. Her confidence about this reflects a fairly widespread empiricist outlook, which is seemingly

indifferent to its lack of ability to explain the organic and developmental *unity* of a human life.

[18] I argue that if the burden of justifying voluntary euthanasia is successfully borne by the judgment that the person to be killed does not have a worthwhile life, that judgment will also serve to justify both non-voluntary and involuntary euthanasia—that is, the euthanasia both of those incapable of consenting and of those capable but unwilling to consent. (I do not confuse these two kinds of euthanasia, as Ms Smoker supposes; I concentrate on non-voluntary euthanasia because, whatever the logic of their position, most propagandists for euthanasia do not have the same kinds of objectives as Nazis.) Ms Smoker is happy to embrace the justification of non-voluntary euthanasia, since she thinks, *inter alia*, that keeping a malformed infant alive amounts to a 'cruel condemnation of the helpless infant to an intolerable life sentence', while, on the other hand, she rejects involuntary euthanasia as plainly murder. This position calls for a number of comments. First, even if Ms Smoker does not see the grave injustice of intentionally killing an innocent human being, she should be less confident that she can know how a person's life will turn out—whether tolerable or intolerable. Second, the idea that parents 'sentence' their children 'to life', as Ms Smoker puts it, is a clamant example of ideological distortion. Human beings who retain a true sense of the mystery of the human person and who therefore do not consider other human beings disposable on the basis of utilitarian calculation, will care for and sustain their children: such care and sustenance are elementary expressions of respect for the child. Third, since Ms Smoker thinks only killing which is unnecessary is unjust (see *n.* 15 above), she has no sure ground for calling involuntary euthanasia 'murder', if by 'murder' she means unjust killing. What you think necessary depends upon what you want, and if you are sufficiently powerful you may arrange on grounds of 'necessity' to kill those whom you judge not to have a worthwhile life, whatever they themselves may think. That is just what the Nazis did, helping themselves to the justifications for euthanasia advanced in the 1920s by non-Nazis like Binding and Hoche, who advocated the killing of those lacking a 'worthwhile life'.

[19] See the Report of the Linacre Centre Working Party *Euthanasia and Clinical Practice* (London, Linacre Centre, 1982, pp. 16–19. See also I van der Sluis, 'The Movement for Euthanasia 1875–1975', *Janus*, 66 (1979) 131–72.

[20] Quoted by Yale Kamisar on p. 139 of the present volume.

[21] 'Dualism' is a slippery term. It may occur to readers that the views of the present writer imply a dualistic conception of man, since he speaks of human beings as 'essentially spiritual as well as essentially fleshly' (1j). This dual character of human life is to be explained, moreover, in the writer's view, by the fact that human animals possess spiritual souls. However, the idea of the soul is not the idea of something distinct from the body; for what it is that makes a body to be a human body is precisely a human soul. A human being is not a soul which possesses a body. It is the view of St Thomas Aquinas that a human person is a human body. 'My soul is not I' (*Anima mea non est ego*), he writes in one place. Hence, even if the human soul is immortal, this does not show that *I* survive my death. Somebody who accepts Aquinas's view of the soul is not to be accused of the kind of dualism which holds that what it is to be a human person is distinct from what it is to be a living human body. Ms Smoker believes I am simply confused in thinking euthanasiasts to be dualists. Her own position is not entirely clear. She seems to hold one or other of the following positions:

(a) What it is to be a person is different from what it is to be a living human body. It resides in the presently exercisable capacity for intellectual activities. The necessary but not sufficient condition for the possession of this capacity is a functioning human cerebral cortex. Among questions which need to be faced by someone holding such a position are the following:

(i) What is the status of somebody with a temporarily non-functioning cerebral cortex?

(ii) Given both that the cerebral cortex develops and that intellectual abilities develop, what kind of capacity must an entity already possess in order to develop in these ways? Or is it a mistake to speak about development *within* a single life, and should we instead understand what are normally referred to as developments as in fact 'accretions'?

(b) Common-sense talk of living human beings is just confused. Among apparently human bodies are some which genuinely are human bodies and others which are not human because they lack a presently functioning cerebral cortex. Among the questions which need to be faced by someone holding such a position are the following:

(i) What kind of entity is the merely apparent living human body?

(ii) What is the status of somebody with a temporarily non-functioning cerebral cortex?

[22] A dualism for which the human person is something other than the living body runs through the writings of Joseph Fletcher. A crudely plain example of it is the penultimate paragraph of his essay 'The Patient's Right to Die' in the present volume, where he contrasts 'mere biological life' and 'personality values', for which 'the flesh' is 'the means rather than the end'. Fletcher compounds his dualism with the false belief that the traditional moral prohibition on intentionally killing the innocent commits those who hold it to striving to prolong life in all circumstances. On that error see *Euthanasia and Clinical Practice* (London, Linacre Centre, 1982), pp. 33–4, 45–53.

[23] For Professor Glanville Williams's most recent contribution on our topic, see 'The Right to Die', *New Law Journal* (Jan. 27, 1984).

[24] Barbara Smoker's observations on suffering well illustrate the incapacity of a utilitarian to think of meaning in human life in anything other than utilitarian terms: suffering is 'meaningless' unless you can compute the benefits to be derived therefrom. Moreover, she provides no argument to show that the suffering of people who see no value in their suffering while they are suffering is irredeemably meaningless. There surely is no argument which could show this, since it is so plainly contrary to experience. Moreover, such experience is not confined to theists. There have been many experiences of 'meaningless suffering' which have been retrospectively recognized—by agnostics among others—as the necessary condition for stripping away fantasy and illusion. The claim that certain forms of suffering are inherently meaningless is an expression of dogmatic prejudice (of a kind characteristic of certain atheists who succeed in being the mirror-images of their own caricatures of religious believers).

[25] I owe to Mary Geach this way of stating the connection between the value of 'mere humanity' and the doctrine of equality invoked against exploitation.

[26] Barbara Smoker, 'The Last Right', *Forum*, 2 (1983) (Council of Europe journal).

[27] The distinction between active and passive euthanasia, understood simply as an application of the distinction between killing and letting die, is not on its own sufficient for making the morally significant discriminations we need in discussing the subject. For one may aim to bring about someone's death simply by refraining from intervening when one *could* and *should* intervene, and save a life in so doing. Desired results can be obtained by intentional omissions as well as by intentional actions. But not every foreseen result of an omission is an intended result. If Ms Smoker wishes to reject the moral significance both of the distinction between what we do and what we allow to

happen and of the distinction between what we aim at (intend) and what we foresee as the result of what we do, she will thereby have jettisoned some quite central parts of morality. If there never is a morally significant distinction between killing and letting die, killing some patients to salvage their organs in order to save others will be regarded as morally equivalent to allowing some patients to die in one's necessarily limited efforts to save some other patients. This bizarre position is indeed adopted by John Harris (see his *Violence and Responsibility*, London: Routledge & Kegan Paul, 1980), and Ms Smoker is perhaps persuaded by his reasoning. Harris's position at least has the merit of bringing out the logic of utilitarianism. It is clear that the denial of moral significance to the distinction between what a man aims at (by act or omission) and what he foresees will be the result of what he does or omits to do, is motivated by prior commitment to utilitarianism and in particular to the view that the whole moral significance of what a person does (or omits to do) derives from the totality of beneficial or harmful consequences which follow from his behaviour. (On this point see Philippa Foot, 'Morality, Action and Outcome' in Ted Honderich [ed.], *Morality and Objectivity* London, Routledge and Kegan Paul 1985, pp. 23-38.) By contrast, the tradition of common morality holds that you can attribute moral goodness or badness only to what is a human action (i.e. to what is under some description *intentional*) and to what falls within the scope of human voluntary control. Hence the attitude of the will and the character of the agent are of quite central importance in understanding the moral significance of human action. It is indeed a crucial feature of human action that we cannot choose only to bring about states of affairs in the world but must also choose *to do* or *to be* such and such in acting with a view to ends; we thereby modify and shape the kind of persons, the kind of moral agents, we become. It is surely utilitarian blindness to this central feature of human agency which has led Barbara Smoker to ignore the central point of my essay in her Rejoinder: the contention that a man would dishonour and corrupt himself in acting unjustly towards another. So the nature and absoluteness of the requirements of justice are a manifestation of the honour due to our numanity and thus of the dignity of all humanity.

[28] See the Report of the Linacre Centre Working Party, *Euthanasia and Clinical Practice*, p. 26. See more generally G.E.M. Anscombe, 'On the Source of the Authority of the State' in her *Collected Philosophical Papers,* Vol. III: *Ethics Religion and Politics* (Oxford: Basil Blackwell, 1981), pp. 130-55.

[29] See Yale Kamisar, p. 112 of the present volume.

Barbara Smoker

*A Rejoinder to Religious and Non-Consequentialist Objections**

The earlier editions of this book included just one main contribution opposed to euthanasia—that of Professor Kamisar, which is retained in the present volume. But the objections set out in that essay rest on consequentialist (utilitarian) principles, not on religious premises. Indeed, its title specifically excludes them. The only contribution written from an explicitly religious viewpoint for the original edition was the one by the late Dean Matthews, who unequivocally comes down in favour of active voluntary euthanasia. Thus, although the objections to euthanasia most usually encountered are those based on religious assumptions, or at least on philosophical attitudes associated with religious assumptions, such objections were not included in the original book at all. It was therefore decided to repair the omission in this present revised version. For that reason, a contribution was invited from Luke Gormally, representing the traditional Roman Catholic viewpoint, this being the religious persuasion that is most rigorously opposed, in general, to euthanasia.

However, whereas non-Catholic opponents of euthanasia tend to express their opposition in specifically religious terms ('life is a gift from God', and so on), and are therefore forced to admit that their conclusions cannot be morally binding on atheists or on those who believe in a different kind of god, the Catholic Church claims moral jurisdiction over all mankind, the ground of this claim being that its moral teaching stems from 'natural law'. This was defined by Thomas Aquinas as the temporal part of eternal law, and held by him to be discernible by man's natural reason from creation itself. Thus, being 'self-evident', Catholic morality is absolute and universally binding. This important strand in traditional Roman Catholic thinking enables

* The notes for this article appear on p. 109.

Catholic theologians and philosophers to express in non-religious ('natural law') terms the ethics of their religion and to insist that the criminal law of the country prohibit practices at variance with the resulting moral code—in this debate, active euthanasia. Mr Gormally is of this school, and, indeed, relies on this line of argument in his essay in order to address himself to non-believers. But in my present essay, largely comprising a rejoinder to Luke Gormally's, I will argue that his whole thesis draws upon essentially religious concepts of what is moral. Secular humanist concepts of morality (my own personal position) are far less rigid—and far more human. It is not true that defenders of euthanasia deny 'the reality of spirit' (p. 79), if by 'spirit' is meant such human qualities as courage and fortitude, but we see no point in deliberately pushing such qualities to the limits of endurance.

Luke Gormally's interpretation of 'utilitarianism' (the humanist school of philosophy which, in Bentham's definition, makes the criterion of morality 'the greatest happiness of the greatest number') is too narrowly Benthamite. Utilitarians since J. S. Mill have embraced many sorts of human values in the concept of happiness, including the values (to take Mr Gormally's example on p. 76) underlying the refusal by Socrates to be a party to murder in order to save his own skin, even though his refusal would not save Leon of Salamis: for Socrates knew that, had he acted otherwise, he could never live comfortably afterwards with his own self-image. So it is untrue that utilitarianism obscures such considerations.

Besides, secular humanists do not derive their morality exclusively from the principles of utilitarianism. Indeed, some humanist philosophers (e.g. Bernard Williams and Thomas Nagel) put greater emphasis on the 'respect for persons' or 'minimum treatment' principle, which asserts that every person has the right to expect certain minimal standards of treatment, however great might be the benefits to humanity in general if these expectations were disregarded. To some extent, all humanists agree with this fundamental moral principle, though the balance between 'minimum treatment' and the calculation of gains in terms of human welfare will vary, one to another.

In humanist thinking, there is no such thing as an absolute principle: various principles compete for pre-eminence according to their relevance in the particular circumstances of the case and to individual priorities. This is, perhaps, the main distinction between religious and non-religious modes of thought, religion being founded on absolutes.

The pre-eminent moral principle with Roman Catholic theologians is justice—or, rather, their idea of justice, complicated by their belief in divine justice—whereas with secular humanists justice is always tempered by compassion.

It would, in fact, be impossible for arguments that depend so heavily on notions of punitive justice, with its implications of total moral responsibility and 'sin', to derive from humanism, which recognizes that human beings, having no control over the genes they were born with or their childhood conditioning, cannot be blamed for their compulsions, or, therefore, to any great extent, for compulsive behaviour. (Even allergies affect human behaviour!)

In any case, true 'justice' must surely entail appropriate treatment: what is unjust is not a decision to kill, *per se*, but a decision to kill unnecessarily,[1] when the victim wishes to live.

Luke Gormally asserts that 'human beings may not be killed simply for some advantage to be gained thereby', with which I wholeheartedly concur, except in the case of a person freely choosing to be killed either in order to avoid great suffering for himself or to bring about some great advantage for others—for example, taking someone else's place in the gas chamber. Paradoxically enough, because Mr Gormally places undue emphasis on justice, his exceptions to the immorality of human killing are far wider than mine. For instance, I do not accept, as he does, that a person could actually *deserve* death. (Though this, after all, is as nothing when compared with the belief that a person may deserve to be punished for all eternity!)

The 'respect for persons' principle, being an important strand in all acceptable ethical systems, is common ground between us. Luke Gormally, indeed, regards it as an absolute. But the 'respect' required in accordance with his essay is directed to life itself, without regard either to the quality of life or the right to choose, whereas I see both these factors as ineluctable. As for what we mean by 'persons', these, in Luke Gormally's thinking, comprise every human entity from the moment of conception to the moment of death, even including an embryo without a functional nervous system (as he has stated elsewhere), or a severely brain-damaged patient in an irreversible coma. He lumps them all together under his phrase 'the nature of human life and human dignity' (p. 72). To most of us, however—and here I refer not only to humanists but to most religionists, including the more moderate members of Luke Gormally's own Church—this is manifest nonsense. In the name of common sense, we should treat all life as it actually is—not as it once was, or as it might, in different circumstances, have been.[2]

As for the contention that it is good for people to suffer, even though they recognize no benefit to themselves in their suffering, this can be justified in only three possible ways, each of which is repudiated by humanist principles. The first way is by invoking a god that desires suffering. The second way is by arguing that the suffering actually benefits the victim, whether or not he or she recognizes it, thus making a high-handed judgment on another's behalf in a matter which most intimately concerns that person. (This usurpation of the autonomy of others who are equally part of the moral domain is rooted in a viewpoint which again is not rationally, but only religiously, defensible.) The third way is by pointing to benefits that the suffering affords *other* people—by, say, giving them the opportunity to gain merit through having sufferers around on whom they can practise good works. This third argument, which really advocates using people for ends not their own is, in effect, a bizarre form of the utilitarian principle!

Far from the victim being ennobled by suffering (as is often alleged by opponents of euthanasia), extreme and perpetual suffering is, for most people, degrading, demoralizing and self-absorbing. Even though there may be exceptions—people who are able to regard their sufferings as a challenge (whether physical or spiritual) and derive some deep satisfaction from transcending them—why should the rest of us be made to feel that such people represent a moral ideal that we should try to live up to?

It is a part of Roman Catholic doctrine (see section III of the Vatican's 1980 *Declaration on Euthanasia*, reproduced here as Appendix 4) that 'suffering has a special place in God's saving plan'; but this can have no significance for anyone who does not believe in a god of that sort with so dubious a plan. Even Catholics often talk about a 'merciful release' when a distressing terminal illness ends in death: supporters of voluntary euthanasia simply want the merciful release to occur before the suffering has been uselessly prolonged, if that is the patient's wish.

No one would deny that for every person there are degrees of short-term suffering that we will readily accept in exchange for 'felt gains'—that is, consequences which we ourselves feel to be gains. These need not be gains in terms of pleasure, but felt gains of some kind there must be—whether simultaneous gains (such as the exhilaration and immediate satisfaction experienced by mountaineers or athletes in testing their endurance to the utmost), or future gains (such as those associated with the suffering endured in childbirth or dental treatment), or altruistic gains (either for the benefit of those we love or for the sake of our own pride or similar satisfaction). But suffering that is disproportionate to the felt gain and is therefore not voluntarily accepted can have no inherent value, and no other person has any moral right to demand it. Even Mr Gormally's ideal of the martyr is surely nullified if martyrdom be imposed, without any choice at all.

To deny the sufferer the right to repudiate his suffering is indefensible, and is totally dependent on the god idea, for whence would the alleged value of chronic suffering and slow deterioration otherwise come? In fact, if one sets aside the notion of divine will, the whole moral argument against euthanasia falls, and, in attempting to set aside religious assumptions as well as consequentialist arguments, Mr Gormally has failed to make out a rational case for adopting the far from 'self-evident' values on which his thesis rests. He contrives to do so by appealing to the general principle of 'respect for persons', suggesting that anyone agreeing to help someone else to cut short his or her life is, in effect, judging that person's life to be 'not worthwhile'. But the judgment that the degree of suffering inherent in the life is such as to make it 'not worthwhile' is essentially that of the one person who is competent to make this judgment, and the actual decision must always rest with the person concerned: the only person who has the right to make it.

At the same time, I agree with Mr Gormally that voluntary euthanasia and assisted suicide have a moral component not present in unilateral suicide: the morality of the assistant's decision to help. Humanist morality recognizes that there is an important moral distinction between, on the one hand, carrying out voluntary euthanasia in circumstances that make it justifiable and, on the other, doing so in the absence of such circumstances. What this demands, however, is not, as Mr Gormally states (p. 76), 'global assessments of the value of a particular human life', but searching assessments both of the subjective rationality of the person who wishes to die and of the objective reasonableness of that wish.

If the judgment of the person wishing to die were obviously impaired—by, say, clinical depression or extremes of emotion—it would certainly be immoral to accede to an impulsive request for the irrevocable act of euthanasia. So it would if the grounds for even a steadfast request were not sufficiently strong. This is not to say, however, that it is morally necessary for the euthanasiast to decide that if he were in the same condition as the patient he himself would choose to die: after all, different people have not only different levels of endurance but different life goals and satisfactions to determine the kinds of disability that would, for them, make life intolerable. But it is morally necessary for the euthanasiast to ascertain that the patient's decision, besides being a steadfast one and one made in a state of reason, is also a justifiable one, in that the cause is sufficiently serious and apparently incurable.

To this extent, therefore, euthanasia certainly does (as Luke Gormally argues) involve an assessment of the 'worthwhileness' of a life, by the euthanasiast as well as by the person who makes the choice to die, but not quite in the sense in which Mr Gormally understands the word 'worthwhileness'. For his use of the phrase 'not worthwhile' is ambiguous: it can either mean (as Mr Gormally intends) 'intrinsically valueless', or (as a supporter of voluntary euthanasia might use the phrase) 'unendurable'—that is, having irremediable negative experiences which far outweigh the positive ones at the present time and in the likely future. Even philosophers (such as Nagel) who assert that all experience, *per se*, has a positive value, irrespective of the content of the experience, would still say that it is possible for that basic positive experience to be outweighed by negative experiences. For instance, who would choose to be conscious so as to experience being burnt alive?

Incidentally, in warfare a soldier may shoot dead a comrade trapped in a burning tank as a simple act of humanity. How does such an act differ essentially from active euthanasia? If the difference resides in the brief span of time that will elapse before death is certain anyway, what is the actual estimated duration that would justify active euthanasia? Ten seconds? Five minutes? Two hours? One day?

Apart from 'worthwhileness', another terminological idiosyncracy in Luke Gormally's essay is his use of the word 'dualism' (p. 82). This term generally refers to metaphysical theories (epitomized in Descartes) that regard body and mind as two distinct entities, thus leaving the way open for belief in disembodied spirits—in gods, ghosts and so on. It is ironic, therefore, that Mr Gormally, who admits to belief in a supreme spirit (with, presumably, thought processes in the absence of a brain), and in some sort of conscious life for individuals after death, should apply the word 'dualist' not to himself but to those advocates of voluntary euthanasia who, like me, have no religious belief and who deny (in line with most modern philosophers—Strawson and others) that there is any dichotomy between body and mind. In fact, when Mr Gormally, after stating quite correctly that dualism is largely discredited in modern philosophy, goes on to remark that this has had little effect on secularist ethics, he is apparently unaware that it was secularist thinking which undermined dualist theories in the first place. What we now call secular humanism used to be known as 'monism'—that is, the opposite of dualism.

It is not dualistic to acknowledge that our essential humanity is identified by our minds—that is, the inner life which is the activity of a functioning fore-brain. But the notion that this activity could continue once the fore-brain is dead has to depend on dualism.

Mr Gormally's misunderstanding of the word arises from a prior mistake: the false assumption that it is necessary to be a dualist in order to recognize that it is possible for a living body to lack certain normal functions. Although we monists do not recognize any possibility of a human mind existing without a body—any more than there could be seeing or hearing without a body—we certainly accept the possibility of there being a (defective) human body without a mind (or inner life).

This raises the question of what constitutes a person, with the status and rights of a person. If a human being lacks such faculties as sight or hearing, this does not, of course, prevent him or her from being a person. But if a human being suffers death of the cerebral brain, and therefore lacks any inner life, he or she is no longer really a person, for consciousness, being a crucial human function, is a necessary (though not of course a sufficient) condition of being a person, as distinct from being a non-sentient biological organism. An irreparably 'vegetative' human body of this kind is manifestly a euthanasia candidate, but one to whom the voluntary principle can hardly apply, except by reference to an advance declaration (or Living Will) or through the next of kin.

In the absence of an advance declaration, it would be non-voluntary euthanasia, not involuntary (such as the Nazi variety?—a euphemism for murder), though Mr Gormally seems to confuse the two. It is true that many of us in the Voluntary Euthanasia Movement are also in favour of non-voluntary (but not involuntary) euthanasia, such as infant euthanasia where there are serious congenital abnormalities—

and, though this is not the direct concern of the Voluntary Euthanasia Society, it is the concern of a kindred organization called Prospect. But it is absurd to suggest that there is any alternative to making decisions on behalf of new-born babies: none would survive without positive steps being taken to keep them alive. And it is a mistake to suppose that making a decision to keep a malformed neonate alive is morally superior to a decision to allow it to die—or to bring about its death without delay. In fact, the last option can be seen as an act of compassion and humanity, and the first as condemnation of the helpless infant to an intolerable life sentence; while a decision to keep it alive until it is old enough to decide for itself must mean a sentence of many years, and would still be a decision made on the child's behalf. And for what reason? Usually out of moral cowardice or squeamishness or for the sake of an ideological theory, for a new-born baby, having no concept of any future, has no stake in life whatsoever.

The issue of infant euthanasia is, however, outside the scope both of the Voluntary Euthanasia Society and of this book, apart from the light it sheds on the philosophical questions it shares with voluntary euthanasia, such as the widespread, though futile, attempts to make a clear moral distinction between active and passive euthanasia.

The Vatican's 1980 *Declaration on Euthanasia* rests heavily on this putative moral distinction. Though completely discredited in secular moral philosophy, this spurious distinction is by no means confined to Catholic, or even religious, teaching. Not only do most religious believers contrive to make this moral distinction between active and passive euthanasia, so does the present secular law in almost every country. The one honourable exception (and that only recently) is the Netherlands.

In the U.S.A., a young woman, Karen Ann Quinlan, was finally allowed to die of untreated pneumonia in June 1985, after ten years in an irreversible coma. Her brain had, they say, long since shrunk to the size of a golf-ball. During the first year, her Catholic adoptive parents had wanted the life-support system to be switched off, but (America being a legalistic country) it took a year for the courts to decide that this could be done. Then, because the brain-stem (as opposed to the cerebral part of the brain) was not dead, the girl's own heart and lungs took over, and so she went on living—if one can call it 'living'—for another nine years. Rotas of nurses fed this living corpse through the nose, pumped out excrement, turned the body, and massaged the limbs, while other people in the same locality were no doubt suffering and dying for lack of adequate medical resources.

The monetary cost of keeping Karen Quinlan breathing for ten years could not possibly have been met by her family, and no medical insurance policy would cover the whole of it. Apparently in such a case universities would probably meet part of the cost, in the hope of extending the frontiers of medical knowledge, while religious charities might also contribute, and newspapers would chip in for the sake of the story.

The Quinlan parents, meanwhile—unable to go through the normal bereavement and mourning experience—continued daily visits to the half-living body all those years; and steadfastly insisted, under the pressures of their religion and of public opinion, that artificial feeding must be continued. They still say that it was manifestly God's will, for some mysterious divine purpose, that Karen should have 'lived' in a coma for ten years.

While I am opposed to the starvation of any conscious patient, there is no reason (apart from anti-euthanasia reasons) why this method should not be used in the condition of irreversible coma. Whether starvation is put in the category of active or of passive euthanasia may be important to lawyers and to some doctors, university researchers and newspapers, as well as to theologians; but, provided the patient does not suffer, the categorization has no (non-religious) moral significance whatsoever.

No distinction is actually made in any non-theological system of ethics between acts of commission and non-acts of omission—in this context, between killing and letting die. That there is logically no such moral distinction—assuming the same intent and same motive—is, indeed, argued irrefutably by leading moral philosophers. Yet both medical practice and the secular law relating to euthanasia still contrive, in the last quarter of the twentieth century, to rest on this putative moral distinction.

The British medical profession quietly encourages its members to sedate seriously defective neonates in order to let them die of starvation over a period of several days, yet recoils in horror from any suggestion of giving these babies a quick lethal injection, which would be less distressing to all concerned, including the nursing staff.

This indirect method of euthanasia—under the pretence that it is not euthanasia at all—is, in fact, increasingly used not only in neonatal wards but in geriatric wards: if the old, terminally ill patient does not ask for food, the likelihood in such cases is that he or she will be given only water. But the idea that withholding sustenance from a patient is in some way less lethal—or more moral—than an honest, direct method of euthanasia is manifestly absurd. Moreover, to employ slow, passive (or indirect) methods of euthanasia, rather than quick, active methods, is to contravene the generally accepted medical principle that a physician should always act in the best interests of his patient.

Since the term 'passive euthanasia' is generally defined as the withholding of life-prolonging medical treatment, I think it makes a useful semantic distinction if we use the different term 'indirect euthanasia' for the withholding of the normal means of sustaining life, such as food.

Pope Pius XII, faced with the situation of rapidly advancing medical technology, declared in 1957 that 'extraordinary means' (or 'heroic means') need not be used to keep people alive; but his Church has since extended this in practice to include quite *ordinary* means. (For one thing, many treatments that seemed 'extraordinary' in 1957 have become quite ordinary since.) The word 'disproportionate' is therefore often substituted nowadays for 'extraordinary'. This amendment seems to leave open the question of who is to decide, and on what criteria, what sorts of treatment would be 'disproportionate' in any particular case—and apparently puts it on a consequentialist footing!

A particular instance of quite ordinary medical treatment that is frequently withheld from patients, with Roman Catholic approval, is the administration of antibiotics when an incidental attack of pneumonia happens to offer a 'merciful release' from an incurable condition. Yet there is no discernible ethical distinction between withholding antibiotics (so as not to cure the pneumonia) and administering a lethal dose or injection (in the absence of pneumonia) —except, perhaps, the implicit principle that you must always give the Almighty a sporting chance!

More disingenuous still is the argument (generally maintained by religious believers, including the most traditional of Roman Catholic theologians) that it is perfectly moral to administer a sufficient quantity of pain-killing drugs to control pain, even if the quantity required be a lethal dose, because the motive is said to be to deal with the pain, not to hasten death. Thus, the argument goes, such an act does not constitute active euthanasia, however certain it may be that the drug will kill the patient! It is as though a man with a loaded gun were to aim it at another person, pull the trigger, and then plead that the ensuing death was merely accidental, since his sole intention had been to test the firing mechanism. This, clearly, is a non-consequentialist argument.

Some modern Catholic theologians, however (especially in the past twenty years, which have seen so many changes in their Church, including the decline of papal authority), do recognize that there is a large, and expanding, grey area between active and passive euthanasia (a part of which, as suggested above, might be termed 'indirect' euthanasia). And if the administering of a known lethal dose of a pain-killer can be placed outside the grey area at all, it surely must come under active, not passive, euthanasia.

One of the most progressive Roman Catholic theologians today, Hans Kung (who seems to have been teetering on the brink of excommunication for many years), has explored the subject of euthanasia from a modernist Catholic standpoint in his book *Eternal Life?** He repudiates, as follows, the attempt made in traditional Catholic teaching (reiterated in the Vatican *Declaration* of 1980) to make a clear distinction in practice between active and passive euthanasia: 'What can be clearly distinguished conceptually often cannot be kept apart in the concrete; here the frontiers of all these ideas of aid—between active and passive, natural and artificial, life-preserving and life-terminating—are obviously fluid.' And though he stops short of a complete vindication of the right to choose the time of one's own death, he does recognize that it is justifiable in certain circumstances:

> Human life is God's 'gift', certainly. But is it not also—according to God's will—man's task?
>
> Human life is God's 'creation', certainly. But is it not—according to the Creator's mandate—also man's responsibility?
>
> Man must hold out to his 'appointed' end. But what is the end appointed?
>
> A 'premature surrender' of life is a human refusal of the divine consent. But what is the meaning of 'premature' when we are

* See pp. 210–13 in the English translation published by Collins (1984).

speaking of a life that has been destroyed physically or psychologically?

Needless to say, this God-centred style of ethical argument is quite foreign to my own way of thinking, but its flexibility does at least manifest some human compassion that is lacking in the blanket prohibition of active euthanasia (however narrowly defined it may be) found in more traditional Catholic teaching, including the Vatican *Declaration* of 1980 and the essay by Luke Gormally.[3]

I should like to make it clear that the views I am expressing in the present essay are my personal ones, which are those of a secular humanist who is also a member of the Voluntary Euthanasia Society. They are representative of neither the entire secular humanist movement nor the entire Voluntary Euthanasia Movement, for there are members of each who do not support the other; and while the humanist outlook is certainly more strongly represented in the Voluntary Euthanasia Society than in the population at large, there are also many religious believers among its members, including some Roman Catholics.

Indeed, we know from opinion surveys that a majority of Roman Catholics in Britain disagree with the official teaching of their Church on the issue of voluntary euthanasia. In nation-wide statistical surveys carried out by National Opinion Polls in May 1976 and again in February 1985, 54 per cent of those respondents describing themselves as Roman Catholics said they agreed with the following statement: 'Some people say that the law should allow adults to receive medical help to an immediate peaceful death if they suffer from an incurable physical illness that is intolerable to them, provided they have previously requested such help in writing.' In fact, these polls show that a majority of the members of *all* the main religious denominations are in agreement with voluntary euthanasia. For instance, of those who described themselves as Church of England or Anglican, 72 per cent in 1976 and 74 per cent in 1985 said they agreed with the statement quoted above.

As might be expected, however, atheists and agnostics come out highest of all, with, respectively, 80 per cent and 87 per cent in favour of voluntary euthanasia in 1976, and 89 per cent and 85 per cent in 1985. The corollary of this is that most of our opponents are religious believers: in 1985 (after eliminating the Don't Knows), only 11 per cent of non-believers were opposed to voluntary euthanasia, compared with 21 per cent of the total population, 23 per cent of all Protestants, and 39 per cent of Roman Catholics. And, more often than not, the arguments that we hear used against voluntary euthanasia are, however rationalized or overlaid with practical problems, based primarily on religious beliefs.

Such religious opposition often insists that God alone is to determine our time of death; humans are not allowed to tamper with God's will. In that case, is it not wrong to intervene to *save* life, as well as to hasten death? But human lives, they tell us, are a 'gift from God'. Even if we accepted this as true, is there no right to decline a gift when it is nothing but a burden?

Another phrase that Christians, and other religionists, are inclined to use against active euthanasia is 'the sanctity of life'. But what exactly does this mean? It has more than one possible connotation. First, it may imply that life has a supernatural aspect which makes it sacrosanct. But how can this be reconciled with the fact that earthquakes and other natural disasters take such a heavy and indiscriminate toll of human life? And if animals are also regarded as God's creatures, how can the sanctity of life apply when one animal cannot survive without eating another? In a different sense, however (in the sense that human beings should have humane consideration, compassion and respect for one another), we secular humanists also accept 'the sanctity of life'. And, of course, the very aims of the voluntary euthanasia movement are based on such consideration, compassion and respect. We firmly deny that people should always have to live as long as possible, whatever their condition. *Our* meaning of the sanctity of life cannot be divorced from the *quality* of life.

Besides, the case for legalizing voluntary euthanasia is primarily that the required change in the law would be merely permissive. We uphold the right of our opponents to decide against active (or even passive) euthanasia for themselves, but not for us. They have no moral right to make laws that impose their views on others, who may not even share the religious beliefs on which those views are based. Believers who uphold the principle of complete freedom of religion often fail to see that, in all logic, this must include freedom *from* religion.

ACKNOWLEDGEMENTS

I cannot attempt to list all the lecturers, writers and personal contacts who have helped, over the past four decades, to rid my ethical thinking of the rigidity of its pre-conciliar Roman Catholic origins and to develop my present secular humanist approach to ethics in general and medical ethics in particular. I should, however, like to thank Rona Gerber (Lecturer in Philosophy at Middlesex Polytechnic) for her direct help with this essay, and H. J. Blackham (author of many philosophy books, including the Penguin *Humanism* and *Six Existentialist Thinkers*) for his constructive criticism of it. I should also like to acknowledge my indebtedness to Charles Wilshaw for the 'sanctity of life' argument put forward in his booklet, *The Right to Die* (British Humanist Association, 1974/1983).

NOTES

[1] Mr Gormally's *n.* 15 and *n.* 18 present a travesty of my position on necessity. In this context, it would entail defending other people's lives.

[2] In his *n.* 21 (b), Mr Gormally suggests that in my view some living human bodies are 'not human because they lack a presently functioning cerebral cortex'. This is incorrect. The words 'not human' here should be replaced by 'not persons' and the words 'presently functioning' by 'functional'.

[3] The discussion is continued by other progressive theologians in the international Catholic publication *Concilium*, ed. J. Pohier and D. Mieth (Edinburgh: T. & T. Clark, 1985).

Yale Kamisar

*Euthanasia Legislation: Some Non-Religious Objections**

A book by Glanville Williams, *The Sanctity of Life and the Criminal Law*,[1] once again brought to the fore the controversial topic of euthanasia, more popularly known as 'mercy-killing'. In keeping with the trend of the euthanasia movement over the past generation, Williams concentrates his efforts for reform on the *voluntary* type of euthanasia, for example the cancer victim begging for death, as opposed to the *involuntary* variety—that is, the case of the congenital idiot, the permanently insane or the senile.

When a legal scholar of Williams's stature joins the ranks of such formidable law thinkers as America's Herbert Wechsler and the late Jerome Michael, and England's Hermann Mannheim in approving voluntary euthanasia at least in certain circumstances, a major exploration of the bases for the euthanasia prohibition seems in order. This need is underscored by the fact that Williams's book arrived on the scene soon after the stir caused by the plea for voluntary euthanasia contained in a book by a brilliant American Anglican clergyman.[2]

The Law on the Books condemns all mercy-killings.[3] That this has a substantial deterrent effect, even its harshest critics admit. Of course, it does not stamp out all mercy-killings, just as murder and rape provisions do not stamp out all murder and rape, but presumably it does impose a substantially greater responsibility on physicians and relatives in a euthanasia situation and turns them away from significantly more doubtful cases than would otherwise be the practice under any proposed euthanasia legislation to date. When a mercy-killing occurs, however, The Law in Action is as malleable as The Law on the Books is uncompromising. The high incidence of failures to indict, acquittals, suspended sentences and reprieves lends considerable

*The notes for this article appear on pp. 142–55.

support to the view that:

> If the circumstances are so compelling that the defendant ought to violate the law, then they are compelling enough for the jury to violate their oaths. The law does well to declare these homicides unlawful. It does equally well to put no more than the sanction of an oath in the way of an acquittal.

The complaint has been registered that 'the prospect of a sentimental acquittal cannot be reckoned as a certainty'.[4] Of course not. The defendant is not always *entitled* to a sentimental acquittal. The few American convictions cited for the proposition that the present state of affairs breeds 'inequality' in application may be cited as well for the proposition that it is characterized by elasticity and flexibility. In any event, if inequality of application suffices to damn a particular provision of the criminal law, we might as well tear up all our codes—beginning with the section on chicken-stealing.

The existing law on euthanasia is hardly perfect. But if it is not too good, neither, as I have suggested, is it much worse than the rest of the criminal law. At any rate, the imperfections of existing law are not cured by Williams's proposal. Indeed, I believe adoption of his views would add more difficulties than it would remove.

Williams strongly suggests that 'euthanasia can be condemned only according to a religious opinion'.[5] He tends to view the opposing camps as Roman Catholics versus Liberals. Although this has a certain initial appeal to me, a non-Catholic and self-styled liberal, I deny that this is the only way the battle lines can, or should, be drawn. I leave the religious arguments to the theologians. I share the view that 'those who hold the faith may follow its precepts without requiring those who do not hold it to act as if they did'.[6] But I do find substantial utilitarian obstacles on the high road to euthanasia. I am not enamoured of the *status quo* on mercy-killing. But while I am not prepared to defend it against all comers, I am prepared to defend it against the proposals for change which have come forth to date.

As an ultimate philosophical proposition, the case for voluntary euthanasia is strong. Whatever may be said for and against suicide generally, the appeal of death is immeasurably greater when it is sought not for a poor reason or just any reason, but for 'good cause', so to speak; when it is invoked not on behalf of a 'socially useful' person, but on behalf of, for example, the pain-racked 'hopelessly incurable' cancer victim. *If* a person is *in fact* (1) presently incurable, (2) beyond the aid of any respite which may come along in his life expectancy, suffering (3) intolerable and (4) unmitigable pain and of a (5) fixed and (6) rational desire to die, I would hate to have to argue that the hand of death should be stayed. But abstract propositions and carefully formed hypotheticals are one thing; specific proposals designed to cover everyday situations are something else again.

In essence, Williams's specific proposal is that death be authorized for a person in the above situation 'by giving the medical practitioner a wide discretion and trusting to his good sense'.[7] This, I submit, raises too great a risk of abuse and mistake to warrant a change in the existing law. That a proposal entails risk of mistake is hardly a conclusive reason against it. But neither is it irrelevant. Under any euthanasia programme the consequences of mistake, of course, are always fatal. As I shall endeavour to show, the incidence of mistake of one kind or another is likely to be quite appreciable. If this indeed be the case, unless the need for the authorized conduct is compelling enough to override it, I take it the risk of mistake *is* a conclusive reason against such authorization. I submit, too, that the possible radiations from the proposed legislation—for example, involuntary euthanasia of idiots and imbeciles (the typical 'mercy-killings' reported by the press)—and the emergence of the legal precedent that there are lives not 'worth living', give additional cause for reflection.

I see the issue, then, as the need for voluntary euthanasia versus (1) the incidence of mistake and abuse; and (2) the danger that legal machinery initially designed to kill those who are a nuisance to themselves may some day engulf those who are a nuisance to others.[8]

The 'freedom to choose a merciful death by euthanasia' may well be regarded as a special area of civil liberties. This is definitely a part of Professor Williams's approach:

> If the law were to remove its ban on euthanasia, the effect would merely be to leave this subject to the individual conscience. This proposal would . . . be easy to defend, as restoring personal liberty in a field in which men differ on the question of conscience. . . . On a question like this there is surely everything to be said for the liberty of the individual.[9]

I am perfectly willing to accept civil liberties as the battlefield, but issues of 'liberty' and 'freedom' mean little until we begin to pin down *whose* 'liberty' and 'freedom' and for *what* need and at *what* price. Williams champions the 'personal liberty' of the dying to die painlessly. I am more concerned about the life and liberty of those who would needlessly be killed in the process or who would irrationally choose to partake of the process. Williams's price on behalf of those who are *in fact* 'hopeless incurables' and *in fact* of a fixed and rational desire to die is the sacrifice of (1) some few, who, though they know it not, because their physicians know it not, need not and should not die; (2) others, probably not so few, who, though they go through the motions of 'volunteering', are casualties of strain, pain or narcotics to such an extent that they really know not what they do. My price on behalf of those who, despite appearances to the contrary, have some relatively normal and reasonably useful life left in them, or who are incapable of making the choice, is the lingering on for awhile of those who, if you will, *in fact* have no desire and no reason to linger on.

1. A Close-up View of Voluntary Euthanasia

A. THE EUTHANASIAST'S DILEMMA AND WILLIAMS'S PROPOSED SOLUTION

As if the general principle they advocate did not raise enough difficulties in itself, euthanasiasts have learned only too bitterly that specific plans of enforcement are often much less palatable than the abstract notions they are designed to effectuate. In the case of voluntary euthanasia, the means of implementation vary from (1) the simple proposal that mercy-killings by anyone, typically relatives, be immunized from the criminal law; to (2) the elaborate legal machinery contained in the early bills of the Euthanasia Society (England) and the Euthanasia Society of America for carrying out euthanasia.

The British Society, in the Bill it originally proposed, would require the eligible patient—that is, a person over twenty-one who is 'suffering from a disease involving severe pain and of an incurable and fatal character',[10] to forward a specially prescribed application, along with two medical certificates, one signed by the attending physician, and the other by a specially qualified physician, to a specially appointed Euthanasia Referee 'who shall satisfy himself by means of a personal interview with the patient and otherwise that the said conditions shall have been fulfilled and that the patient fully understands the nature and purpose of the application'; and, if so satisfied, shall then send a euthanasia permit to the patient; which permit shall, seven days after receipt, become 'operative' in the presence of an official witness; unless the nearest relative manages to cancel the permit by persuading a court of appropriate jurisdiction that the requisite conditions have not been met.

The American Society would have the eligible patient—that is, one over twenty-one 'suffering from severe physical pain caused by a disease for which no remedy affording lasting relief or recovery is at the time known to medical science',[11] petition for euthanasia in the presence of two witnesses and file same, along with the certificate of an attending physician, in a court of appropriate jurisdiction; said court then to appoint a committee of three, of whom at least two must be physicians, 'who shall forthwith examine the patient and such other persons as they deem advisable or as the court may direct and within five days after their appointment, shall report to the court whether or not the patient understands the nature and purpose of the petition and comes within the [act's] provisions'; whereupon, if the report is in the affirmative, the court shall—'unless there is some reason to believe that the report is erroneous or untrue'—grant the petition; in which event euthanasia is to be administered in the presence of the committee, or any two members thereof.

As will be seen, and as might be expected, the simple negative proposal to remove 'mercy-killings' from the ban of the criminal law is strenuously resisted on the ground that it offers the patient far too little protection from not-so-necessary or not-so-merciful killings. On the other hand, the elaborate affirmative proposals of the Euthanasia Societies meet much pronounced eye-blinking, not a few guffaws, and sharp criticism that the legal machinery is so drawn-out, so complex, so formal and so tedious as to offer the patient far too little solace.

The naked suggestion that mercy-killing be made a good defence against a charge of criminal homicide appears to have no prospect of success in the foreseeable future. Only recently, the Royal Commission on Capital Punishment 'reluctantly' concluded that such homicides could not feasibly be taken out of the category of murder, let alone completely immunized:

[Witnesses] thought it would be most dangerous to provide that 'mercy-killings' should not be murder, because it would be impossible to define a category which could not be seriously abused. Such a definition could only be in terms of the motive of the offender . . . which is notoriously difficult to establish and cannot, like intent, be inferred from a person's overt actions. Moreover, it was agreed by almost all witnesses, including those who thought that there would be no real difficulty in discriminating between genuine and spurious suicide pacts, that, even if such a definition could be devised, it would in practice often prove extremely difficult to distinguish killings where the motive was merciful from those where it was not. How, for example, were the jury to decide whether a daughter had killed her invalid father from compassion, from a desire for material gain, from a natural wish to bring to an end a trying period of her life, or from a combination of motives?[12]

While the appeal in simply taking 'mercy-killings' off the books is dulled by the likelihood of abuse, the force of the idea is likewise substantially diminished by the encumbering protective features proposed by the American and British Societies. Thus, Lord Dawson, an eminent medical member of the House of Lords and one of the great leaders of the British medical profession, protested that the British Bill 'would turn the sick-room into a bureau', that he was revolted by 'the very idea of the sick-chamber being visited by officials and the patient, who is struggling with this dire malady, being treated as if it was a case of insanity'.[13] Dr A. Leslie Banks, then Principal Medical Officer of the Ministry of Health, reflected that the proposed machinery would 'produce an atmosphere quite foreign to all accepted notions of dying in peace'.[14] Dr I. Phillips Frohman has similarly objected to the American Bill as one whose 'whole procedure is so lengthy that it does not seem consonant either with the "mercy" motive on which presumably it is based, or with the "bearableness" of the pain'.[15]

The extensive procedural concern of the euthanasia bills has repelled many, but perhaps the best evidence of its psychological misconception is that it has distressed sympathizers with the movement as well. The very year the British Society was organized and a proposed bill drafted, Dr Harry Roberts observed:

We all realize the intensified horror attached to the death-penalty by its accompanying formalities—from the phraseology of the

> judge's sentence, and his black cap, to the weight-gauging visit of the hangman to the cell, and the correct attendance at the final scene of the surpliced chaplain, the doctor and the prison governor. This is not irrelevant to the problem of legalized euthanasia.[16]

After discussing the many procedural steps of the British Bill Dr Roberts observed, 'I can almost hear the cheerful announcement: "please, ma'am, the euthanizer's come".'

At a meeting of the Medico-Legal Society, Dr Kenneth McFadyean, after reminding the group that 'some time ago I stated from a public platform that I had practised euthanasia for twenty years and I do not believe I am running risks because I have helped a hopeless sufferer out of this life', commented on the British Bill that

> There was no comparison between being in a position to make a will and making a patient choose his own death at any stated moment. The patient had to discuss it—not once with his own doctor, but two, three, or even four times with strangers, which was no solace or comfort to people suffering intolerable pain.[17]

Nothing rouses Professor Glanville Williams's ire more than the fact that opponents of the euthanasia movement argue that euthanasia proposals offer either inadequate protection or over-elaborate safeguards. Williams appears to meet this dilemma with the insinuation that because arguments are made in the antithesis *they must each be invalid, each be obstructionist, and each be made in bad faith.*[18]

It just may be, however, that each alternative argument is quite valid, that the trouble lies with the euthanasiasts themselves in seeking a goal which is *inherently inconsistent*: a procedure for death which *both* (1) provides ample safeguards against abuse and mistake, and (2) is 'quick' and 'easy' in operation. Professor Williams meets the problem with more than bitter comments about the tactics of the opposition. He makes a brave try to break through the dilemma:

> [T]he reformers might be well advised, in their next proposal, to abandon all their cumbrous safeguards and to do as their opponents wish, giving the medical practitioner a wide discretion and trusting to his good sense.
>
> [T]he essence of the bill would then be simple. It would provide

> that no medical practitioner should be guilty of an offence in respect of an act done intentionally to accelerate the death of a patient who is seriously ill, unless it is proved that the act was not done in good faith with the consent of the patient and for the purpose of saving him from severe pain in an illness believed to be of an incurable and fatal character. Under this formula it would be for the physician, if charged, to show that the patient was seriously ill, but for the prosecution to prove that the physician acted from some motive other than the humanitarian one allowed to him by law.[19]

Evidently, the presumption is that the general practitioner is a sufficient buffer between the patient and the restless spouse, or overwrought or overreaching relative, as well as a depository of enough general scientific know-how and enough information about current research developments and trends, to assure a minimum of error in diagnosis and anticipation of new measures of relief. Whether or not the general practitioner will accept the responsibility Williams would confer on him is itself a problem of major proportions.[20] Putting that question aside, the soundness of the underlying premises of Williams's 'legislative suggestion' will be examined in the course of the discussion of various aspects of the euthanasia problem.

B. THE 'CHOICE'

Under current proposals to establish legal machinery, elaborate or otherwise, for the administration of a quick and easy death, it is not enough that those authorized to pass on the question decide that the patient, in effect, is 'better off dead'. The patient must concur in this opinion. Much of the appeal in the current proposal lies in this so-called 'voluntary' attribute.

But is the adult patient really in a position to concur?[21] Is he truly able to make euthanasia a 'voluntary' act? There is a good deal to be said, is there not, for Dr Frohman's pithy comment that the 'voluntary' plan is supposed to be carried out 'only if the victim is both sane and crazed by pain'.[22]

By hypothesis, voluntary euthanasia is not to be resorted to until narcotics have long since been administered and the patient has developed a tolerance to them. *When*, then, does the patient make the choice? While heavily drugged?[23] Or is narcotic relief to be withdrawn for the time of decision? But if heavy dosage no longer deadens pain, indeed, no longer makes it bearable, how overwhelming is it when whatever relief narcotics offer is taken away too?

'Hypersensitivity to pain after analgesia has worn off is nearly always noted'.[24] Moreover, 'the mental side-effects of narcotics, unfortunately for anyone wishing to suspend them temporarily without unduly tormenting the patient, appear to outlast the analgesic effect' and 'by many hours'.[25] The situation is further complicated by the fact that 'a person in terminal stages of cancer who had been given morphine steadily for a matter of weeks would certainly be dependent upon it physically and would probably be addicted to it and react with the addict's response'.[26]

The narcotics problem aside, Dr Benjamin Miller, who probably has personally experienced more pain than any other commentator on the euthanasia scene, observes:

> Anyone who has been severely ill knows how distorted his judgment became during the worst moments of the illness. Pain and the toxic effect of disease, or the violent reaction to certain surgical procedures may change our capacity for rational and courageous thought.[27]

Undoubtedly, some euthanasia candidates will have their lucid moments. How they are to be distinguished from fellow-sufferers who do not, or how these instances are to be distinguished from others when the patient is exercising an irrational judgment, is not an easy matter. Particularly is this so under Williams's proposal, where no specially qualified persons, psychiatrically trained or otherwise, are to assist in the process.

Assuming, for purposes of argument, that the occasion when a euthanasia candidate possesses a sufficiently clear mind can be ascertained and that a request for euthanasia is then made, there remain other problems. The mind of the pain-racked may occasionally be clear, but is it not also likely to be uncertain and variable? This point was pressed hard by the great physician, Lord Horder, in the House of Lords debates:

> During the morning depression he [the patient] will be found to favour the application under this Bill, later in the day he will think

> quite differently, or will have forgotten all about it. The mental clarity with which noble Lords who present this Bill are able to think and to speak must not be thought to have any counterpart in the alternating moods and confused judgments of the sick man.[28]

The concept of 'voluntary' in voluntary euthanasia would have a great deal more substance to it if, as is the case with voluntary admission statutes for the mentally ill, the patient retained the right to reverse the process within a specified number of days after he gives written notice of his desire to do so—but unfortunately this cannot be. The choice here, of course, is an irrevocable one.

The likelihood of confusion, distortion or vaccilation would appear to be serious drawbacks to any voluntary plan. Moreover, Williams's proposal is particularly vulnerable in this regard, since as he admits, by eliminating the fairly elaborate procedure of the American and British Societies' plans, he also eliminates a time period which would furnish substantial evidence of the patient's settled intention to avail himself of euthanasia.[29] But if Williams does not always choose to slug it out, he can box neatly and parry gingerly:

> [T]he problem can be exaggerated. Every law has to face difficulties in application, and these difficulties are not a conclusive argument against a law if it has a beneficial operation. The measure here proposed is designed to meet the situation where the patient's consent to euthanasia is clear and incontrovertible. The physician, conscious of the need to protect himself against malicious accusations, can devise his own safeguards appropriate to the circumstances; he would normally be well advised to get the patient's consent in writing, just as is now the practice before operations. Sometimes the patient's consent will be particularly clear because he will have expressed a desire for ultimate euthanasia while he is still clear-headed and before he comes to be racked by pain; if the expression of desire is never revoked, but rather is reaffirmed under the pain, there is the best possible proof of full consent. If, on the other hand, there is no such settled frame of mind, and if the physician chooses to administer euthanasia when the patient's mind is in a variable state, he will be walking in the margin of the law and may find himself unprotected.[30]

If consent is given at a time when the patient's condition has so degenerated that he has become a fit candidate for euthanasia, when, if ever, will it be 'clear and incontrovertible'? Is the suggested alternative of consent in advance a satisfactory solution? Can such a consent be deemed an informed one? Is this much different from holding a man to a prior statement of intent that if such and such an employment opportunity would present itself he would accept it, or if such and such a young woman were to come along he would marry her? Need one marshal authority for the proposition that many an 'iffy' inclination is disregarded when the actual facts are at hand?

Professor Williams states that where a pre-pain desire for 'ultimate euthanasia' is 'reaffirmed' under pain, 'there is the best possible proof of full consent'. Perhaps. But what if it is alternately renounced and reaffirmed under pain? What if it is neither affirmed or renounced? What if it is only renounced? Will a physician be free to go ahead on the ground that the prior desire was 'rational', but the present desire 'irrational'? Under Williams's plan, will not the physician frequently 'be walking in the margin of the law'—just as he is now? Do we really accomplish much more under this proposal than to put the euthanasia principle on the books?

Even if the patient's choice could be said to be 'clear and incontrovertible', do not other difficulties remain? Is this the kind of choice, assuming that it can be made in a fixed and rational manner, that we want to offer a gravely ill person? Will we not sweep up, in the process, some who are not really tired of life, but think others are tired of them; some who do not really want to die, but who feel they should not live on, because to do so when there looms the legal alternative of euthanasia is to do a selfish or a cowardly act? Will not some feel an obligation to have themselves 'eliminated' in order that funds allocated for their terminal care might be better used by their families or, financial worries aside, in order to relieve their families of the emotional strain involved?

It would not be surprising for the gravely ill person to seek to inquire of those close to him whether he should avail himself of the legal alternative of euthanasia. Certainly, he is likely to wonder about their attitude in the matter. It is quite possible, is it not, that he will not exactly be gratified by any inclination on their part—however noble their motives may be in fact—that he resort to the new procedure? At this stage, the patient-family relationship may well be a good deal less than it ought to be.

And what of the relatives? If their views will not always influence the patient, will they not at least influence the attending physician? Will a physician assume the risks to his reputation, if not his pocketbook, by administering the *coup de grâce* over the objection—however irrational—of a close relative. Do not the relatives, then, also have a 'choice'? Is not the decision on their part to do nothing and say nothing *itself* a 'choice'? In many families there will be some, will there not, who will consider a stand against euthanasia the only proof of love, devotion and gratitude for past events? What of the stress and strife if close relatives differ over the desirability of euthanatizing the patient?

At such a time, members of the family are not likely to be in the best state of mind, either, to make this kind of decision. Financial stress and conscious or unconscious competition for the family's estate aside,

> The chronic illness and persistent pain in terminal carcinoma may place strong and excessive stresses upon the family's emotional ties with the patient. The family members who have strong emotional attachment to start with are most likely to take the patient's fears, pains and fate personally. Panic often strikes them. Whatever guilt feelings they may have toward the patient emerge to plague them.
>
> If the patient is maintained at home, many frustrations and physical demands may be imposed on the family by the advanced illness. There may develop extreme weakness, incontinence and bad odors. The pressure of caring for the individual under these circumstances is likely to arouse a resentment and, in turn, guilt feelings on the part of those who have to do the nursing.[31]

Nor should it be overlooked that while Professor Williams would remove the various procedural steps and personnel contemplated in the British and American Bills and bank his all on the 'good sense' of the general practitioner, no man is immune to the fear, anxieties and frustrations engendered by the apparently helpless, hopeless patient. Not even the general practitioner:

> Working with a patient suffering from a malignancy causes special problems for the physician. First of all, the patient with a malignancy is most likely to engender anxiety concerning death,

> even in the doctor. And at the same time, this type of patient constitutes a serious threat or frustration to medical ambition. As a result, a doctor may react more emotionally and less objectively than in any other area of medical practice. . . . His deep concern may make him more pessimistic than is necessary. As a result of the feeling of frustration in his wish to help, the doctor may have moments of annoyance with the patient. He may even feel almost inclined to want to avoid this type of patient.[32]

Putting aside the problem of whether the good sense of the general practitioner warrants dispensing with other personnel, there still remain the problems posed by *any* voluntary euthanasia programme: the aforementioned considerable pressures on the patient and his family. Are these the kind of pressures we want to inflict on any person, let alone a very sick person? Are these the kind of pressures we want to impose on any family, let alone an emotionally shattered family? And if so, why are they not also proper considerations for the crippled, the paralyzed, the quadruple amputee, the iron-lung occupant and their families?

Might it not be said of the existing ban on euthanasia, as Professor Herbert Wechsler has said of the criminal law in another connection:

> It also operates, and perhaps more significantly, at anterior stages in the patterns of conduct, the dark shadow of organized disapproval eliminating from the ambit of consideration alternatives that might otherwise present themselves in the final competition of choice.[33]

C. THE 'HOPELESSLY INCURABLE' PATIENT AND THE FALLIBLE DOCTOR

Professor Williams notes as 'standard argument' the plea that 'no sufferer from an apparently fatal illness should be deprived of his life because there is always the possibility that the diagnosis is wrong, or else that some remarkable cure will be discovered in time'.[34] But he does not reach the issue until he has already dismissed it with this prefatory remark:

> It has been noticed before in this work that writers who object to a practice for theological reasons frequently try to support their

condemnation on medical grounds. With euthanasia this is difficult, but the effort is made.[35]

Does not Williams, while he pleads that euthanasia be not theologically prejudged, at the same time invite the inference that non-theological objections to euthanasia are simply camouflage?

It is no doubt true that many theological opponents employ medical arguments as well, but it is also true that the doctor who has probably most forcefully advanced medical objections to euthanasia of the so-called incurables, Cornell University's world-renowned Foster Kennedy, a former President of the Euthanasia Society of America, *advocates* euthanasia in other areas where error in diagnosis and prospect of new relief or cures are much reduced—that is, for the 'congenitally unfit'.[36] In large part for the same reasons, Great Britain's Dr A. Leslie Banks, then Principal Medical Officer of the Ministry of Health, maintained that a better case could be made for the destruction of congenital idiots and those in the final stages of dementia, particularly senile dementia, than could be made for the doing away of the pain-stricken incurable.[37] Surely, such opponents of voluntary euthanasia cannot be accused of wrapping theological objections in medical dressing!

Until the Euthanasia Societies of Great Britain and America had been organized and a party decision reached, shall we say, to advocate euthanasia only for incurables on their request, Dr Abraham L. Wolbarst, one of the most ardent supporters of the movement, was less troubled about putting away 'insane or defective people [who] have suffered mental incapacity and tortures of the mind for many years' than he was about the 'incurables'.[38] He recognized the 'difficulty involved in the decision as to incurability' as one of the 'doubtful aspects of euthanasia': 'Doctors are only human beings, with few if any supermen among them. They make honest mistakes, like other men, because of the limitations of the human mind.'[39]

He noted further that 'it goes without saying that, in recently developed cases with a possibility of cure, euthanasia should not even be considered', that 'the law might establish a limit of, say, ten years in which there is a chance of the patient's recovery'.[40]

Dr Benjamin Miller is another who is unlikely to harbour an ulterior theological motive. His interest is more personal. He himself was left to die the death of a 'hopeless' tuberculosis victim, only to discover that he was suffering from a rare malady which affects the lungs in much the same manner but seldom kills. Five years and sixteen hospitalizations later, Dr Miller dramatized his point by recalling the last diagnostic clinic of the brilliant Richard Cabot, on the occasion of his official retirement:

> He was given the case records [complete medical histories and results of careful examinations] of two patients and asked to diagnose their illnesses. . . . The patients had died and only the hospital pathologist knew the exact diagnosis beyond doubt, for he had seen the descriptions of the postmortem findings. Dr Cabot, usually very accurate in his diagnosis, that day missed both.
>
> The chief pathologist who had selected the cases was a wise person. He had purposely chosen two of the most deceptive to remind the medical students and young physicians that even at the end of a long and rich experience one of the greatest diagnosticians of our time was still not infallible.[41]

Richard Cabot was the John W. Davis, the John Lord O'Brian, of his profession. When one reads the account of his last clinic, one cannot help but think of how fallible the *average* general practitioner must be, how fallible the *young doctor just starting practice* must be—and this, of course, is all that some small communities have in the way of medical care—how fallible the *worst* practitioner, young or old, must be. If the range of skill and judgment among licensed physicians approaches the wide gap between the very best and the very worst members of the bar—and I have no reason to think it does not—then the minimally competent physician is hardly the man to be given the responsibility for ending another's life.[42] Yet, under Williams's proposal at least, the marginal physician, as well as his more distinguished brethren, would have legal authorization to make just such decisions. Under Williams's proposal, euthanatizing a patient or two would all be part of the routine day's work.

Perhaps it is not amiss to add as a final note, that no less a euthanasiast than Dr C. Killick Millard[43] had such little faith in the average general practitioner that as regards the *mere administering* of the *coup de grâce*, he observed:

> In order to prevent any likelihood of bungling, it would be very

> necessary that only medical practitioners who had been specially licensed to euthanize (after acquiring special knowledge and skill) should be allowed to administer euthanasia. Quite possibly, the work would largely be left in the hands of the official euthanizors who would have to be appointed specially for each area.[44]

True, the percentage of correct diagnosis is particularly high in cancer.[45] The short answer, however, is that euthanasiasts most emphatically do not propose to restrict mercy-killing to cancer cases. Dr Millard has maintained that 'there are very many diseases besides cancer which tend to kill "by inches", and where death, when it does at last come to the rescue, is brought about by pain and exhaustion'.[46] Furthermore, even if mercy-killings were to be limited to cancer, however relatively accurate the diagnosis in these cases, here, too, 'incurability of a disease is never more than an estimate based upon experience, and how fallacious experience may be in medicine only those who have had a great deal of experience fully realize'.[47]

Dr Daniel Laszlo, Chief of Division of Neoplastic Diseases, Montefiore Hospital, New York City, and three other physicians have observed:

> The mass crowding of a group of patients labeled 'terminal' in institutions designated for that kind of care carries a grave danger. The experience gathered from this group makes it seem reasonable to conclude that a fresh evaluation of any large group in mental institutions, in institutions for chronic care, or in homes for the incurably sick, would unearth a rewarding number of salvageable patients who can be returned to their normal place in society. . . . For purposes of this study we were especially interested in those with a diagnosis of advanced cancer. In a number of these patients, major errors in diagnosis or management were encountered.[48]

Faulty diagnosis is only one ground for error. Even if the diagnosis is correct, a second ground for error lies in the possibility that some measure of relief, if not a full cure, may come to the fore within the life expectancy of the patient. Since Glanville Williams does not deign this objection to euthanasia worth more than a passing reference,[49] it is necessary to turn elsewhere to ascertain how it has been met. One answer is: 'It must be little comfort to a man slowly coming apart from multiple sclerosis to think that fifteen years from now, death might not be his only hope.'[50]

To state the problem this way is of course, to avoid it entirely. How do we know that fifteen *days* or fifteen *hours* from now, 'death might not be [the incurable's] only hope'?

A second answer is: '[N]o cure for cancer which might be found "tomorrow" would be of any value to a man or woman "so far advanced in cancerous toxemia as to be an applicant for euthanasia".'[51]

As I shall endeavour to show, this approach is a good deal easier to formulate than it is to apply. For one thing, it presumes that we know today *what* cures will be found tomorrow. For another, it overlooks that if such cases can be said to exist, the patient is likely to be *so far* advanced in cancerous toxemia as to be no longer capable of understanding the step he is taking and hence *beyond* the stage when euthanasia ought to be administered.[52]

Thirty-six years ago, Dr Haven Emerson, then President of the American Public Health Association, made the point that 'no one can say today what will be incurable tomorrow. No one can predict what disease will be fatal or permanently incurable until medicine becomes stationary and sterile'. Dr Emerson went so far as to say that 'to be at all accurate we must drop altogether the term "incurables" and substitute for it some such term as "chronic illness"'.[53]

At that time Dr Emerson did not have to go back more than a decade to document his contention. Before Banting and Best's insulin discovery, many a diabetic had been doomed. Before the Whipple-Minot-Murphy liver treatment made it a relatively minor malady, many a pernicious anaemia sufferer had been branded 'hopeless'. Before the uses of sulphanilomide were disclosed, a patient with widespread streptococcal blood-poisoning was a condemned man.[54]

Today, we may take even that most resolute disease, cancer, and we need look back no further than the last two decades of research in this field to document the same contention.[55] True, many types of cancer still run their course virtually unhampered by man's arduous efforts to inhibit them. But the number of cancers coming under some control is ever increasing. With medicine attacking on so many fronts with so many weapons, who would bet a man's life on when and how the next type of cancer will yield, if only just a bit? Of course, we would not be betting much of a life. For even in those areas where gains have been registered, the life is not 'saved', death is only postponed. In a sense this is the case with every 'cure' for every ailment. But it may be urged that, after all, there is a great deal of difference between the typical 'cure' which achieves an indefinite postponement, more or less, and the cancer respite which results in only a brief intermission, so to speak, of rarely more than six months or a year. Is this really long enough to warrant all the bother?

Well, how long *is* long enough? In many recent cases of cancer respite, the patient, though experiencing only temporary relief, underwent sufficient improvement to retake his place in society. Six or twelve or eighteen months is long enough to do most of the things which socially justify our existence, is it not? Long enough for a nurse to care for more patients, a teacher to impart learning to more classes, a judge to write a great opinion, a novelist to write a stimulating book, a scientist to make an important discovery and, after all, for a factory-hand to put the wheels on another year's Cadillac.

D. 'MISTAKES ARE ALWAYS POSSIBLE'

Under Professor Williams's 'legislative suggestion' a doctor could 'refrain from taking steps to prolong the patient's life by medical means' solely on his own authority. Only when disposition by affirmative 'mercy-killing' is a considered alternative, need he do so much as, and only so much as, consult another general practitioner.[56] There are no other safeguards: no 'euthanasia referee' no requirement that death be administered in the presence of an official witness, as in the British Society's bill; no court to petition, no committee to investigate and report back to the court, as in the American Society's bill. Professor Williams's view is:

> It may be allowed that mistakes are always possible, but this is so in any of the affairs of life. And it is just as possible to make a mistake by doing nothing as by acting. All that can be expected of any moral agent is that he should do his best on the facts as they appear to him.[57]

That mistakes are always possible, that mistakes are always made, does not, it is true, deter society from pursuing a particular line of conduct—if the line of conduct is *compelled* by needs which override the risk of mistake. A thousand *Convicting the Innocent's*[58] or *Not Guilty's*[59] may stir us, may spur us to improve the administration of the criminal law, but they cannot and should not bring the business of deterring and incapacitating dangerous criminals or would-be dangerous criminals to an abrupt and complete halt.

A relevant question, then, is what is the need for euthanasia which leads us to tolerate the mistakes, the very fatal mistakes, which will inevitably occur? What is the compelling force which requires us to tinker with deeply entrenched and almost universal precepts of criminal law?

Let us first examine the qualitative need for euthanasia.

Proponents of euthanasia like to present for consideration the case of the surgical operation, particularly a highly dangerous one: risk of death is substantial, perhaps even more probable than not; in addition, there is always the risk that the doctors have misjudged the situation and that no operation was needed at all. Yet it is not unlawful to perform the operation.

The short answer is the witticism that whatever the incidence of death in connection with different types of operations, 'no doubt, it is in all cases below 100 per cent, which is the incidence rate for euthanasia'.[60] But this may not be the full answer. There are occasions where the law permits action involving about a 100 per cent incidence of death—for example, self-defence. There may well be other instances where the law should condone such action—for example, the 'necessity' cases illustrated by the overcrowded lifeboat,[61] the starving survivors of a shipwreck[62] and—perhaps best of all—by Professor Lon Fuller's penetrating and fascinating tale of the trapped cave explorers.[63]

In all these situations, death for some may well be excused, if not justified, yet the prospect that some deaths will be unnecessary is a real one. He who kills in self-defence may have misjudged the facts. They who throw passengers overboard to lighten the load may no sooner do so than see 'masts and sails of rescue . . . emerge out of the fog'.[64] But no human being will ever find himself in a situation where he knows for an absolute certainty that one or several must die that he or others may live. 'Modern legal systems . . . do not require divine knowledge of human beings.'[65]

Reasonable mistakes, then, may be tolerated if, as in the above circumstances and as in the case of the surgical operation, these mistakes are the inevitable by-products of efforts to save one or more human lives.[66]

The need the euthanasiast advances, however, is a good deal less compelling. It is only to ease pain.

Let us next examine the quantitative need for euthanasia.

No figures are available, so far as I can determine, as to the number of, say, cancer victims, who undergo intolerable or overwhelming pain. That an appreciable number do suffer such pain, I have no doubt. But that anything approaching this number, whatever it is, need suffer such pain, I have—viewing the many sundry palliative measures now available—considerable doubt. The whole field of severe pain and its management in the terminal stage of cancer is, according to an eminent physician, 'a subject neglected far too much by the medical profession'.[67] Other well-qualified commentators have recently noted the 'obvious lack of interest in the literature about the problem of cancer pain'[68] and have scored 'the deplorable attitude of defeatism and therapeutic inactivity found in some quarters'.[69]

The picture of the advanced cancer victim beyond the relief of morphine and like drugs is a poignant one, but apparently no small number of these situations may have been brought about by premature or excessive application of these drugs. Psychotherapy 'unfortunately . . . has barely been explored'[70] in this area, although a survey conducted on approximately three hundred patients with advanced cancer disclosed that 'over 50 per cent of patients who had received analgesics for long periods of time could be adequately controlled by placebo medication'.[71] Nor should it be overlooked that nowadays drugs are only one of many ways—and by no means always the most effective way—of attacking the pain problem. Radiation, Röntgen and X-ray therapy; the administration of various endocrine substances; intrathecal alcohol injections and other types of nerve blocking; and various neurosurgical operations such as spinothalmic chordotomy and spinothalmic tractomy, have all furnished striking relief in many cases. These various formidable non-narcotic measures, it should be added, are conspicuously absent from the prolific writings of the euthanasiasts.

That of those who do suffer and must necessarily suffer the requisite pain, many *really* desire death, I have considerable doubt.[72] Further, that of those who may desire death at a given moment, many have a fixed and rational desire for death, I likewise have considerable doubt. Finally, taking those who may have such a desire, again I must register a strong note of scepticism that many cannot do the job themselves.[73] It is not that I condone suicide. It is simply that I find it easier to prefer a *laissez-faire* approach in such matters over an approach aided and sanctioned by the state.

The need is only one variable. The incidence of mistake is another. Can it not be said that although the need is not very great it is great enough to outweigh the few mistakes which are likely to occur? I think not. The incidence of error may be small in euthanasia, but as I have endeavoured to show, and as Professor Williams has not taken pains to deny, under our present state of knowledge appreciable error is inevitable.

Even if the need for voluntary euthanasia could be said to outweigh the risk of mistake, this is not the end of the matter. That 'all that can be expected of any moral agent is that he should do his best on the facts as they appear to him'[74] may be true as far as it goes, but it would seem that where the consequence of error is so irreparable it is not too much to expect of society that there be *a good deal more than one moral agent* 'to do his best on the facts as they appear to him'.

2. *A Long-range View of Euthanasia*

A. VOLUNTARY VERSUS INVOLUNTARY EUTHANASIA

Ever since the 1870s, when what was probably the first euthanasia debate of the modern era took place,[75] most proponents of the movement—at least when they are pressed—have taken considerable pains to restrict the question to the plight of the unbearably suffering incurable who *voluntarily seeks* death, while most of their opponents have striven equally hard to frame the issue in terms which would encompass certain involuntary situations as well, e.g. the 'congenital idiots', the 'permanently insane', and the senile.

Glanville Williams reflects the outward mood of many euthanasiasts when he scores those who insist on considering the question from a broader angle:

> The [British Society's] bill [debated in the House of Lords in 1936 and 1950] excluded any question of compulsory euthanasia, even for hopelessly defective infants. Unfortunately, a legislative proposal is not assured of success merely because it is worded in a studiously moderate and restrictive form. The method of attack, by those who

dislike the proposal, is to use the 'thin end of the wedge' argument. . . . There is no proposal for reform on any topic, however conciliatory and moderate, that cannot be opposed by this dialectic.[76]

Why was the bill 'worded in a studiously moderate and restrictive form'? If it were done as a matter of principle, if it were done in recognition of the ethico-moral-legal 'wall of separation' which stands between voluntary and compulsory 'mercy-killings', much can be said for the euthanasiasts' lament about the methods employed by the opposition. But if it were done as a matter of political expediency—with great hopes and expectations of pushing through a second and somewhat less restrictive bill as soon as the first one had sufficiently 'educated' public opinion and next a third, still less restrictive bill—what standing do the euthanasiasts then have to attack the methods of the opposition? No cry of righteous indignation could ring more hollow, I would think, than the protest from those utilizing the 'wedge' principle themselves that their opponents are making the wedge objection.

In this regard the words and action of the euthanasiasts are not insignificant.

In the 1936 debate in the House of Lords, Lord Ponsonby of Shulbrede, who moved the second reading of the Voluntary Euthanasia Bill, described two appealing actual cases, one where a man drowned his four-year-old daughter 'who had contracted tuberculosis and had developed gangrene in the face',[77] and another where a woman killed her mother who was suffering from 'general paralysis of the insane'.[78] Both cases of course were of the compulsory variety of euthanasia. True, Lord Ponsonby readily admitted that these cases were not covered by the proposed bill, but the fact remains that they were the *only* specific cases he chose to describe.

In 1950, Lord Chorley once again called the Voluntary Euthanasia Bill to the attention of the House of Lords. He was most articulate, if not too discreet, on excluding compulsory euthanasia cases from coverage:

> . . . Another objection is that the Bill does not go far enough, because it applies only to adults and does not apply to children who come into the world deaf, dumb and crippled, and who have a

much better cause than those for whom the Bill provides. That may be so, but we must go step by step.[79]

In 1938, two years after the British Society was organized and its bill had been introduced into the House of Lords, the Euthanasia Society of America was formed.[80] At its first annual meeting the following year, it offered proposed euthanasia legislation:

Infant imbeciles, hopelessly insane persons . . . and any person not requesting his own death would not come within the scope of the proposed act. Charles E. Nixdorff, New York lawyer and treasurer of the society, who offered the bill for consideration, explained to some of the members who desired to broaden the scope of the proposed law, that it was *limited purposely to voluntary euthanasia because public opinion is not ready to accept the broader principle.* He said, however, that *the society hoped eventually to legalize the putting to death of nonvolunteers* beyond the help of medical science.[81]

At a meeting of the Society of Medical Jurisprudence held several weeks after the American Society's Voluntary Euthanasia Bill had been drafted, Dr Foster Kennedy, newly elected President of the Society, urged 'the legalizing of euthanasia primarily in cases of born defectives who are doomed to remain defective, rather than for normal persons who have become miserable through incurable illness' and scored the 'absurd and misplaced sentimental kindness' that seeks to preserve the life of a 'person who is not a person'. 'If the law sought to restrict euthanasia to those who could speak out for it, and thus overlooked these creatures who cannot speak, then, I say as Dickens did, "The law's an ass".'[82] As pointed out elsewhere, *while President* of the Society, Dr Kennedy not only eloquently advocated involuntary euthanasia but strenuously *opposed* the voluntary variety.[83] Is it any wonder that opponents of the movement do not always respect the voluntary-involuntary dichotomy?

In 1950, the 'mercy-killings' perpetrated by Dr Herman N. Sander on his cancer-stricken patient and by Miss Carol Ann Paight on her cancer-stricken father put the euthanasia question on page one.[84] In the midst of the fervour over these cases, Dr Clarence Cook Little, one of the leaders in the movement and a former President of the American Society, suggested specific safeguards for a law legalizing 'mercy-killings' for the 'incurably ill but mentally fit' *and* for 'mental defectives'.[85] The Reverend Charles Francis Potter, the founder and first president of the American Society, hailed Dr Sander's action as 'morally right' and hence that which 'should be legally right'.[86] Shortly thereafter, at its annual meeting, the American Society 'voted to continue support' of both Dr Sander and Miss Paight.[87]

Now, one of the interesting, albeit underplayed, features of these cases—and this was evident all along—was that both were *involuntary* 'mercy-killings'. There was considerable conflict in the testimony at the Sander Trial as to whether or not the victim's *husband* had pleaded with the doctor to end her suffering,[88] but nobody claimed that the victim herself had done such pleading. There was considerable evidence in the *Paight* case to the effect that the victim's *daughter* had a 'cancer phobia', the cancer deaths of two aunts having left a deep mark on her,[89] but nobody suggested that the victim had a 'cancer phobia'.

It is true that Mother Paight said approvingly of her mercy-killing daughter that 'she had the old Paight guts',[90] but it is no less true that Father Paight had no opportunity to pass judgment on the question. He was asleep, still under the anaesthetic of the exploratory operation which revealed the cancer in his stomach when his daughter, after having taken one practice shot in the woods, fired into his left temple.[91] Is it not just possible that Father Paight would have preferred to have had the vaunted Paight intestinal fortitude channelled in other directions, e.g. by his daughter bearing to see him suffer?[92]

The *Sander* and *Paight* cases amply demonstrate that to the press, the public, and many euthanasiasts, the killing of one who does not or cannot speak is no less a 'mercy-killing' than the killing of one who asks for death. Indeed, the overwhelming majority of known or alleged 'mercy-killings' have occurred without the consent of the victim. If the *Sander* and *Paight* cases are typical at all, they are so only in that the victims were not ill or retarded children, as in the *Simpson*,[93] *Brownhill*[94] and *Long*[95] English cases, and the *Greenfield, Repouille, Noxon* and *Braunsdorf* American cases.[96]

These situations are all quite moving. So much so that two of the strongest presentations of the need for *voluntary* euthanasia, free copies of which may be obtained from the American Society, lead off with sympathetic discussions of the *Brownhill* and *Greenfield* cases.[97] This, it need hardly be said, is not the way to honour the voluntary-involuntary boundary; not the way to ease the pressure to legalize at least this type of involuntary euthanasia as well, if any changes in the broad area are to be made at all.

Nor, it should be noted, is Williams free from criticism in this regard. In his discussion of 'the present law', apparently a discussion of voluntary euthanasia, he cites only one case, *Simpson*, an involuntary situation.[98] In his section on 'the administration of the law' he describes only the *Sander* case and the 'compassionate acquittal' of a man who drowned his four-year-old daughter, a sufferer of tuberculosis and gangrene of the face.[99] Again, both are involuntary cases. For 'some other' American mercy-killing cases, Williams refers generally to an article by Helen Silving,[100] but two of the three cases he seems to have in mind are likewise cases of involuntary euthanasia.[101]

That the press and general public are not alone in viewing an act as a 'mercy-killing', lack of consent on the part of the victim notwithstanding, is well evidenced by the deliberations of the Royal Commission on Capital Punishment.[102] The report itself described 'mercy-killings' as 'for example, where a mother has killed her child or a husband has killed his wife from merciful motives of pity and humanity'.[103] The only specific proposal to exclude 'mercy-killings' from the category of murder discussed in the report is a suggestion by the Society of Labour Lawyers which disregards the voluntary-involuntary distinction:

> If a person who has killed another person proves that he killed that person with the compassionate intention of saving him physical or mental suffering, he shall not be guilty of murder.[104]

Another proposal, one by Hector Hughes, M.P., to the effect that only those who 'maliciously' cause the death of another shall be guilty of murder,[105] likewise treated the voluntary and involuntary 'mercy-killer' as one and the same.

Testimony before the Commission underscored the great appeal of the *involuntary* 'mercy-killings.' Thus, Lord Goddard, the Lord Chief Justice, referred to the famous *Brownhill* case, which he himself had tried some fifteen years earlier, as 'a dreadfully pathetic case'.[106] 'The son,' he pointed out, 'was a hopeless imbecile, more than imbecile, a mindless idiot.'[107]

Mr Justice Humphreys recalled 'one case that was the most pathetic sight I ever saw',[108] a case which literally had the trial judge, Mr

Justice Hawkins, in tears. It involved a young father who smothered his infant child to death when he learned the child had contracted syphilis from the mother (whose morals turned out to be something less than represented) and would be blind for life. 'That,' Mr Justice Humphreys told the Commission, 'was a real "mercy-killing".'[109]

The boldness and daring which characterize most of Glanville Williams's book dim perceptibly when he comes to involuntary euthanasia proposals. As to the senile, he states:

> At present the problem has certainly not reached the degree of seriousness that would warrant an effort being made to change traditional attitudes towards the sanctity of life of the aged. Only the grimmest necessity could bring about a change that, however cautious in its approach, would probably cause apprehension and deep distress to many people, and inflict a traumatic injury upon the accepted code of behaviour built up by two thousand years of the Christian religion. It may be, however, that as the problem becomes more acute it will itself cause a reversal of generally accepted values.[110]

To me, this passage is the most startling one in the book. On page 310 Williams invokes 'traditional attitudes towards the sanctity of life' and 'the accepted code of behaviour built up by two thousand years of the Christian religion' to check the extension of euthanasia to the senile, but for 309 pages he had been merrily rolling along debunking both. Substitute 'cancer victim' for 'the aged' and Williams's passage is essentially the argument of many of his *opponents* on the voluntary euthanasia question.

The unsupported comment that 'the problem [of senility] has certainly not reached the degree of seriousness' to warrant euthanasia is also rather puzzling, particularly coming as it does after an observation by Williams on the immediately preceding page that 'it is increasingly common for men and women to reach an age of "second childishness and mere oblivion", with a loss of almost all adult faculties except that of digestion'.[111]

How 'serious' does a problem have to be to warrant a change in these 'traditional attitudes'? If, as the statement seems to indicate, 'seriousness' of the problem is to be determined numerically, the problem of the cancer victim does not appear to be as substantial as the problem of the senile. For example, taking just the 95,837 first admissions to 'public prolonged-care hospitals' for mental diseases in the United States in 1955, 23,561—or one-fourth—were cerebral arteriosclerosis or senile brain disease cases. I am not at all sure that there are twenty thousand cancer victims per year who die *unbearably painful* deaths. Even if there were, I cannot believe that among their ranks are some twenty thousand per year who, when still in a rational state, so long for a quick and easy death that they would avail themselves of legal machinery for euthanasia.

If the problem of the incurable cancer victim has reached 'the degree of seriousness that would warrant an effort being made to change traditional attitudes towards the sanctity of life', as Williams obviously thinks it has, then so has the problem of senility. In any event, the senility problem will undoubtedly soon reach even Williams's requisite degree of seriousness:

> A decision concerning the senile may have to be taken within the next twenty years. The number of old people are increasing by leaps and bounds. Pneumonia, 'the old man's friend', is now checked by antibiotics. The effects of hardship, exposure, starvation and accident are now minimized. Where is this leading us? . . . What of the drooling, helpless, disorientated old man or the doubly incontinent old woman lying log-like in bed? Is it here that the real need for euthanasia exists?[112]

If, as Williams indicates, 'seriousness' of the problem is a major criterion for euthanatizing a category of unfortunates, the sum total of mentally deficient persons would appear to warrant high priority, indeed.[113]

When Williams turns to the plight of the 'hopelessly defective infants', his characteristic vim and vigour are, as in the senility discussion, conspicuously absent:

> While the Euthanasia Society of England has never advocated this, the Euthanasia Society of America did include it in its original programme. The proposal certainly escapes the chief objection to the similar proposal for senile dementia: it does not create a sense of insecurity in society, because infants cannot, like adults, feel anticipatory dread of being done to death if their condition should

worsen. Moreover, the proposal receives some support on eugenic grounds, and more importantly on humanitarian grounds—both on account of the parents, to whom the child will be a burden all their lives, and on account of the handicapped child itself. (It is not, however, proposed that any child should be destroyed against the wishes of its parents.) Finally, the legalization of euthanasia for handicapped children would bring the law into closer relation to its practical administration, because juries do not regard parental mercy-killing as murder. For these various reasons the proposal to legalize humanitarian infanticide is put forward from time to time by individuals. They remain in a very small minority, and the proposal may at present be dismissed as politically insignificant.[114]

It is understandable for a reformer to limit his present proposals for change to those with a real prospect of success. But it is hardly reassuring for Williams to cite the fact that only 'a very small minority' has urged euthanasia for 'hopelessly defective infants' as the *only* reason for not pressing for such legislation now. If, as Williams sees it, the only advantage voluntary euthanasia has over the involuntary variety lies in the organized movements on its behalf, that advantage can readily be wiped out.

In any event, I do not think that such 'a very small minority' has advocated 'humanitarian infanticide'. Until the organization of the British and American societies led to a concentration on the voluntary type, and until the by-products of the Nazi euthanasia programme somewhat embarrassed, if only temporarily, most proponents of involuntary euthanasia, about as many writers urged one type as another.[115] Indeed, some euthanasiasts have taken considerable pains to demonstrate the superiority of defective infant euthanasia over incurably ill euthanasia.[116]

As for dismissing euthanasia of defective infants as 'politically insignificant', the only poll that I know of which measured the public response to both types of euthanasia revealed that *45 per cent favoured euthanasia for defective infants under certain conditions while only 37.3 per cent approved euthanasia for the incurably and painfully ill under any conditions.*[117] Furthermore, of those who favoured the mercy-killing cure for incurable adults, some 40 per cent would require only family permission or medical board approval, but not the patient's permission.[118]

Nor do I think it irrelevant that while public resistance caused Hitler to yield on the adult euthanasia front, the killing of malformed and idiot children continued unhindered to the end of the war, the definition of 'children' expanding all the while.[119] Is it the embarrassing experience of the Nazi euthanasia programme which has rendered destruction of defective infants presently 'politically insignificant'? If so, is it any more of a jump for the incurably and painfully ill to the unorthodox political thinker than it is from the hopelessly defective infant to the same 'unsavoury character'? Or is it not so much that the euthanasiasts are troubled by the Nazi experience as it is that they are troubled that the public is troubled by the Nazi experience?

I read Williams's comments on defective infants for the proposition that there are some very good reasons for euthanatizing defective infants, but the time is not yet ripe. When will it be? When will the proposal become politically significant? After a voluntary euthanasia law is on the books and public opinion is sufficiently 'educated'?

Williams's reasons for not extending euthanasia—once we legalize it in the narrow 'voluntary' area—to the senile and the defective are much less forceful and much less persuasive than his arguments for legalizing voluntary euthanasia in the first place. I regard this as another reason for not legalizing voluntary euthanasia in the first place.

B. THE PARADE OF HORRORS

'Look, when the messenger cometh, shut the door, and hold him fast at the door: *is* not the sound of his master's feet behind him?'[120]

This is the 'wedge principle', the 'parade of horrors' objection, if you will, to voluntary euthanasia. Glanville Williams's peremptory retort is:

> This use of the 'wedge' objection evidently involves a particular determination as to the meaning of words, namely the words 'if raised to a general line of conduct'. The author supposes, for the sake of argument, that the merciful extinction of life in a suffering patient is not in itself immoral. Still it is immoral, because if it were permitted this would admit 'a most dangerous wedge that might eventually put all life in a precarious condition'. It seems a sufficient reply to say that this type of reasoning could be used to condemn

> any act whatever, because there is no human conduct from which evil cannot be imagined to follow if it is persisted in when some of the circumstances are changed. All moral questions involve the drawing of a line, but the 'wedge principle' would make it impossible to draw a line, because the line would have to be pushed farther and farther back until all action became vetoed.[121]

I agree with Williams that if a first step is 'moral' it is moral wherever a second step may take us. The real point, however, the point that Williams sloughs, is that whether or not the first step is precarious, is perilous, is worth taking, rests in part on what the second step is likely to be.

It is true that the 'wedge' objection can always be advanced, the horrors can always be paraded. But it is no less true that on some occasions the objection is much more valid than it is on others. One reason why the 'parade of horrors' cannot be too lightly dismissed in this particular instance is that Miss Voluntary Euthanasia is not likely to be going it alone for very long. Many of her admirers, as I have endeavoured to show in the preceding section, would be neither surprised nor distressed to see her joined by Miss Euthanatize the Congenital Idiots and Miss Euthanatize the Permanently Insane and Miss Euthanatize the Senile Dementia. And these lasses—whether or not they themselves constitute a 'parade of horrors'—certainly make excellent majorettes for such a parade:

> Some are proposing what is called euthanasia; at present only a proposal for killing those who are a nuisance to themselves; but soon to be applied to those who are a nuisance to other people.[122]

Another reason why the 'parade of horrors' argument cannot be too lightly dismissed in this particular instance, it seems to me, is that the parade *has* taken place in our time and the order of procession has been headed by the killing of the 'incurables' and the 'useless':

> Even before the Nazis took open charge in Germany, a propaganda barrage was directed against the traditional compassionate nineteenth-century attitudes toward the chronically ill, and for the adoption of a utilitarian, Hegelian point of view. . . . Lay opinion was not neglected in this campaign. Adults were propagandized by

> motion pictures, one of which, entitled 'I Accuse', deals entirely with euthanasia. This film depicts the life history of a woman suffering from multiple sclerosis; in it her husband, a doctor, finally kills her to the accompaniment of soft piano music rendered by a sympathetic colleague in an adjoining room. Acceptance of this ideology was implanted even in the children. A widely used high-school mathematics text . . . included problems stated in distorted terms of the cost of caring for and rehabilitating the chronically sick and crippled. One of the problems asked, for instance, how many new housing units could be built and how many marriage-allowance loans could be given to newly wedded couples for the amount of money it cost the state to care for 'the crippled, the criminal and the insane. . . .' The beginnings at first were merely a subtle shift in emphasis in the basic attitude of the physicians. *It started with the acceptance of the attitude, basic in the euthanasia movement, that there is such a thing as life not worthy to be lived.* This attitude in its early stages concerned itself merely with the severely and chronically sick. Gradually the sphere of those to be included in this category was enlarged to encompass the socially unproductive, the ideologically unwanted, the racially unwanted and finally all non-Germans. But it is important to realize that the infinitely small wedged-in lever from which this entire trend of mind received its impetus was the attitude toward the non-rehabilitatable sick.[123]

The apparent innocuousness of Germany's 'small beginnings' is perhaps best shown by the fact that German Jews were at first excluded from the programme. For it was originally conceived that 'the blessing of euthanasia should be granted only to [true] Germans'.[124]

Relatively early in the German programme, Pastor Braune, Chairman of the Executive Committee of the Domestic Welfare Council of the German Protestant Church, called for a halt to euthanasia measures 'since they strike sharply at the moral foundations of the nation as a whole. The inviolability of human life is a pillar of any social order'.[125] And the pastor raised the same question which euthanasia opponents ask today, as well they might, considering the disinclination of many in the movement to stop at voluntary 'mercy-killings': Where do we, how do we, draw the line? The good pastor asked:

> How far is the destruction of socially unfit life to go? The mass-methods used so far have quite evidently taken in many people who are to a considerable degree of sound mind. . . . Is it intended to strike only at the utterly hopeless cases—the idiots and imbeciles? The instruction sheet, as already mentioned, also lists senile diseases. The latest decree by the same authorities requires that children with serious congenital disease and malformation of every kind be registered, to be collected and processed in special institutions. This necessarily gives rise to grave apprehensions. Will a line be drawn at the tubercular? In the case of persons in custody by court order, euthanasia measures have evidently already been initiated. Are other abnormal or anti-social persons likewise to be included? Where is the borderline? Who is abnormal, anti-social, hopelessly sick?[126]

Williams makes no attempt to distinguish or minimize the Nazi Germany experience. Apparently he does not consider it worthy of mention in a euthanasia discussion.

A Final Reflection

There have been and there will continue to be compelling circumstances when a doctor or relative or friend will violate The Law on the Books and, more often than not, receive protection from The Law in Action. But this is not to deny that there are other occasions when The Law on the Books operates to stay the hand of all concerned, among them situations where the patient is in fact (1) presently incurable, (2) beyond the aid of any respite which may come along in his life expectancy, suffering (3) intolerable and (4) unmitigable pain and of a (5) fixed and (6) rational desire to die. That any euthanasia programme may only be the opening wedge for far more objectionable practices, and that even within the bounds of a 'voluntary' plan such as Williams's the incidence of mistake or abuse is likely to be substantial, are not much solace to one in the above plight.

It may be conceded that in a narrow sense it is an 'evil' for such a patient to have to continue to suffer—if only for a little while. But in a narrow sense, long-term sentences and capital punishment are 'evils', too.[127] If we can justify the infliction of imprisonment and death by the state 'on the ground of the social interests to be protected', then surely we can similarly justify the postponement of death by the state. The objection that the individual is thereby treated not as an 'end' in himself but only as a 'means' to further the common good was, I think, aptly disposed of by Holmes long ago: 'If a man lives in society, he is likely to find himself so treated.'[128]

NOTES

[1] First published in the U.S. in 1957, by arrangement with the Columbia Law School. Page references in the notes following relate to the British edition (Faber & Faber, 1958).

[2] Joseph Fletcher, *Morals and Medicine* (1954; Gollancz, 1955). Subsequent page references (*n.* 19, 20) relate to the U.S. edition.

[3] In a number of countries, e.g. Germany, Norway, Switzerland, a compassionate motive and/or 'homicide upon request' operates to reduce the penalty. See generally Silving, 'Euthanasia: A Study in Comparative Criminal Law', *Univ. of Pennsylvania Law Review*, 103 (1954), 350. However, apparently only Uruguayan law completely immunizes a homicide characterized by both of the above factors. The Silving article also contains an interesting and fairly extensive comparative study of assisted suicide and the degree to which it is treated differently from a direct 'mercy-killing'. In this regard see also Friedman, 'Suicide, Euthanasia and the Law', *Medical Times*, 85 (1957), 681.

[4] Williams, p. 293.

[5] Id., p. 278. This seems to be the position taken by Bertrand Russell in reviewing Williams's book: 'The central theme of the book is the conflict in the criminal law between the two divergent systems of ethics which may be called respectively utilitarian and taboo morality. . . . Utilitarian morality in the wide sense in which I am using the word, judges actions by their effects. . . . In taboo morality . . . forbidden actions are sin, and they do not cease to be so when their consequences are such as we should all welcome.' (*Stanford Law Review*, 10 [1958], 382) I trust Russell would agree, should he read this article, that the issue is not quite so simple. At any rate, I trust he would agree that I stay within the system of utilitarian ethics.

[6] Wechsler and Michael, 'A Rationale of the Law of Homicide', *Columbia Law Review*, 37 (1937).

[7] Williams, p. 302.

[8] Cf. G. K. Chesterton, 'Euthanasia and Murder', *American Law Review*, 8 (1937), 486, 490.

[9] Williams, pp. 304, 309.

[10] Section 2 (1) of the British Bill. The full text is set forth in H. Roberts, *Euthanasia and Other Aspects of Life and Death* (1936), pp. 21-6. For the Bill now favoured by the Society, see Appendix to the present volume.

[11] Section 301 of the American Bill. The full text is set forth in Sullivan, *The Morality of Mercy Killing* (1950), pp. 25-8.

[12] *Royal Commission on Capital Punishment*, Report (1953), Cmd No. 8932, para. 179. Cf. Bentham, *The Theory of Legislation* (Ogden edn, 1931), p. 256: 'Let us recollect that there is no room for considering the motive except when it is manifest and palpable. It would often be very difficult to discover the true or dominant motive, when the action might be

equally produced by different motives, or where motives of several sorts might have co-operated in its production. In the interpretation of these doubtful cases it is necessary to distrust the malignity of the human heart, and that general disposition to exhibit a brilliant sagacity at the expense of good nature. We involuntarily deceive even ourselves as to what puts us into action. In relation even to our own motives we are wilfully blind, and are always ready to break into a passion against the occulist who desires to remove the cataract of ignorance and prejudice.' Cf. Roberts, op. cit., pp. 10–11: 'Self-deception as to one's motives, what the psychologists call "rationalization", is one of the most powerful of man's self-protective mechanisms. It is an old observation of criminal psychologists that the day-dreamers and the rationalizers account for a very large proportion of the criminal population; whilst, in murderers, this habit of self-deception is often carried to incredible lengths.' It should be noted, however, that the likelihood of faked mercy-killings would seem to be substantially reduced when such acts are not completely immunized but only categorized as a lesser degree of criminal homicide. If mercy-killings were simply taken out of the category of murder, a second line of defence might well be the appearance of a mercy-killing, but in planned murders generally the primary concern of the murderer must surely be to escape all punishment whatever, not to give a serious, but not the most serious, appearance to his act, not to substitute a long period of imprisonment for execution. Cf. the discussion of faked suicide pacts in the Royal Commission findings, op. cit., Minutes of Evidence, paras 804–7. This paper deals with proposals to legalize 'mercy-killing' completely, not with the advisability of removing it from the category of murder.

[13] *House of Lords Debates*, 103, 5th series (1936), cols 484–5.

[14] Banks, 'Euthanasia', *General Practitioner*, 161 (1948), 101, 104.

[15] Frohman, 'Vexing Problems in Forensic Medicine: A Physician's View' *New York Univ. Law Review*, 31 (1956), 1215, 1222.

[16] Roberts, op. cit. (*n.* 10 above), pp. 14–15.

[17] Earengey, 'Voluntary Euthanasia', *Medico-Legal and Criminal Review*, 8 (1940), 91, 106 (discussion following the reading of Judge Earengey's paper).

[18] 'The promoters of the bill hoped that they might be able to mollify the opposition by providing stringent safeguards. Now, they were right in thinking that if they had put in no safeguards—if they had merely said that a doctor could kill his patient whenever he thought it right—they would have been passionately opposed on this ground. So they put in the safeguards. . . . Did the opposition like these elaborate safeguards? On the contrary, they made them a matter of complaint. The safeguards would, it was said, bring too much formality into the sick-room, and destroy the relationship between doctor and patient. So the safeguards were wrong, but not one of the opposition speakers said that he would have voted for the bill without the safeguards.' (Williams, p. 298)

[19] Id., pp. 302 ff. The desire to give doctors a free hand is expressed *passim* numerous times, e.g.: '[T]here should be no formalities and . . . everything should be left to the discretion of the doctor.' (p. 303) '. . . the bill would merely leave this question to the discretion and conscience of the individual medical practitioner'. (p. 304) 'It would be the purpose of the proposed legislation to set doctors free from the fear of the law so that they can think only of the relief of their patients.' (p. 305) 'It would bring the whole subject within ordinary medical practice.' (Ibid.) Williams suggests that the pertinent provisions might be worded as follows:

> '1. For the avoidance of doubt, it is hereby declared that it shall be lawful for a physician whose patient is seriously ill . . . 'b. to refrain from taking steps to prolong the patient's life by medical means; . . . unless it is proved that . . . the omission was not made, in good faith for the purpose of saving the patient from severe pain in an illness believed to be of an incurable and fatal character.

> '2. It shall be lawful for a physician, after consultation with another physician, to accelerate by any merciful means the death of a patient who is seriously ill, unless it is proved that the act was not done in good faith with the consent of the patient and for the purpose of saving him from severe pain in an illness believed to be of an incurable and fatal character.' (p. 308)

The completely unrestricted authorization to kill by omission may well be based on Williams's belief that, under existing law, ' "mercy-killing" by omission to prolong life is probably lawful' since the physician is 'probably exempted' from the duty to use reasonable care to conserve his patient's life 'if life has become a burden'. (p. 291) And he adds—as if this settles the legal question—that 'the morality of an omission in these circumstances is conceded by Catholics'. (Ibid.) If Williams means, as he seems to, *that once a doctor has undertaken treatment and the patient is entrusted solely to his care* he may sit by the bedside of the patient whose life has 'become a burden' and let him die—e.g. by not replacing the oxygen bottle—I submit that he is quite mistaken.

The outer limits of criminal liability for inaction are hardly free from doubt, but it seems fairly clear under existing law that the special and traditional relationship of physician and patient imposes a 'legal duty to act', particularly where the patient is helpless and completely dependent on the physician, and that the physician who withholds life-preserving medical means of the type described above commits criminal homicide by omission. In this regard, see Burdick, *Crimes*, 2 (1946), § 466c; Hall, *Principles of Criminal Law* (1947), pp. 272–8; Kenny, *Outlines of Criminal Law* (16th edn: Turner, 1952), pp. 14–15, 107–9; Perkins, *Criminal Law* (1957), pp. 513–27; Russell, *Crime*, 1 (10th edn: Turner, 1950), pp. 449–66; Hughes, 'Criminal Omissions', *Yale Law Journal*, 67 (1958), 590, 599–600, 621–6, 630 *n*. 142; Kirchheimer, 'Criminal Omissions', *Harvard Law Review*, 55 (1942), 615, 625–8; Wechsler and Michael, op. cit. (*n*. 6 above), 724–5. Nor am I at all certain that the Catholics do 'concede' this point. Williams's reference is to Sullivan, op. cit. (*n*. 11 above), p. 64. But Sullivan considers therein what might be viewed as relatively remote and indirect omissions, e.g. whether to call in a very expensive specialist, whether to undergo a very painful or very drastic operation.

The Catholic approach raises nice questions and draws fine lines, e.g. how many limbs must be amputated before an operation is to be regarded as non-obligatory 'extraordinary', as opposed to 'ordinary', means; but they will not be dwelt upon herein. Suffice to say that apparently there has never been an indictment, let alone a conviction, for a 'mercy-killing' by omission, not even one which directly and immediately produces death. This, of course, is not to say that no such negative 'mercy-killings' have ever occurred. There is reason to think that not too infrequently this is the fate of the defective newborn infant. Williams simply asserts that the 'beneficient tendency of nature [in that 'monsters' usually die quickly after birth] is assisted, in Britain at any rate, by the practice of doctors and nurses, who, when an infant is born seriously malformed, do not "strive officiously to keep alive"'. (p. 32) Fletcher makes a similar and likewise undocumented observation that 'it has always been a quite common practice of midwives and, in modern times doctors, simply to fail to respirate monstrous babies at birth'. (op. cit [*n*. 2 above], p. 207 *n*. 54) A supposition to the same effect was made twenty years earlier in Gregg, 'The Right to Kill', *N. American Review*, 237 (1934), 239, 242. A noted obstetrician and gynaecologist, Dr Frederick Loomis, has told of occasions where expectant fathers have, in effect, asked him to destroy the child, if born abnormal. (Loomis, *Consultation Room* [1946], p. 53) For an eloquent presentation of the problem raised by the defective infant, see id., pp. 53–64.

It is difficult to discuss the consultation feature of Williams's proposal for affirmative 'mercy-killing', because Williams himself never discusses it. This fact, plus the fact that Williams's recurrent theme is to give the general practitioner a free hand, indicates that he himself does not regard consultation as a significant feature of his plan. The attending physician need only consult another general practitioner and there is no requirement that there be any concurrence in his diagnosis. There is no requirement of a written report. There is no indication as to what point in time there need be consultation. Probably consultation would be thought necessary only in regard to diagnosis of the disease and from that point in respect of the extent and mitigatory nature of the pain, the firmness and rationality of the desire to die to be judged solely by the attending physician. For the view that even under rather elaborate consultation requirements, in many thinly staffed communities the consultant doctor would merely reflect the view of the attending physician, see 'Life and Death', *Time Magazine* (March 13, 1950), p. 50. After reviewing eleven case-histories of patients wrongly diagnosed as having advanced cancer—diagnoses that stood uncorrected over long periods of time and after several admissions at leading hospitals—Drs Laszlo, Colmer, Silver and Standard conclude: '[I]t became increasingly clear that the original error was one easily made, but that the continuation of that error was due to an acceptance of the original data without exploring their verity and completeness.' ('Errors in Diagnosis and Management of Cancer', *Annals of Internal Medicine*, 33 [1950], 670)

[20] In 1950 the General Assembly of the World Medical Association approved a resolution recommending to all national associations that they 'condemn the practice of euthanasia under any circumstances'. (*New York Times* [Oct. 18, 1950], p. 22) Earlier that year the Medical Society of the State of New York went on record as being 'unalterably opposed to euthanasia and to any legislation which will legalize euthanasia'. (Ibid. [May 10, 1950], p. 29).

On the other hand, euthanasiasts claim their movement finds great support in the medical profession. The most impressive and most frequently cited piece of evidence is the formation, in 1946, of a committee of 1,776 physicians for the legalization of voluntary euthanasia in New York. (See Williams, p. 296; Fletcher, op. cit. [*n.* 2 above], p. 187) Williams states that of 3,272 physicians who replied to a questionnaire in New York State in 1946, 80 per cent approved voluntary euthanasia and the Committee of 1,776 came from among this favourable group. I have been unable to find any authority for the 80 per cent figure, and Williams cites none. Some years ago, Gertrude Anne Edwards, then editor of the *Euthanasia Society Bulletin*, claimed 3,272 physicians—apparently *all* who replied—favoured legalizing voluntary euthanasia. (Edwards, 'Mercy Death for Incurables Should Be Made Legal', *Daily Compass* [Aug. 24, 1949], p. 8) Presumably, as in the case of the recent New Jersey questionnaire discussed below, *every* physician in New York was sent a questionnaire. If so, then the figure cited, whether Williams's or Edwards's, would mean a great deal more (and support the euthanasiasts a great deal less) if it were added that 88 or 89 per cent of the physicians in the state did not reply at all. In 1940, there were over 26,000 physicians in the State of New York (U.S. Dept of Commerce, Bureau of the Census: *The Labor Force*, Pt 4, p. 366); and in 1950 there were over 30,000 (id.: *Characteristics of the Population*, Pt 32, p. 260).

In 1957 a petition for legalized euthanasia was signed by 166 New Jersey physicians, urging in effect the adoption of the American Society's Bill. (See Anderson, 'Who Signed for Euthanasia?', *America*, 96 [1957], 573). About 98 per cent of the state medical profession *declined* to sign such a petition. The Medical Society of New Jersey immediately issued a statement that 'euthanasia has been and continues to be in conflict with accepted principles of morality and sound medical practice'. When their names were published in a state newspaper, many of the 166 claimed they had not signed the petition or that they had misunderstood its purpose or that, unknown to them, it had been handled by a secretary as a routine matter.

[21] It should be noted that under what might be termed the 'family plan' feature of Williams's proposal, minors might be euthanatized too. Their fate is to be 'left to the

good sense of the doctor, taking into account, as he always does, the wishes of parents as well as those of the child'. (Williams, p. 303 *n.* 1) The dubious quality of the 'voluntariness' of euthanasia in these circumstances need not be laboured.

[22] Frohman, loc. cit. (*n.* 15 above).

[23] The disturbing mental effects of morphine, 'the classic opiate for the relief of severe pain' (Schiffrin and Gross, 'Systematic Analgetics', *Management of Pain in Cancer* [Schiffrin edn, 1956], p. 22), and 'still the most commonly used potent narcotic analgesic in treatment of cancer pain' (Bonica, 'The Management of Cancer Pain', *General Practitioner* [Nov. 1954], pp. 35, 39), have been described in considerable detail by Drs Wolff, Hardy and Goodell in 'Studies on Pain: Measurement of the Effect of Morphine, Codeine and Other Opiates on the Pain Threshold and an Analysis of Their Relation to the Pain Experience', *Journal of Clinical Investigation*, 19 (1940), 659, 664. The increasing use of ACTH or cortisone therapy in cancer palliation presents further problems. Such therapy 'frequently' leads to a 'severe degree of disturbance in capacity for rational, sequential thought'. (Lindemann and Clark, 'Modifications in Ego Structure and Personality Reactions under the Influence of the Effects of Drugs', *American Journal of Psychiatry*, 108 [1952], 561, 566)

[24] Goodman and Gilman, *The Pharmacological Basis of Therapeutics* (2nd edn, 1955), p. 235. To the same effect is Seevers and Pfeiffer, 'A Study of the Analgesia, Subjective Depression and Euphoria Produced by Morphine, Heroin, Dilaudid and Codeine in the Normal Human Subject', *Journal of Pharmacological and Experimental Therapy,* 56 (1936), 166, 182, 187.

[25] Sharpe, 'Medication as a Threat to Testamentary Capacity', *N. Carolina Law Review*, 35 (1957), 380, 392, and medical authorities cited therein. In the case of ACTH or cortisone therapy, the situation is complicated by the fact that 'a frequent pattern of recovery' from psychoses induced by such therapy is 'by the occurrence of lucid intervals of increasing frequency and duration, punctuated by relapses in psychotic behavior'. (Clark *et al.*, 'Further Observations on Mental Disturbances Associated with Cortisone and ACTH Therapy', *New England Journal of Medicine*, 249 [1953], 178, 183).

[26] Sharpe, op. cit., 384. Goodman and Gilman observe that while 'different individuals require varying periods of time before the repeated administration of morphine results in tolerance . . . as a rule . . . after about two to three weeks of continued use of the same dose of alkaloid the usual depressant effects fail to appear', whereupon 'phenomenally large doses may be taken'. (Op. cit. [*n.* 24 above], p. 234) For a discussion of 'the nature of addiction', see Maurer and Vogel, *Narcotics and Narcotic Addiction* (1954), pp. 20–31.

[27] 'Why I Oppose Mercy Killings', *Woman's Home Companion* (June 1950), pp. 38, 103.

[28] *House of Lords Debates*, 103, 5th series (1936), cols 466, 492–3. To the same effect is Lord Horder's speech in the 1950 debates (op. cit., 169, 5th series [1950], cols 551, 569). See also Gumpert, 'A False Mercy', *The Nation*, 170 (1950), 80: 'Even the incapacitated, agonized patient in despair most of the time, may still get some joy from existence. His mood will change between longing for death and fear of death. Who would want to decide what should be done on such unsafe ground?'

[29] Williams, pp. 306–7.

[30] Id., p. 307.

[31] Zarling, 'Psychological Aspects of Pain in Terminal Malignancies', *Management of Pain in Cancer* (Schiffrin edn, 1956), pp. 211–12.

[32] Id., pp. 213–14. See also Dr Benjamin Miller to the effect that cancer 'can be a "horrible experience" for the doctor too' and that 'a long, difficult illness may emotionally exhaust the relatives and physician even more than the patient' (op. cit. [*n.* 27 above], p. 103); and Stephen, commenting on the disclosure by a Dr Thwing that he had practised euthanasia: 'The boldness of this avowal is made particularly conspicuous by Dr Thwing's express admission that the only person for whom the lady's death, if she had been allowed to die naturally, would have been in any degree painful was not the

lady herself, but Dr Thwing.' ('Murder from the Best of Motives', *Law Quarterly Review*, 5 [1889], 188)

[33] Wechsler, 'The Issues of the Nuremberg Trial', *Political Science Quarterly*, 62 (1947), 11, 16. Cf. Cardozo, 'What Medicine Can Do for Law', *Law and Literature* (1931), pp. 88–9: 'Punishment is necessary, indeed, not only to deter the man who is a criminal at heart, who has felt the criminal impulse, who is on the brink of indecision, but also to deter others who in our existing social organization have never felt the criminal impulse and shrink from crime in horror. Most of us have such a scorn and loathing of robbery or forgery that the temptation to rob or forge is never within the range of choice; it is never a real alternative. There can be little doubt, however, that some of this repugnance is due to the ignominy that has been attached to these and like offenses through the sanctions of the criminal law. If the ignominy were withdrawn, the horror might be dimmed.'

[34] Williams, p. 283.

[35] Ibid.

[36] 'What to do with the hopelessly unfit? I had thought at a younger time of my life that the legalizing of euthanasia—a soft gentle-sounding word—was a thing to be encouraged; but as I pondered, and as my experience in medicine grew, I became less sure. Now my face is set against the legalization of euthanasia for any person, who, having been well, has at last become ill, for however ill they be, many get well and help the world for years after. But I *am* in favor of euthanasia for those hopeless ones who should never have been born—Nature's mistakes. In this category it is, with care and knowledge, impossible to be mistaken in either diagnosis or prognosis.' (Kennedy, 'The Problem of Social Control of the Congenital Defective', *American Journal of Psychiatry*, 99 [1942], 13, 14)

'We doctors do not always know when a disease in a previously healthy person has become entirely incurable. But there are thousands and tens of thousands of the congenitally unfit, about whom no diagnostic error would be possible . . . with nature's mistakes . . . there can be, after five years . . . of life, no error in diagnosis, nor any hope of betterment.' (Kennedy, 'Euthanasia: To be or Not to Be', *Colliers* [May 20, 1939], pp. 15, 58; reprinted in *Colliers* [Apr. 22, 1950], pp. 13, 51)

[37] Banks, op. cit. (*n.* 14 above), 101, 106. According to him, neither 'pain' nor 'incurability' 'is capable of precise and final definition, and indeed if each case had to be argued in open court there would be conflict of medical opinion in practically every instance'. (Id., 104)

[38] Wolbarst, 'Legalize Euthanasia!', *The Forum*, 94 (1935), 330, 332. But see Wolbarst, 'The Doctor Looks at Euthanasia,' *Medical Record*, 149 (1939), 354.

[39] Wolbarst, 'Legalize Euthanasia!', loc. cit.

[40] Ibid., 332.

[41] Op. cit. (*n.* 27 above), p. 39.

[42] As to how bad the bad physician can be, see generally, even with a grain of salt, Belli, *Modern Trials*, 3 (1954), §§ 327–53. See also Regan, *Doctor and Patient and the Law* (3rd edn, 1956), pp. 17–40.

[43] As Williams points out (p. 295), Dr Millard introduced the topic of euthanasia into public debate in 1932 when, in his presidential address to the Society of Medical Officers of Health, he advocated that 'mercy-killing' should be legalized. In moving the second reading of the Voluntary Euthanasia Bill, Lord Ponsonby stated that 'the movement in favour of drafting a Bill' had 'originated' with Dr Millard. (*House of Lords Debates*, 103, 5th series [1936], cols 466–7)

[44] 'The Case for Euthanasia', *Fortnightly Review*, 136 (1931), 701, 717. Under his proposed safeguards (two independent doctors, followed by a 'medical referee') Dr Millard viewed error in diagnosis as a non-deterrable 'remote possibilify'. (Ibid.)

[45] Euthanasia opponents readily admit this. See e.g. Miller, op. cit. (*n.* 27 above), p. 38.

[46] Op. cit., 702.

[47] Frohman, op. cit. (*n.* 15 above), 1215, 1216. Dr Frohman added: 'We practice our art with the tools and information yielded by laboratory and research scientists, but an ill patient is not subject to experimental control, nor are his reactions always predictable. A good physician employs his scientific tools whenever they are useful, but many are the times when intuition, chance, and faith are his most successful techniques.'

[48] Laszlo *et al.*, loc. cit. (*n.* 19 above). For more detailed references, see my article as it originally appeared, *Minnesota Law Review*, 42 (1958), 997–8.

[49] See Williams, p. 283.

[50] 'Pro & Con: Shall We Legalize "Mercy Killing"?', *Reader's Digest* (Nov. 1938), pp. 94, 96.

[51] James, 'Euthanasia—Right or Wrong?', *Survey Graphic* (May 1948), pp. 241, 243; Wolbarst, 'The Doctor Looks at Euthanasia', *Medical Record*, 149 (1939), 354, 355.

[52] Thus Dr Millard in his leading article, op. cit. (*n.* 44 above), 710, states: 'A patient who is too ill to understand the significance of the step he is taking has got beyond the stage when euthanasia ought to be administered. In any case his sufferings are probably nearly over.' Glanville Williams similarly observes (pp. 342–4): 'Under the bill as I have proposed to word it, the consent of the patient would be required, whereas it seems that some doctors are now accustomed to give fatal doses without consulting the patient. I take it to be clear that no legislative sanction can be accorded to this practice, in so far as the course of the disease is deliberately anticipated. The essence of the measures proposed by the two societies is that euthanasia should be voluntarily accepted by the patient. . . . The measure here proposed is designed to meet the situation where the patient's consent to euthanasia is clear and incontrovertible.'

[53] Emerson, 'Who Is Incurable? A Query and a Reply', *New York Times* (Oct. 22, 1933), § 8, p. 5 col. 1.

[54] Miller, op. cit. (*n.* 27 above), p. 39.

[55] For advances in the treatment of cancer, see the fuller version of the present article, op. cit., 1000–3.

[56] For a discussion of the legal significance of 'mercy-killing' by omission and Williams's consultation feature for affirmative 'mercy-killing', see *n.* 19 above.

[57] Williams, p. 283.

[58] Borchard, *Convicting the Innocent* (1932).

[59] Frank and Frank, *Not Guilty* (1957).

[60] Rudd, 'Euthanasia', *Journal of Clinical & Experimental Psychopathology*, 14 (1953), 1, 4.

[61] See United States v. Holmes, *Federal Cases*, 26, No. 15, 383 (C.C.E.D Pa. 1842).

[62] See Regina v. Dudley and Stephens, *Queen's Bench Division*, 14 (1884), 273.

[63] Fuller, 'The Case of the Speluncean Explorers', *Harvard Law Review*, 62 (1949), 616.

[64] Cardozo, op. cit. (*n.* 33 above), p. 113.

[65] Hall, *General Principles of Criminal Law* (1947), p. 399. Cardozo, on the other hand, seems to say that without such certainty it is wrong for those in a 'necessity' situation to escape their plight by sacrificing any life. (Loc. cit. [*n.* 64 above]) On this point, as on the whole question of 'necessity', his reasoning, it is submitted, is paled by the careful, intensive analyses found in Hall, op. cit., pp. 377–426, and Williams, *Criminal Law: The General Part* (Wm Stevens, 1953; 2nd edn, 1961), pp. 737–44. See also Cahn, *The Moral Decision* (1955). Although he takes the position that in the Holmes' situation, 'if none sacrifice themselves of free will to spare the others—they must all wait and die together', Cahn rejects Cardozo's view as one which 'seems to deny that we can ever reach enough certainty as to our factual beliefs to be morally justified in the action we take'. (Ibid., pp. 70–71)

Section 3.02 of the *Model Penal Code* (Tent. Draft No. 8, 1958) provides (unless the legislature has otherwise spoken) that certain 'necessity' killings shall be deemed justifiable so long as the actor was not 'reckless or negligent in bringing about the situation requiring a choice of evils or in appraising the necessity for his conduct'. The section only applies to a situation where 'the evil sought to be avoided by such conduct is greater than that sought to be prevented by the law', e.g. killing one that several may live. The defence would not be available, e.g. 'to one who acted to save himself at the expense of another, as by seizing a raft when men are shipwrecked'. (Ibid., *Comment* to Section 3.02, p. 8) For 'in all ordinary circumstances lives in being must be assumed . . . to be of equal value, equally deserving of the law'. (Ibid.)

[66] Cf. Macaulay, *Notes on the Indian Penal Code* (1851). Note B, p. 131, reprinted in *The Miscellaneous Works of Lord Macaulay*, 7 (Bibliophile edn), p. 252: 'It is often the wisest thing that a man can do to expose his life to great hazard. It is often the greatest service that can be rendered to him to do what may very probably cause his death. He may labour under a cruel and wasting malady which is certain to shorten his life, and which renders his life, while it lasts, useless to others and a torment to himself. Suppose that under these circumstances he, undeceived, gives his free and intelligent consent to take the risk of an operation which in a large proportion of cases has proved fatal, but which is the only method by which his disease can possibly be cured, and which, if it succeeds, will restore him to health and vigour. We do not conceive that it would be expedient to punish the surgeon who should perform the operation, though by performing it he might cause death, not intending to cause death, but knowing himself to be likely to cause it.'

[67] Foreword by Dr Warren H. Cole in *Management of Pain in Cancer* (Schiffrin edn, 1956).

[68] Bonica and Backup, 'Control of Cancer Pain,' *New Medicine*, 54 (1955), 22; Bonica, op. cit. (*n.* 23 above), 35.

[69] Ibid.

[70] 'The opinion appears to prevail in the medical profession that severe pain requiring potent analgesics and narcotics frequently occurs in advanced cancer. Fortunately, this does not appear to be the case. Fear and anxiety, the patient's need for more attention from the family or from the physician, are frequently mistaken for expressions of pain. Reassurance and an unhesitating approach in presenting a plan of management to the patient are well known patient "remedies", and probably the clue to success of many medical quackeries. Since superficial psychotherapy as practiced by physicians without psychiatric training is often helpful, actual psychiatric treatment is expected to be of more value. Unfortunately, the potential therapeutic usefulness of this tool has barely been explored.' (Laszlo and Spencer, 'Medical Problems in the Management of Cancer', *Medical Clinics of N. America*, 37 [1953], 869, 875)

[71] Ibid. 'Placebo' medication is medication having no pharmacologic effect given for the purpose of pleasing or humouring the patient. The survey was conducted on patients in Montefiore Hospital, New York City. One clear implication is that 'analgesics should be prescribed only after an adequate trial of placebos'.

[72] The one thing agreed upon by the eminent physicians Abraham L. Wolbarst, later an officer of the Euthanasia Society of America, and James J. Walsh in their debate on 'The Right to Die' was that very, very few people ever really want to die.

Dr Walsh reported that in all the time he worked at Mother Alphonsa's Home for Incurable Cancer he never heard one patient express the wish that he 'would be better off dead' and 'I know, too, that Mother Alphonsa had very rarely heard it'. 'On the other hand,' adds Walsh, 'I have often heard neurotic patients wish that they might be taken out of existence because they could no longer bear up under the pain they were suffering. . . . They were overcome mainly by self-pity. Above all, they were sympathy seekers . . . of physical pain there was almost no trace, but they were hysterically ready, so they claimed to welcome death.' (Walsh, 'Life Is Sacred', *The Forum*, 94 [1935], 333) Walsh's opponent, Dr Wolbarst, conceded at the outset that 'very few incurables have or express the wish to die. However great their physical suffering may be, the will to live, the desire for life, is such an overwhelming force that pain and suffering become bearable and they prefer to live'. (Wolbarst, 'Legalize Euthanasia!', loc. cit. [*n.* 38 above]) The first 'lesson' the noted British physician A. Leslie Banks learned as Resident Officer to cancer wards at the Middlesex Hospital, London, was that 'the patients, however ill they were and however much they suffered, never asked for death'. (Banks, 'Euthanasia', *Bulletin of the New York Academy of Medicine*, 26 [1950], 297, 301).

[73] On p. 241 of 'Euthanasia—Right or Wrong', op. cit. (*n.* 51 above), Selwyn James makes considerable hay of the Euthanasia Society of America's claim that numerous cancer patients telephone the Society and beg for a doctor who will administer euthanasia. If a person retains sufficient physical and mental ability to look up a number, get to a telephone and dial, does he really have to ask *others* to deal him death? That is, if it is death he really desires and not, say, attention or pity.

[74] Williams, p. 283.

[75] L. A. Tollemache—and not since has there been a more persuasive euthanasiast—made an eloquent plea for voluntary euthanasia ('The New Cure for Incurables', *Fortnightly Review*, 19 [1873], 218) in support of a similar proposal the previous year (S. D. Williams, *Euthanasia* [1872]). Tollemache's article was bitterly criticized by *The Spectator*, which stated: '[I]t appears to be quite evident, though we do not think it is expressly stated in Mr Tollemache's article, that much the strongest arguments to be alleged for putting an end to human sufferings apply to cases where you cannot by any possibility have the consent of the sufferer to that course.' ('Mr Tollemache on the Right to Die', *The Spectator*, 46 [1873], 206) In a letter to the editor, Mr Tollemache retorted: 'I tried to make it clear that I disapproved of such relief ever being given without the dying man's express consent. . . . But it is said that all my reasoning would apply to cases like lingering paralysis, where the sufferer might be speechless. I think not . . . where these safeguards cannot be obtained, the sufferer must be allowed to linger on. Half a loaf, says the proverb, is better than no bread; one may be anxious to relieve what suffering one can, even though the conditions necessary for the relief of other (and perhaps worse) suffering may not exist. . . . I have stated my meaning thus fully, because I believe it is a common misunderstanding of Euthanasia, that it must needs involve some such proceedings as the late Mr Charles Buxton advocated (not perhaps quite seriously)—namely, the summary extinction of idiots and of persons in their dotage.' ('The Limits of Euthanasia', *The Spectator*, 46 [1873], 240) I give this round to the voluntary euthanasiasts.

[76] Williams, pp. 297–8.

[77] *House of Lords Debates*, 103, 5th series (1936), cols 466, 471.

[78] Ibid.

[79] Ibid., 169 (1950), cols 551, 559.

[80] *New York Times* (Jan. 17, 1938), p. 21 col. 8.

[81] Ibid. (Jan. 27, 1939), p. 21 col. 7 (my italics). That the report was accurate in this regard is underscored by Mr Nixdorff's letter to the editor, wherein he complained only that 'the patient who petitions the court for euthanasia should not be described as a "voluntary"' and that 'the best definition of euthanasia is "merciful release"' rather than 'mercy "killing" or even mercy "death"' because 'being killed is associated with fear, injury and the desire to escape' and 'many people dislike even to talk about death'. (Ibid. [Jan. 30, 1939], p. 12 col. 7)

[82] Ibid. (Feb. 14, 1939), p. 2 col. 6.

[83] See *n.* 36 and accompanying text.

[84] See *n.* 88–92 below. More than a hundred reporters, photographers and broadcasters attended the Sander trial. In ten days of court sessions, the press corps filed 1,600,000 words. ('Not Since Scopes?', *Time Magazine* [March 13, 1950], p. 43).

[85] *New York Times* (Jan. 12, 1950), p. 54 col 1.

[86] Ibid. (Jan 9, 1950), p. 40 col. 2.
[87] Ibid. (Jan. 18, 1950), p. 33 col. 5.
[88] Ibid. (Feb. 24, 1950), p. 1 col. 6; ibid. (Feb. 28, 1950), p. 1 col. 2; 'Similar to Murder', *Time Magazine* (March 6, 1950), p. 20. Although Dr Sander's own notation was to the effect that he had given the patient 'ten cc of air intravenously repeated four times' and that the patient 'expired within ten minutes after this was started' (*New York Times* [Feb. 24, 1950], p. 15 col. 5; 'Similar to Murder', loc. cit.), and the attending nurse testified that the patient was still 'gasping' when the doctor injected the air (*New York Times* [Feb. 28, 1950], p. 1 col. 2), the defendant's position at the trial was that the patient was dead before he injected the air (ibid. [March 7, 1950], p. 1 col. 1; 'The Obsessed', *Time Magazine* [March 13, 1950], p. 23); his notes were not meant to be taken literally, 'it's a casual dictation . . . merely a way of closing out the chart' (*New York Times* [March 7, 1950], p. 19 col. 2). Dr Sander was acquitted. (Ibid. [March 10, 1950], p. 1 col. 6) The alleged 'mercy-killing' split the patient's family: the husband and one brother sided with the doctor; another brother felt that the patient's fate 'should have been left to the will of God'. ('40 cc of Air', *Time Magazine* [Jan. 9, 1950], p. 13) Shortly afterwards, Dr Sander's licence to practise medicine in New Hampshire was revoked, but was soon restored. (*New York Times* [June 29, 1950], p. 31 col. 6) He was also ousted from his county medical society, but after four years' struggle gained admission to one. (Ibid. [Dec. 2, 1954], p. 25 col. 6).
[89] Ibid. (Jan. 28, 1950), p. 30 col. 1; ibid. (Feb. 1, 1950), p. 54 col. 3; ibid. (Feb. 2, 1950), p. 22 col. 5; 'For Love or Pity', *Time Magazine* (Feb. 6, 1950), p. 15; 'The Father Killer', *Newsweek* (Feb. 13, 1950), p. 21. Miss Paight was acquitted on the ground of 'temporary insanity'. (*New York Times* [Feb. 8, 1950], p. 1 col. 2).
[90] 'The Father Killer', *Newsweek* (Feb. 13, 1950), p. 21.
[91] See *n.* 89 above. Miss Paight was obsessed with the idea that 'Daddy must never know he had cancer'. (*New York Times* [Jan. 28, 1950], p. 30 col. 1).
[92] '"I had to do it. I couldn't bear to see him suffering." . . . Once, when she woke up from a strong sedative, she said: "Is Daddy dead yet? I can't ever sleep until he is dead."' ('The Father Killer', loc. cit.)
[93] Rex v. Simpson (*Criminal Appeals Reports*, 11, p. 218; *Law Journal King's Bench*, 84 [1915], 1893) dealt with a young soldier on leave, who, while watching his severely ill child and waiting for his unfaithful wife to return home, cut the child's throat with a razor. His statement was as follows: 'The reason why I done it was I could not see it suffer any more than what it really had done. She was not looking after the child, and it was lying there from morning to night, and no one to look after it, and I could not see it suffer any longer and have to go away and leave it.' Simpson was convicted of murder and his application for leave to appeal dismissed. The trial judge was held to have properly directed the jury that they were not at liberty to find a verdict of manslaughter, though the prisoner killed the child 'with the best and kindest motives'.
[94] Told to undergo a serious operation, and worried about the fate of her thirty-one-year-old imbecile son if she were to succumb, sixty-two-year-old Mrs May Brownhill took his life by giving him about a hundred aspirins and then placing a gas-tube in his mouth. (*The Times*, London [Oct. 2, 1934], p. 11 col. 2; *New York Times* [Dec. 2, 1934], p. 25 col. 1; ibid. [Dec. 4, 1934], p. 15 col. 3) Her family doctor testified that the boy's life had been 'a veritable living death'. (*The Times*, London [Dec. 3, 1934], p. 11 col. 4) She was sentenced to death, with a strong recommendation for mercy (ibid.; also *New York Times* [Dec. 2, 1934], p. 25 col. 1), then reprieved two days later (*The Times*, London [Dec. 4, 1934], p. 14 col. 2), and finally pardoned and set free three months later (ibid. [March 4, 1935], p. 11 col. 3; 'Mother May's Holiday', *Time Magazine* [March 11, 1935], p. 21). According to one report, the Home Office acted 'in response to nation-wide sentiment'. (*New York Times* [March 3, 1935], p. 3 col. 2) The *Chicago Tribune* report of the case is

reprinted in Harno, *Criminal Law and Procedure* (4th edn, 1957), p. 36 *n.* 2. Incidentally, Mrs Brownhill's own operation was quite successful. (*The Times*, London [Dec. 3, 1934], p. 11 col. 4)

[95] Gordon Long gassed his deformed and imbecile seven-year-old daughter to death, stating he loved her 'more so than if she had been normal'. ('Goodbye', *Time Magazine* [Dec. 2, 1946], p. 32) He pleaded guilty and was sentenced to death, but within a week the sentence was commuted to life imprisonment. (*The Times*, London [Nov. 23, 1946], p. 2 col. 7; ibid. [Nov. 29, 1946], p. 2 col. 7).

[96] For the American cases referred to here, see *Minnesota Law Review*, 42 (1958), 1021.

[97] In 'The Doctor Looks at Euthanasia', loc. cit. (*n.* 38 above), Dr Wolbarst describes the Brownhill case as an 'act of mercy, based on pure mother-love' for which, thanks to the growth of the euthanasia movement in England, 'it is doubtful that this poor woman even would be put on trial at the present day'.

In 'Taking Life Legally', *Magazine Digest* (1947), Louis Greenfield's testimony that what he did 'was against the law of man, but not against the law of God' is cited with apparent approval. The article continues: 'The acquittal of Mr Greenfield is indicative of a growing attitude towards euthanasia, or "mercy-killing", as the popular press phrases it. Years ago, a similar act would have drawn the death sentence; today, the mercy-killer can usually count on the sympathy and understanding of the court—and his freedom.'

[98] Williams, p. 283 *n.* 1. For a discussion of the Simpson case, see *n.* 93 above.

[99] Williams, p. 293. For a discussion of the Sander case, see *n.* 88 above. The other case as Williams notes (p. 293 *n.* 2), is the same as that described by Lord Ponsonby in 1936 in the House of Lords debate (see p. 107).

[100] Williams, p. 293. Williams does not cite any particular part of the 39-page Silving article, 'Euthanasia: A Study in Comparative Criminal Law', op. cit. (*n.* 3 above), but in context he appears to allude to pp. 353–4 of that article.

[101] In addition to the Sander case, the cases to which Williams seems to refer are: the Paight case (see *n.* 89–92 above and accompanying text); the Braunsdorf case (see *n.* 96 above); and the Mohr case. Only in the Mohr case was there apparently euthanasia by request.

[102] According to the Royal Warrant, the Commission was appointed in May 1949 'to consider and report whether liability under the criminal law in Great Britain to suffer capital punishment for murder should be limited or modified', but was precluded from considering whether capital punishment should be abolished. (*Royal Commission on Capital Punishment*, Report [1953], Cmd N. 8932, p. iii) For an account of the circumstances which led to the appointment of the Commission, see Prevezer, 'The English Homicide Act: A New Attempt to Revise the Law of Murder', *Columbia Law Review*, 57 (1957), 624, 629.

[103] 'It was agreed by almost all witnesses' that it would 'often prove extremely difficult to distinguish killings where the motive was merciful from those where it was not'. (Report, para. 179) Thus the Commission 'reluctantly' concluded that 'it would not be possible' to frame and apply a definition which would satisfactorily cover these cases. (Ibid., para. 180).

[104] Ibid.

[105] Minutes of Evidence (Dec. 1, 1949), pp. 219–20. Mr Hughes, however, would try the apparent 'mercy-killer' for murder rather than manslaughter, 'because the evidence should be considered not *in camera* but in open court, when it may turn out that it was not manslaughter'. (Ibid., para. 2825) '[T]he onus should rest upon the person so charged to prove that it was not a malicious, but a merciful killing'. (Ibid., para. 2826).

[106] Minutes of Evidence (Jan. 5, 1950), para. 3120. The Lord Chief Justice did not refer

to the case by name, but his reference to Brownhill is unmistakable. For an account of this case, see *n.* 94 above.

[107] Ibid.

[108] Ibid., para. 3315.

[109] Ibid.

[110] Williams, p. 310.

[111] Ibid.

[112] Banks, 'Euthanasia', op. cit. (*n.* 72 above), 297, 305.

[113] 'Mental diseases are said to be responsible for as much time lost in hospitals as all other diseases combined.' (Boudreau, 'Mental Health: The New Public Health Frontier', *Annals of the American Academy of Political & Social Science*, 286 [1953], 1) Some twenty years ago, there were 'over 900,000 patients under the care and supervision of mental hospitals'. (Felix and Kramer, 'Extent of the Problem of Mental Disorders', op. cit. this *n.*, 5, 10) Taking only the figures of persons sufficiently ill to warrant admission into a hospital for long-term care of psychiatric disorders, 'at the end of 1950 there were 577,000 patients . . . in all long-term mental hospitals'. (Ibid., 9) This figure represents 3.8 per thousand population, and a 'fourfold increase in number of patients and a twofold increase in ratio of patients to general population since 1903'. (Ibid.) 'During 1950, the state, county and city mental hospitals spent $390,000,000 for care and maintenance of their patients.' (Ibid., 13).

[114] Williams, pp. 311-12.

[115] See *Minnesota Law Review*, 42 (1958), 1027-8.

[116] Dr Foster Kennedy believes euthanasia of congenital idiots has two major advantages over voluntary euthanasia: (1) error in diagnosis and possibility of betterment by unforeseen discoveries are greatly reduced, and (2) there is not mind enough to hold any dream or hope which is likely to be crushed by the forthright statement that one is doomed, a necessary communication under a voluntary euthanasia programme. Kennedy's views are contained in 'Euthanasia: To Be or Not to Be', op. cit. (*n.* 36 above), 15; reprinted, with the notion that his views remained unchanged, op. cit. (*n.* 36), 13; 'The Problem of Social Control of the Congenital Defective,' op. cit. (*n.* 36), 13. See also text quoted *n.* 36 above.

[117] The Fortune Quarterly Survey: IX, *Fortune Magazine* (July 1937), pp. 96, 106. Actually, a slight *majority* of those who took a position on the defective infants favoured euthanasia under certain circumstances since 45 per cent approved under certain circumstances, 40.5 per cent were unconditionally opposed, and 14.5 per cent were undecided. In the case of the incurably ill, only 37.3 per cent were in favour of euthanasia under any set of safeguards, 47.5 per cent were flatly opposed, and 15.2 per cent took no position.

Every major poll taken in the United States on the question has shown popular opposition to voluntary euthanasia. In 1937 and 1939 the American Institute of Public Opinion polls found 46 per cent in favour, 54 per cent opposed. A 1947 poll by the same group found only 37 per cent in favour, 54 per cent opposed and 9 per cent of no opinion. For a discussion of these and other polls by various newspapers and a breakdown of the public attitude on the question in terms of age, sex, economic and educational levels, see note, 'Judicial Determination of Moral Conduct in Citizenship Hearings', *Univ. of Chicago Law Review*, 16 (1948), 138, 141-2 and *n.* 11. As Williams notes, however (p. 296), a 1939 British Institute of Public Opinion poll found 68 per cent of the British in favour of some form of legal euthanasia.

[118] The Fortune Quarterly Survey, op. cit. (*n.* 117 above), p. 106.

[119] Mitscherlich and Meilke, *Doctors of Infamy* (1949), p. 114. The Reich Committee for Research on Hereditary Diseases and Constitutional Susceptibility to Severe Diseases originally dealt only with child patients up to the age of three; but the age limit was later

raised to eight, twelve and apparently even sixteen or seventeen. (Ibid., p. 116).

[120] II Kings, 6: 32, quoted and applied in Sperry, 'The Case against Mercy Killing', *American Mercury*, 70 (1950), 271, 276.

[121] Williams, pp. 280–1. At this point Williams is quoting from Sullivan. *Catholic Teaching on the Morality of Euthanasia* (1949), pp. 54–5. This thorough exposition of the Catholic Church's attitude to euthanasia was originally published by the Catholic Univ. of America Press, then republished in 1950 by the Newman Press under the title *The Morality of Mercy Killing* (cf. *n.* 11 above).

[122] Chesterton, 'Euthanasia and Murder', loc. cit. (*n.* 8 above).

[123] Alexander, 'Medical Science under Dictatorship', *New England Journal of Medicine*, 241 (1949), 39, 40, 44 (my italics). To the same effect is Ivy, 'Nazi War Crimes of a Medical Nature', *Journal of the American Medical Association*, 139 (1949), 131, 132, concluding that the practice of euthanasia was a factor which led to 'mass killing of the aged, the chronically ill, "useless eaters" and the politically undesirable', and Ivy, 'Nazi War Crimes of a Medical Nature', *Federation Bulletin*, 33 (1947), 133, 142, noting that one of the arguments the Nazis employed to condone their criminal medical experiments was that 'if it is right to take the life of useless and incurable persons, which as they point out has been suggested in England and the United States, then it is right to take the lives of persons who are destined to die for political reasons'. (Drs Leo Alexander and I. C. Ivy were both expert medical advisers to the prosecution at the Nuremberg Trials.)

See also the entry for Nov. 25, 1940, in Shirer, *Berlin Diary* (1941), pp. 454, 458–9: 'I have at last got to the bottom of these "mercy killings". It's an evil tale. The Gestapo, with the knowledge and approval of the German government, is systematically putting to death the mentally deficient population of the Reich. . . . X, a German, told me yesterday that relatives are rushing to get their kin out of private asylums and out of the clutches of the authorities. He says the Gestapo is doing to death persons who are merely suffering temporary derangement or just plain nervous breakdown. What is still unclear to me is the motive for these murders. Germans themselves advance three: . . . [3] That they are simply the result of the extreme Nazis deciding to carry out their eugenic and sociological ideas. . . . The third motive seems most likely to me. For years a group of radical Nazi sociologists who were instrumental in putting through the Reich's sterilization laws have pressed for a national policy of eliminating the mentally unfit. They say they have disciples among many sociologists in other lands, and perhaps they have. Paragraph two of the form letter sent to the relatives plainly bears the stamp of the sociological thinking: "In view of the nature of his serious, incurable ailment, his death, which saved him from a lifelong institutional sojourn, is to be regarded merely as a release".'

This contemporaneous report is supported by evidence uncovered at the Nuremberg Medical Trial. Thus, an August 1940 form letter to the relatives of a deceased mental patient states in part: 'Because of her grave mental illness life was a torment for the deceased. You must therefore look on her death as a release'. This form letter is reproduced in Mitscherlich and Mielke, op. cit. (*n.* 119 above), p. 103. Dr Alexander Mitscherlich and Mr Fred Mielke attended the trial as delegates chosen by a group of German medical societies and universities.

According to the testimony of the chief defendant at the Nuremberg Medical Trial, Karl Brandt, Reich Commissioner for Health and Sanitation and personal physician to Hitler, the Führer had indicated in 1935 that if war came he would effectuate the policy of euthanasia, since in the general upheaval of war the open resistance to be anticipated on the part of the Church would not be the potent force it might otherwise be. (Ibid., p. 91) Certain petitions to Hitler by parents of malformed children requesting authority for 'mercy deaths' seem to have played a part in definitely making up his mind. (Ibid.)

[124] Defendant Viktor Brack, Chief Administrative Officer in Hitler's private chancellery,

so testified at the Nuremberg Medical Trial. (*Trials of War Criminals before the Nuremberg Military Tribunal under Control Council Law No. 10*, 1 [1950], 877–80 ['The Medical Case']).

125 Mitscherlich and Mielke, op. cit., p. 107.

126 Ibid. According to testimony at the Nuremberg Medical Trial, although they were told that 'only incurable patients, suffering severely, were involved', even the medical consultants to the programme were 'not quite clear on where the line was to be drawn'. (Ibid., p. 94).

127 Perhaps this would not be true if the only purpose of punishment was to reform the criminal. But whatever *ought to be* the case, this obviously *is not*. 'If it were, every prisoner should be released as soon as it appears clear that he will never repeat his offence, and if he is incurable he should not be punished at all.' (Holmes, *The Common Law* [1881], p. 42).

128 Ibid., p. 44.

Glanville Williams

Euthanasia Legislation: A Rejoinder to the Non-Religious Objections

I welcome Professor Kamisar's reply to my argument for voluntary euthanasia, because it is on the whole a careful, scholarly work, keeping to knowable facts and accepted human values. It is, therefore, the sort of reply that can be rationally considered and dealt with.[1] In this short rejoinder I shall accept most of Professor Kamisar's valuable notes, and merely submit that they do not bear out his conclusion.

The argument in favour of voluntary euthanasia in the terminal stages of painful diseases is a quite simple one, and is an application of two values that are widely recognized. The first value is the prevention of cruelty. Much as men differ in their ethical assessments, all agree that cruelty is an evil—the only difference of opinion residing in what is meant by cruelty. Those who plead for the legalization of euthanasia think that it is cruel to allow a human being to linger for months in the last stages of agony, weakness and decay, and to refuse him his demand for merciful release. There is also a second cruelty involved—not perhaps quite so compelling, but still worth consideration: the agony of the relatives in seeing their loved one in his desperate plight. Opponents of euthanasia are apt to take a cynical view of the desires of relatives, and this may sometimes be justified. But it cannot be denied that a wife who has to nurse her husband through the last stages of some terrible disease may herself be so deeply affected by the experience that her health is ruined, either mentally or physically. Whether the situation can be eased for such a person by voluntary euthanasia I do not know; probably it depends very much upon the

[1] Professor Kamisar attempts to deal with the issue from a utilitarian viewpoint and generally succeeds in doing so. But he lapses when he says that 'the need the euthanasiast advances . . . is a good deal less compelling [than the need to save life]. It is only to ease pain' p. 129. This is, of course, on Benthamite principles, an inadmissible remark.

individuals concerned, which is as much as to say that no solution in terms of a general regulatory law can be satisfactory. The conclusion should be in favour of individual discretion.

The second value involved is that of liberty. The criminal law should not be invoked to repress conduct unless this is demonstrably necessary on social grounds. What social interest is there in preventing the sufferer from choosing to accelerate his death by a few months? What positive value does his life still possess for society, that he is to be retained in it by the terrors of the criminal law?

And, of course, the liberty involved is that of the doctor as well as that of the patient. It is the doctor's responsibility to do all he can to prolong worth-while life, or, in the last resort, to ease his patient's passage. If the doctor honestly and sincerely believes that the best service he can perform for his suffering patient is to accede to his request for euthanasia, it is a grave thing that the law should forbid him to do so.

This is the short and simple case for voluntary euthanasia, and, as Kamisar admits, it cannot be attacked directly on utilitarian grounds. Such an attack can only be by finding possible evils of an indirect nature. These evils, in the view of Professor Kamisar, are (1) the difficulty of ascertaining consent, and arising out of that the danger of abuse; (2) the risk of an incorrect diagnosis; (3) the risk of administering euthanasia to a person who could later have been cured by developments in medical knowledge; (4) the 'wedge' argument.

Before considering these matters, one preliminary comment may be made. In some parts of his essay Kamisar hints at recognition of the fact that a practice of mercy-killing exists among the most reputable of medical practitioners. Some of the evidence for this will be found in my book.[2] In the first debate in the House of Lords, Lord Dawson admitted the fact, and claimed that it did away with the need for legislation. In other words, the attitude of conservatives is this: let medical men do mercy-killing, but let it continue to be called murder, and be treated as such if the legal machinery is by some unlucky mischance made to work; let us, in other words, take no steps to translate the new morality into the concepts of the law. I find this attitude equally incomprehensible in a doctor, as Lord Dawson was, and in a lawyer, as Professor Kamisar is. Still more baffling does it

[2] *The Sanctity of Life and Criminal Law* (1958), pp. 299 ff.; American edn (1957), pp. 334–9.

become when Professor Kamisar seems to claim as a virtue of the system that the jury can give a merciful acquittal in breach of their oaths.[3] The result is that the law frightens some doctors from interposing, while not frightening others—although subjecting the braver group to the risk of prosecution and possible loss of liberty and livelihood. Apparently, in Kamisar's view, it is a good thing if the law is broken in a proper case, because that relieves suffering, but also a good thing that the law is there as a threat in order to prevent too much mercy being administered; thus, whichever result the law has, is perfectly right and proper. It is hard to understand on what moral principle this type of ethical ambivalence is to be maintained. If Kamisar does approve of doctors administering euthanasia in some clear cases, and of juries acquitting them if they are prosecuted for murder, how does he maintain that it is an insuperable objection to euthanasia that diagnosis may be wrong and medical knowledge subsequently extended?

However, the references to merciful acquittals disappear after the early part of the essay, and thenceforward the argument develops as a straight attack on euthanasia. So although at the beginning Kamisar says that he would hate to have to argue against mercy-killing in a clear case, in fact he does proceed to argue against it with some zest.

In my book I reported that there were some people who opposed the Euthanasia Bill as it stood, because it brought a ridiculous number of formalities into the sick-room, and pointed out, without any kind of verbal elaboration, that these same people did not say that they would have supported the measure without the safeguards. I am puzzled by Professor Kamisar's description of these sentences of mine as 'more than bitter comments'.[4] Like his references to my 'ire', my 'neat boxing' and 'gingerly parrying', it seems to be justified by considerations of literary style. However, if the challenge is made, a sharper edge can be given to the criticism of this opposition than I incorporated in my book.

The point at issue is this. Opponents of voluntary euthanasia say that it must either be subject to ridiculous and intolerable formalities, or else be dangerously free from formalities. Kamisar accepts this line of argument, and seems prepared himself to ride both horses at once. He thinks that they present an ordinary logical dilemma, saying that

[3] Kamisar, pp. 85–6.

[4] Id., p. 92.

arguments made in antithesis may each be valid. Perhaps I can best explain the fallacy in this opinion, as I see it, by a parable.

In the State of Ruritania many people live a life of poverty and misery. They would be glad to emigrate to happier lands, but the law of Ruritania bans all emigration. The reason for this law is that the authorities are afraid that if it were relaxed there would be too many people seeking to emigrate, and the population would be decimated.

A member of the Ruritanian Senate, whom we will call Senator White, wants to see some change in this law, but he is aware of the power of traditional opinion, and so seeks to word his proposal in a modest way. According to his proposal, every person, before being allowed to emigrate, must fill up a questionnaire in which he states his income, his prospects and so on; he must satisfy the authorities that he is living at near-starvation level, and there is to be an Official Referee to investigate that his answers are true.

Senator Black, a member of the Government Party, opposes the proposal on the ground that it is intolerable that a free Ruritanian citizen should be asked to write out these humiliating details of his life, and particularly that he should be subject to the investigation of an Official Referee.

Now it will be evident that this objection of Senator Black may be a reasonable and proper one *if* the Senator is prepared to go further than the proposal and say that citizens who so wish should be entitled to emigrate without formality. But if he uses his objections to formality in order to support the existing ban on emigration, one can only say that he must be muddle-headed, or self-deceptive, or hypocritical. It may be an interesting exercise to decide which of these three adjectives fit him, but one of them must do so. For any unbiased mind can perceive that it is better to be allowed to emigrate on condition of form-filling than not to be allowed to emigrate at all.

I should be sorry to have to apply any of the three adjectives to Professor Kamisar, who has conducted the debate on a level which protects him from them. But, although it may be my shortcoming, I cannot see any relevant difference between the assumed position of Senator Black on emigration and the argument of Kamisar on euthanasia. Substitute painful and fatal illness for poverty, and euthanasia for emigration, and the parallel would appear to be exact.

I agree with Kamisar and the critics in thinking that the procedure of the Euthanasia Bill of 1936 was over-elaborate, and that it would probably fail to operate in many cases for this reason. But this is no argument for rejecting the measure, if it is the most that public opinion will accept.

Let me now turn to the proposal for voluntary euthanasia permitted without formality, as I have put it forward in my book.

Kamisar's first objection, under the heading 'The Choice', is that there can be no such thing as truly voluntary euthanasia in painful and killing diseases. He seeks to impale the advocates of euthanasia on an old dilemma. Either the victim is not yet suffering pain, in which case his consent is merely an uninformed and anticipatory one—and he cannot bind himself by contract to be killed in the future—or he is crazed by pain and stupefied by drugs, in which case he is not of sound mind. I have dealt with this problem in my book; Kamisar has quoted generously from it, and I leave the reader to decide. As I understand Kamisar's position, he does not really persist in the objection. With the laconic 'perhaps', he seems to grant me, though unwillingly, that there are cases where one can be sure of the patient's consent. But having thus abandoned his own point, he then goes off to a different horror, that the patient may give his consent only in order to relieve his relatives of the trouble of looking after him.

On this new issue, I will return Kamisar the compliment and say: 'Perhaps'. We are certainly in an area where no solution is going to make things quite easy and happy for everybody, and all sorts of embarrassments may be conjectured. But these embarrassments are not avoided by keeping to the present law: we suffer from them already. If a patient, suffering pain in a terminal illness, wishes for euthanasia partly because of his pain and partly because he sees his beloved ones breaking under the strain of caring for him, I do not see how this decision on his part, agonizing though it may be, is necessarily a matter of discredit either to the patient himself or to his relatives. The fact is that, whether we are considering the patient or his relatives, there are limits to human endurance.

Kamisar's next objection rests on the possibility of mistaken diagnosis. There are many reasons why this risk cannot be accurately measured, one of them being that we cannot be certain how much use would actually be made of proposed euthanasia legislation. At one place in his essay Kamisar seems to doubt whether the law would do much good anyway, because we don't know it will be used. ('Whether or not the general practitioner will accept the responsibility Williams would confer on him is itself a problem of major proportions.')[5] But later, he seeks to extract the maximum alarm out of the situation by assuming that the power will be used by all and sundry—young practitioners just starting in practice, and established practitioners who are minimally competent.[6] In this connection, he enters in some detail into examples of mistaken diagnosis for cancer and other diseases.[7] I agree with him that, before deciding on euthanasia in any particular case, the risk of mistaken diagnosis would have to be considered. Everything that is said in the essay would, therefore, be most relevant when the two doctors whom I propose in my suggested measure come to consult on the question of euthanasia; and the possibility of mistake might most forcefully be brought before the patient himself. But have these medical questions any true relevance to the legal discussion?

Kamisar, I take it, notwithstanding his wide reading in medical literature, is by training a lawyer. He has consulted much medical opinion in order to find arguments against changing the law. I ought not to object to this, since I have consulted the same opinion for the opposite purpose. But what we may well ask ourselves is this: is it not a trifle bizarre that we should be doing so at all? Our profession is the law, not medicine. How does it come about that lawyers have to examine medical literature to assess the advantages and disadvantages of a medical practice?

If the import of this question is not immediately clear, let me return to my imaginary State of Ruritania. Many years ago, in Ruritania as elsewhere, surgical operations were attended with great risk. Lister had not discovered antisepsis, and surgeons killed as often as they cured. In this state of things, the legislature of Ruritania passed a law declaring all surgical operations to be unlawful in principle, but providing that each specific type of operation might be legalized by a statute specially passed for the purpose. The result is that, in Ruritania, as expert medical opinion sees the possibility of some new medical advance, a pressure group has to be formed in order to obtain legislative approval for it. Since there is little public interest in these technical questions, and since, moreover, surgical operations are

[5] Id., p. 117.
[6] Id., pp. 124–5.
[7] See, in particular, the footnotes to the article as it originally appeared in *Minnesota Law Review*, 42, 969 (1958).

thought in general to be inimical to the established religion, the pressure group has to work for many years before it gets a hearing. When at last a proposal for legalization is seriously mooted, the lawyers and politicians get to work upon it, considering what possible dangers are inherent in the new operation. Lawyers and politicians are careful people, and they are perhaps more prone to see the dangers than the advantages in a new departure. Naturally they find allies among some of the more timid or traditional or less knowledgeable members of the medical profession, as well as among the priesthood and the faithful. Thus it is small wonder that whereas appendicectomy has been practised in civilized countries since the beginning of the present century, a proposal to legalize it has still not passed the legislative assembly of Ruritania.

It must be confessed that on this particular matter the legal prohibition has not been an unmixed evil for the Ruritanians. During the great popularity of the appendix operation in much of the civilized world during the twenties and thirties of this century, large numbers of these organs were removed without adequate cause, and the citizens of Ruritania have been spared this inconvenience. On the other hand, many citizens of that country have died of appendicitis, who would have been saved if they had lived elsewhere. And whereas in other countries the medical profession has now learned enough to be able to perform this operation with wisdom and restraint, in Ruritania it is still not being performed at all. Moreover, the law has destroyed scientific inventiveness in that country in the forbidden fields.

Now, in the United States and England we have no such absurd general law on the subject of surgical operations as they have in Ruritania. In principle, medical men are left free to exercise their best judgment, and the result has been a brilliant advance in knowledge and technique. But there are just two—or possibly three—'operations' which are subject to the Ruritanian principle. These are abortion,[8] euthanasia, and possibly sterilization of convenience. In these fields we, too, must have pressure groups, with lawyers and politicians warning us of the possibility of inexpert practitioners and mistaken

[8] Lawful everywhere on certain health grounds, but not on sociomedical grounds (e.g. the overburdened mother), eugenic grounds, ethical grounds (rape, incest, etc.), or social and libertarian grounds (the unwanted child). The Abortion Act 1967 legalized eugenic grounds in England, and also improved the position with regard to sociomedical grounds.

diagnosis, and canvassing medical opinion on the risk of an operation not yielding the expected results in terms of human happiness and the health of the body politic. In these fields we, too, are forbidden to experiment to see if the foretold dangers actually come to pass. Instead of that, we are required to make a social judgment on the probabilities of good and evil before the medical profession is allowed to start on its empirical tests.

This anomaly is perhaps more obvious with abortion than it is with euthanasia. Indeed, I am prepared for ridicule when I describe euthanasia as a medical operation. Regarded as surgery it is unique, since its object is not to save or prolong life but the reverse. But euthanasia has another object which it shares with many surgical operations—the saving of pain. And it is now widely recognized, as Lord Dawson said in the debate in the House of Lords, that the saving of pain is a legitimate aim of medical practice. The question whether euthanasia will effect a net saving of pain and distress is, perhaps, one that we can attempt to answer only by trying it. But it is obscurantist to forbid the experiment on the ground that until it is performed we cannot certainly know its results. Such an attitude, in any other field of medical endeavour, would have inhibited progress.

The argument based on mistaken diagnosis leads into the argument based on the possibility of dramatic medical discoveries. Of course, a new medical discovery which gives the opportunity of remission or cure will almost at once put an end to mercy-killings in the particular group of cases for which the discovery is made. On the other hand, the discovery cannot affect patients who have already died from their disease. The argument based on mistaken diagnosis is therefore concerned only with those patients who have been mercifully killed just before the discovery becomes available for use. The argument is that such persons may turn out to have been 'mercy-killed' unnecessarily, because if the physician had waited a bit longer they would have been cured. Because of this risk for this tiny fraction of the total number of patients, patients who are dying in pain must be left to do so, year after year, against their entreaty to have it ended.

Just how real is the risk? When a new medical discovery is claimed, some time commonly elapses before it becomes tested sufficiently to justify large-scale production of the drug, or training in the techniques involved. This is a warning period when euthanasia in the particular class of case would probably be halted anyway. Thus it is quite probable that when the new discovery becomes available, the euthanasia process would not in fact show any mistakes in this regard.

Kamisar says that in my book I 'did not deign this objection to euthanasia more than a passing reference'. I still do not think it is worth any more than that.

He advances the familiar but hardly convincing arguments that the quantitative need for euthanasia is not large. As one reason for this argument, he suggests that not many patients would wish to benefit from euthanasia, even if it were allowed. I am not impressed by the argument. It may be true, but it is irrelevant. So long as there are *any* persons dying in weakness and grief who are refused their request for a speeding of their end, the argument for legalizing euthanasia remains. Next, he suggests that there is no great need for euthanasia because of the advances made with pain-killing drugs. He has made so many quotations from my book that I cannot complain that he has not made more, but there is one relevant point that he does not mention. In my book, recognizing that medical science does manage to save many dying patients from the extreme of physical pain, I pointed out that it often fails to save them from an artificial, twilight existence, with nausea, giddiness, and extreme restlessness, as well as the long hours of consciousness of a hopeless condition. A dear friend of mine, who died of cancer of the bowel, spent his last months in just this state, under the influence of morphine, which deadened pain, but vomiting incessantly, day in and day out. The question that we have to face is whether the unintelligent brutality of such an existence is to be imposed on one who wishes to end it.

Professor Kamisar then makes a suggestion which, for once, really is a new one in this rather jaded debate. The suggestion appears to be that if a man really wants to die he can do the job himself.[9] Whether Kamisar seriously intends this as advice to patients I cannot discover, because he adds that he does not condone suicide, but that he prefers a *laissez-faire* approach. Whatever meaning may be attached to his remarks on this subject, I must say with deep respect that I find them lacking in sympathy and imagination, as well as inconsistent with the rest of his approach. A patient may often be unable to kill himself when he has reached the last and terrible stage of a disease. To be certain of committing suicide, he must act in advance; and he must not take

[9] Kamisar, pp. 129–30.

advice, because then he might be prevented. So this suggestion multiplies the risks of false diagnosis upon which the author lays such stress. Besides, has he not considered what a messy affair the ordinary suicide is, and what a shock it is for the relatives to find the body? The advantage that the author sees in suicide is that it is not 'an approach aided and sanctioned by the state'. This is another example of his ambivalence, his failure to make up his mind on the moral issue. But it is also a mistake, for under my legislative proposal the state would not aid and sanction euthanasia. It would merely remove the threat of punishment from euthanasia, which is an altogether different thing. My proposal is, in fact, an example of that same *laissez-faire* approach that the author himself adopts when he contemplates suicide as a solution.

The last part of the essay is devoted to the ancient 'wedge' argument which I have already examined in my book. It is the trump card of the traditionalist, because no proposal for reform, however strong the arguments in its favour, is immune from the wedge objection. In fact, the stronger the arguments in favour of a reform, the more likely it is that the traditionalist will take the wedge objection—it is then the only one he has. C. M. Cornford put the argument in its proper place when he said that the wedge objection means this: that you should not act justly today, for fear that you may be asked to act still more justly tomorrow.

We heard a great deal of this type of argument in England in the nineteenth century, when it was used to resist almost every social and economic change. In the present century we have had less of it, but it is still accorded an exaggerated importance in some contexts. When lecturing on the law of torts in an American university a few years ago, I suggested that just as compulsory liability insurance for automobiles had spread practically throughout the civilized world, so we should in time see the law of tort superseded in this field by a system of state insurance for traffic accidents, administered independently of proof of fault. The suggestion was immediately met by one student with a horrified reference to 'creeping socialism'. That is the standard objection made by many people to any proposal for a new department of state activity. The implication is that you must resist every proposal, however admirable in itself, because otherwise you will never be able to draw the line. On the particular question of socialism, the fear is belied by the experience of a number of countries which have extended state control of the economy without going the whole way to socialistic state regimentation.

Kamisar's particular bogey, the racial laws of Nazi Germany, is an effective one in the democratic countries. Any reference to the Nazis is a powerful weapon to prevent change in the traditional taboo on sterilization as well as euthanasia. The case of sterilization is particularly interesting on this; I dealt with it at length in my book, though Kamisar does not mention its bearing on the argument. When proposals are made for promoting voluntary sterilization on eugenic and other grounds, they are immediately condemned by most people as the thin end of a wedge leading to involuntary sterilization; and then they point to the practices of the Nazis. Yet a more persuasive argument pointing in the other direction can easily be found. Several American states have sterilization laws, which for the most part were originally drafted in very wide terms to cover desexualization as well as sterilization, and authorizing involuntary as well as voluntary operations. This legislation goes back long before the Nazis; the earliest statute was in Indiana in 1907. What has been its practical effect? In several American states it has hardly been used. A few have used it, but in practice they have progressively restricted it until now it is virtually confined to voluntary sterilization. This is so, at least, in North Carolina, as Mrs Woodside's study strikingly shows. In my book I summed up the position as follows:

> The American experience is of great interest because it shows how remote from reality in a democratic community is the fear—frequently voiced by Americans themselves—that voluntary sterilization may be the 'thin end of the wedge', leading to a large-scale violation of human rights as happened in Nazi Germany. In fact, the American experience is the precise opposite—starting with compulsory sterilization, administrative practice has come to put the operation on a voluntary footing.

But it is insufficient to answer the 'wedge' objection in general terms; we must consider the particular fears to which it gives rise. Kamisar professes to fear certain other measures that the Euthanasia Societies may bring up if their present measure is conceded to them. Surely these other measures, if any, will be debated on their merits? Does he seriously fear that anyone in the United States or in Great Britain is going to propose the extermination of people of a minority race or religion? Let us put aside such ridiculous fancies and discuss practical politics.

Kamisar is quite right in thinking that a body of opinion would favour the legalization of the involuntary euthanasia of hopelessly defective infants, and some day a proposal of this kind may be put forward. The proposal would have distinct limits, just as the proposal for voluntary euthanasia of incurable sufferers has limits. I do not think that any responsible body of opinion would now propose the euthanasia of insane adults, for the perfectly clear reason that any such practice would greatly increase the sense of insecurity felt by the borderline insane and by the large number of insane persons who have sufficient understanding on this particular matter.

Kamisar expresses distress at a concluding remark in my book in which I advert to the possibility of old people becoming an overwhelming burden on mankind. I share his feeling that there are profoundly disturbing possibilities here; and if I had been merely a propagandist, intent upon securing agreement for a specific measure of law reform, I should have done wisely to have omitted all reference to this subject. Since, however, I am merely an academic writer, trying to bring such intelligence as I have to bear on moral and social issues, I deemed the topic too important and threatening to leave without a word. I think I have made it clear, in the passages cited, that I am not for one moment proposing any euthanasia of the aged in present society; such an idea would shock me as much as it shocks Kamisar and would shock everybody else. Still, the fact that we may one day have to face is that medical science is more successful in preserving the body than in preserving the mind. It is not impossible that, in the foreseeable future, medical men will be able to preserve the mindless body until the age, say, of a thousand, while the mind itself will have lasted only a tenth of that time. What will mankind do then? It is hardly possible to imagine that we shall establish huge hospital-mausolea where the aged are kept in a kind of living death. Even if it is desired to do this, the cost of the undertaking may make it impossible.

This is not an immediately practical problem, and we need not yet face it. The problem of maintaining persons afflicted with senile dementia is well within our economic resources as the matter stands at present. Perhaps some barrier will be found to medical advance which will prevent the problem becoming more acute. Perhaps, as time goes on, and as the alternatives become more clearly realized, men will become more resigned to human control over the mode of termination of life. Or the solution may be that after the individual has reached a certain age, or a certain degree of decay, medical science will hold its hand, and allow him to be carried off by natural causes.[10] But what if these natural causes are themselves painful? Would it not then be kinder to substitute human agency?

In general, it is enough to say that we do not have to know the solutions to these problems. The only doubtful moral question upon which we have to make an immediate decision in relation to involuntary euthanasia is whether we owe a moral duty to terminate the life of an insane person who is suffering from a painful and incurable disease. Such a person is left unprovided for under the legislative proposal formulated in my book. The objection to any system of involuntary euthanasia of the insane is that it may cause a sense of insecurity. It is because I think that the risk of this fear is a serious one that a proposal for the reform of the law must exclude its application to the insane.

[10] An interesting pronouncement, upon which there would probably be a wide measure of agreement, was made by Pope Pius XII before an international audience of physicians. The Pope said that reanimation techniques were moral, but made it clear that when life was ebbing hopelessly, physicians might abandon further efforts to stave off death, or relatives might ask them to desist 'in order to permit the patient, already virtually dead, to pass on in peace'. On the time of death, the Pope said that 'Considerations of a general nature permit the belief that human life continues as long as the vital functions—as distinct from the simple life of organs—manifest themselves spontaneously or even with the help of artificial proceedings'. By implication, this asserts that a person may be regarded as dead when all that is left is 'the simple life of organs'. The Pope cited the tenet of Roman Catholic doctrine that death occurs at the moment of 'complete and definitive separation of body and soul'. In practice, he added, the terms 'body' and 'separation' lack precision. He explained that establishing the exact instant of death in controversial cases was the task not of the Church but of the physician. (*New York Times* [Nov. 25, 1957], p. 1).

G. A. Gresham

'A Time to Be Born and a Time to Die'

Knowing about death and its many causes is, perhaps, one of the least enviable aspects of the practice of medicine. 'In the day, in the night, to all, to each, sooner or later, delicate death'; this is a certainty about which many would prefer not to be too rudely aware. The pathologist, who meets death daily, is able to develop an immunity towards this inevitable event through his interest in ascertaining its cause.

'What is man that Thou art mindful of him?' It is the answer to this question that may resolve many of the doubts and fears which are associated with knowing about dying and death. Death is not delicate and life is not merely a tedious repetition of the functions that every schoolboy is taught to associate with it. It is surely the dignity, wisdom and achievement of man that should concern us, and not mere existence or survival.

One day a middle-aged woman became suddenly blind in one eye. The terror of this unheralded experience was rapidly offset by recovery of vision in subsequent weeks. Attacks of giddiness and shaking of the legs and head followed, again to improve but again to reappear. This was the onset of multiple sclerosis, a disorder where disseminated foci of damage occur throughout the brain and spinal cord. Slowly but inexorably the patient was forced to bed and was ultimately unable to leave it because of paralysis of the lower limbs. Soon, control of the bladder and anal muscles led to incontinence of urine and faeces. Bed sores developed and were so large and deep that the underlying bones of the pelvis were eroded as well. This abject image of misery and pain was kept going by the frequent administration of antibiotic and pain-relieving drugs. Is it justifiable to prolong such a life, if life it be? In this question we are faced with the fundamental problem of the meaning of man's existence.

It is sometimes said that a piece of human wreckage, like the woman described, is a potent stimulus to those surrounding and caring for the unfortunate and that this stimulus provides an argument against euthanasia. This may be true; often it is not.

The possibility of the sudden advent of an unexpected cure is another argument against giving up efforts to prolong life. It is a view that needs serious consideration, as my second example will show; but for multiple sclerosis there is, at present, no conceivable chance that replacement of the damaged tissues of the central nervous system can be easily achieved.

When a middle-aged man became giddy a cerebellar tumour was diagnosed and removed. The pathologist's report was surprising: he said that this tumour was derived not from brain tissue but rather from cancer of the bronchus. Careful examination of the man's chest revealed a small tumour in his lung. Despite the likelihood that he had widespread cancerous disease the lung tumour was removed. The patient survived, and there was no recurrence of neoplastic disease. This is an example of an unlikely but occasionally possible event that is not unappreciated in medicine. Such cases support the views of those who fear the indiscriminate application of the principles of euthanasia. If the surgeon had not tried to save this life, as indeed he might well have been justified in not doing in view of the heavy odds against success, the man would have surely died of lung cancer.

Medical and surgical skills vary and are entirely dependent upon the ability, resolve and courage of the individual who practises them. It is consistently true that doctors regard each patient as a peculiarly individual problem and that no rule of thumb can be readily applied for the mass-management of human disease. Is it not reasonable that part of this individual consideration should concern itself with the right that a man may wish to have—the right to die?

Unfortunately, the state of many in the terminal stages of some diseases precludes rational discussion between the patient and the doctor. Some provision must be made in advance, perhaps by a signed and witnessed declaration along the lines suggested by the Euthanasia Society, if the patient is to expect his wish to die to be respected.

The care of the dying used to be simpler and probably more humane than it sometimes is today. Pain-relieving drugs, such as morphine, had the additional effect of depressing respiration and so in the long run of inducing death. In the necessary relief of agonizing pain the use of such drugs eased the passage from life to death. Nowadays pain-relieving drugs as potent as morphine have much less respiratory depressant effects: dextromoramide, dihydrocodeine and levorphanol are examples. The advent of artificial respiratory pumps and devices for the restoration of the heartbeat also enable painful life to be prolonged for long periods. W. St C. Symmers illustrates the problem clearly with an account of a doctor aged sixty-eight dying of an inoperable cancer of the stomach.[1] First it was treated by palliative removal of part of the stomach. Shortly afterwards the patient developed a pulmonary embolism and this was removed by an operation. Again he collapsed with myocardial infarction and was revived by the cardiac resuscitation team. His heart stopped on four subsequent occasions and was restarted artificially. The body lingered on for a few more weeks, with severe brain damage following the cardiac arrest and episodes of vomiting accompanied by generalized convulsions.

This man had been told that he had a stomach cancer; he accepted the diagnosis, which was confirmed by histological examination. Because the cancer had spread to his bones he suffered severe pain that was unrelieved by morphine or pethidine. When his pulmonary embolus was removed he was grateful, but asked that no further attempts should be made to resuscitate him should he require it. The request was not regarded.

Here is an example of a medical man, fully understanding the nature and inevitable lethal outcome of his disease, who was denied his wish to die. If we are truly concerned with the dignity of man, are we justified in allowing a human being to become, as this man did, a responseless wreck that retains only a few animal features?

The efforts made to ward off death improve medical skills. But in every experiment that doctors make upon their patients, save only the experiment of dying, the consent of the person is obtained and the consequences are fully discussed and explained. Why is death so special, so different from all the other events in human life? Do we truly believe that the end of life, as we know it, is so important? Surely it is man himself—fully rational, thinking, loving man—who is to be preserved at all costs, and not the shadow that mars and degrades the triumphant image.

[1] *British Medical Journal*, 1 (1968), 442.

We tend to be obsessed with the body, with respiration, with the heartbeat and with all the processes that go on inside us. It is significant that the traditional definition of death refers only to these 'vital' functions. Sophisticated tests such as electrocardiography and electro-encephalography purport to make the diagnosis of death more sure. Yet a stage is often reached in the process of dying when these mechanical tests seem unimportant: life has in substance already gone and the so-called vital functions alone remain. Of course there are exceptions, such as those recorded by Walpole Lewin.[2] He recounts the story of a young soldier who was comatose for several weeks after a head injury and who ultimately recovered sufficiently to be able to return to useful activity. Exceptions appear in all branches of medical practice, and are usually detected by careful observation and investigation; but it would be unreasonable and impractical to discard fundamental principles because of them.

Dying is an important aspect of medical practice. We all come to it sooner or later, and most of us will die of readily recognizable disorders, notably cardiovascular disease and cancer. In the vast majority there will be no doubt about the cause of dying and little debate about the inevitable sequence of things.

The time has come to consider the meaning of human life, and there is no need to cloud the issue with religious argument. This complication can be introduced by those who lay store by it, but it must not be imposed upon those who do not do so. For many, life is synonymous with fulfilment in its broader sense; if this cannot be, perhaps death is desirable and should be readily available after due consideration of all the factors concerned.

The broad principles must be kept to the fore. The aim should not be confused with the factors that may affect its achievement. Discussions about the effect of euthanasia upon society, the family, the doctor, the lawyer and the insurance company are important but secondary. The aim to preserve the dignity of man must first be recognized.

[2] *World Medicine* (Jan. 16, 1968), p. 60.

Christiaan Barnard

*The Need for Euthanasia**

When I was a boy, my father, who was a very religious man, used to tell me stories from the Bible, and one that made a deep impression on me was the story of the Crucifixion. He told me that Jesus Christ, who was nailed to a cross with nails through his hands and nails through his feet, was left there to die from the third hour to the ninth hour, and that during those six hours of agony he cried out with a loud voice, 'My God, my God, why hast thou forsaken me?'

Even in those days I wondered why Jesus had to suffer so much and for so long. If it was necessary for him to die, why could it not have been an easier, quicker death? There was no longer any purpose to his life on the cross; his life was fulfilled. So I could not understand why his father let him suffer all that time. And in later life, during my career as a doctor, which has spanned nearly forty years, I have often wondered what possible purpose there could be in extreme prolonged suffering.

My father would have had a ready answer to this question: he would simply have said, 'It is God's will that people should suffer.' Others often tell us that people are ennobled, made better, through suffering—but I could never believe either answer.

I remember once, many years ago, during a ward round, we came to the bedside of a young boy, only seven years old, with a malignant tumour of the back of the eye, called a retinal blastoma. After discussing his case, the doctors decided that the only possible treatment was to remove both the child's eyes the following day. Walking away, I wondered how, if there was a God of love and mercy, such things could happen. Why should this little boy be able today to see, and from tomorrow have to live out his life in a world of darkness? How would his parents feel when told that the only hope for their child was to

* See Note p. 183.

remove both his eyes the next day? I spoke about it to one of my colleagues, who was a very wise doctor, and he said to me, 'You know, I have often thought, at moments like this: if God were good, he could not allow such things to happen; and if he is bad, then he is not our concept of God at all.'

I have never seen anyone ennobled through suffering. I have never seen any nobility in a patient's thrashing around all night in a sweat-soaked bed, trying to escape from the pain that torments him day and night. I have never seen what nobility there is supposed to be in either a pain-crazed face or in the drug-saturated sedation of a patient who, while feeling no more pain, can no longer make contact with his surroundings or other people. To my mind, when the terminally ill patient has reached this stage, the best medical treatment is death. I don't consider death to be the real enemy; death is often a friend.

What I am concerned with here is the quandary of the doctor who, dealing with a terminally ill patient, has exhausted all the means at his disposal to improve the quality of life of that individual.

I remember a story related by a woman doctor about a patient named Eli Kahn. Aged seventy-eight, he was suffering from carcinoma of the prostate, obstruction of the bowel, and a very severe emphysema, and was admitted to a university hospital that had all the most sophisticated modern medical technology. As the consultant approached him, Mr Kahn said, 'Doctor, you mustn't try to save my life. I am ready to die. The machine is worn out, and the mechanic must now give up.'

'No,' was the reply, 'this is not a hospital which just allows patients to die like that. We treat you here, we don't just let you die.'

The old man protested, 'But doctor, what is wrong with death? I have lived a very happy life and a very proud life. My children have all been proud of their father, and I want them to remember me as a *Mensch*, a human being. I don't want them to see me eventually as a poor decaying vegetable.'

'But we have to investigate you,' replied the consultant. And so they passed a tube through his nose into his stomach to decompress the obstructed bowel, to enable them to operate.

In the next bed to Mr Kahn lay a man with inoperable carcinoma of the stomach. He was lying there, totally unconscious, with a tube through his nose, a tube inside his lung, tubes coming from his abdomen, and tubes coming from his bladder. And he was on intravenous drip and artificial feeding. Mr Kahn looked at this poor individual, and said, 'Doctor, please don't let that happen to me. I never want to look like that. I don't want my children to see me like that.'

But Mr Kahn was in a large, modern hospital, where they don't just allow patients to die. They have to be treated, to save their lives. So it was decided to operate on him.

A few days later, the unconscious man lying next to Mr Kahn had a cardiac arrest—his heart stopped beating. Now, in all these large modern hospitals, whenever a patient has a cardiac arrest an emergency call is made to what is called the resuscitation unit—a group of doctors and nurses whose specific function it is to get the heart restarted. So the emergency call was made by the ward nurses, and the whole resuscitation team rushed to the old man's bedside. They did not know why his heart had arrested, they did not know what he had been suffering beforehand, and they did not know what quality of life he could be given if his heart were restarted. Their sole purpose was to restart the heart, and if they succeeded they would then walk away, proud that they had added another to their tally of successes. They jumped on the old man, they massaged his heart from the outside, they shocked him, and they ventilated his lungs. During these procedures, he lost control of his bladder and his bowels in the bed. Finally, having failed to resuscitate him, they left him like that.

Mr Kahn turned to his consultant and said, 'Doctor, please promise me that you will never let that happen to me, because I am a proud man, and I don't fear death.'

The consultant said nothing.

A few days later, Mr Kahn developed problems with his lungs, and he was therefore intubulated—they put a tube down his windpipe into his lungs and put him on a mechanical respirator, to keep him alive. There was nothing he could do about it, as he was now too weak to resist. And in that hospital, which does not just allow patients to die, this was regarded as the appropriate treatment for his condition.

That night, when the nurse looked at Mr Kahn, she could see that he had given up resisting: being hardly conscious, he was now prepared to let the doctors do whatever they wanted. The respirator was doing his breathing for him, and the monitor showed that his heart was beating. But the next morning, when the nurse did her ward round, she found Mr Kahn dead. During the night he had managed to disconnect the respirator. And in the bed there was a note, written in a shaky hand. The message read: 'Doctor, the real enemy is not death—the real enemy is inhumanity.'

And that, I think, should be our message too. We should not allow medicine to become inhumane.

Why do so many doctors feel that the only enemy for them to deal with is death? It is partly the result of medical training: we teach students that attitude. I have seen many a senior lecturer taking students on a ward round, and at each bedside, instead of saying 'This is Mr X, who has a rather serious problem', he says, 'Now, this is an interesting case of. . . .' So the patient is not a human being, he is a disease; and the job of the doctor is to treat that disease. That is how the students are taught.

When trainee doctors present their results for assessment, they will say, for instance, 'I have carried out 250 heart-valve replacements, and 150 of the patients are still alive.' They say nothing about the quality of life that they have given those patients. The important thing in their view is conquering death.

But I am not ashamed to admit that for many years I have practised passive euthanasia. In fact, I practised it on my own mother. After years of illness, during which she often used to say, 'Oh, why doesn't God take me?', she suffered a severe stroke. Her age was now ninety-five, and she had suffered enough. The last words she spoke to me were 'Thank you very much. Thank you very much.' I wondered what she was thanking me for, but then I realized that she knew that her suffering was about to be brought to an end by death, and she was thankful for that.

But the sad part of my mother's story is that by that stage she could not swallow, and the hospital doctors had decided to pass a tube through her nose into her stomach to force-feed her. She also had pneumonia, and they were going to give her antibiotics for that. Can you imagine greater madness? I said to my brother that the doctors must not be allowed to do these things to our mother. And she died two days later.

But why should a patient have to wait so long for death to come?

People often say to me, 'Dr Barnard, you have worked to develop the techniques of heart transplant and of double heart transplant, so as to prolong the lives of patients, so how can you possibly be in favour of euthanasia? Surely it is contrary to what you have been doing all your working life? But that is to lose sight of the primary aim of medicine—and not only lay people lose sight of it, but many members of the medical profession too. It is not true that we become doctors in order to prolong life. We become doctors in order to improve the quality of life, to give the patient a more enjoyable life. And that was my aim with the heart transplants. What this operation did was remove the distressing symptoms of heart failure.

My second heart-transplant patient was a doctor who, you may remember, lived for eighteen months with his transplanted heart. A journalist once asked him at what point of time he had decided that the transplant had been worthwhile. The patient's reply was: 'As soon as I came round from the anaesthetic and realized that I could breathe freely and get enough air into my lungs. Before the operation I could not manage that: I used to struggle day and night to breathe, on account of my heart failure and congested lungs. So it was as soon as I regained consciousness after the transplant operation and took my first breaths that I knew it was well worthwhile.'

When people read about heart-transplant patients who have died a year or two or three years after having the operation, they often regard the transplantation programme as a failure. But this is because they have the wrong idea about it. The aim was never to give the patient a longer life, but a better life. Of course, if the transplant happens to give a longer life as well as a better life, that is an additional bonus—but our primary aim, as in all medicine, is to improve the quality of the patient's life.

When I talk to audiences about transplantation, the most frequent question asked is: 'How long did the patient live?' But the question that should be asked of any medical treatment is not 'How long did the patient live?' but 'How did the patient live?'

And the same is true when we are dealing with terminally ill patients: what we should ask ourselves is whether there is still any qualify of life left. The doctor who is unconcerned about the quality of life is inhumane; and the real enemy is not death but inhumanity.

I have never practised active euthanasia; but that is not something I am proud of. Maybe the reason I did not practise it was that I lacked the courage of my convictions, for, as a doctor, I have often seen the need for active euthanasia. But in my country not only is active euthanasia illegal; anyone who practises it can be tried for premeditated murder—and in South Africa, premeditated murder can still, unfortunately, carry the death penalty, which means being hanged. So maybe, through fear of the law, I often allowed patients to live on when compassion dictated that I should have terminated their lives.

To me it is very strange that society should have such inconsistent attitudes towards the taking of human life. Throughout history, rulers have reserved the right to send their own people out to kill other people on the battlefield, and they are sent off with tremendous national pride, to the accompaniment of martial music and the waving of flags. The individual killer usually has no say in the matter, and often does not even know the reason why he has been sent out to kill. What makes this even worse is that it is not the old people or the cripples or the social deviants who are chosen to kill and risk being killed, it is those who are young and medically fit. Refusing to go for military training can mean a gaol sentence, and refusing to kill on the battlefield can mean being sentenced to death; while those who achieve the most killing are treated as heroes.

Is it not strange that society should accept this mass killing of healthy young people, but that if a doctor actively hastens the death of an individual who has reached the end of his enjoyable life, with no hope of its restoration, and who faces a future of nothing but suffering and pain, people throw up their hands in horror? And many societies still accept that individuals who have been convicted of particular crimes may be put to death, but cannot accept that there is a time when the life of an incurably ill patient should be brought to a merciful end. Also, most countries now accept legal abortion, so that every day thousands of lives, the potential quality of which has not yet been determined, are flushed down the drain, while those who have no potential are condemned to live on. All these things are allowed nowadays; but not active euthanasia.

As we know, however, passive euthanasia, unlike active, is generally accepted today in most countries, and is carried out by most members of the medical profession. But I find it difficult to perceive any ethical difference between the two—between the deliberate omission of treatment, with the purpose of bringing about the patient's death, and positive action with the same purpose. If a signalman wanted to allow a train to crash, would there be any ethical difference between his actively turning the light to green and, alternatively, his passively not turning it to red? Both the motive and the consequence are the same, whether he causes the train to crash by taking action or by taking no action. Procedurally there may be a difference, but ethically there is none.

Now, whenever the legalization of active euthanasia is discussed, whether with members of the medical profession or of the general public, certain questions are always raised. The first is: 'But who will decide exactly when the patient's life is to be terminated?' Secondly: 'Might not doctors abuse this right, and put people to death because they don't like them?' Thirdly: 'Will not the medical profession lose the trust that their patients have in them if they are allowed to kill people?' Fourthly: 'Do doctors have the right to play God?' And finally: 'Surely it is for God to be the arbiter as to when a life is to end?'

Let me start by answering the last two questions—which, by the way, could just as well be asked about war, capital punishment and abortion.

About doctors 'playing God': by intervening, as we do, with the natural course of illness, are we not already doing so? If a terminally ill patient develops pneumonia and we cure that pneumonia with antibiotics, we prevent him from dying, though God might have given him the pneumonia so as to bring about his death. And if we should decide to intervene sometimes in the opposite direction—to curtail suffering, pain and hell on earth—I cannot think that God would mind very much if we were to play God in that way now and then.

As for God being the arbiter, how do we know what God's interpretation of life is? Can we assume that, to God, life is merely the presence of certain vital functions? In the terminal phase of a distressing illness, I think life has already ended—it is not life, only existence that is left at that stage—and in those circumstances I cannot believe that it would be acting against God's will to stop the vital functions.

What about the medical profession supposedly losing the trust of their patients if they were allowed to kill people? There are trades and professions in many parts of the world where a word of honour is as binding as any signed piece of paper. In the same way, a patient with confidence in his doctor will know that the doctor will never abuse that trust.

Now I come to the first and most difficult of the five questions: who will decide when the patient's life is to be terminated? It is interesting that this question, which we hear so frequently with regard to active euthanasia, was also frequently asked in the early days of organ transplants: who should decide when the potential donor was really dead and his organs could justifiably be removed for transplantation? Many people said that this decision should not be left to the medical profession alone, but members of the general public should be brought in. Mr Walter Mondale, at that time chairman of a congressional investigating committee on this subject, was firmly of that opinion, and anxious to push it through. I remember discussing it with him, backwards and forwards. I insisted that the decision that a person was dead could be made only by doctors, since they are the people trained to make it. When a plane has to make a forced landing, it would be absurd if the pilot were expected to ask the passengers what he should do about it, for they are not qualified to make such a decision. Similarly, only doctors are qualified to decide when a patient is dead. Eventually, unable to budge me from this position, Mr Mondale asked who paid for transplant operations in my country. When I replied that the hospitals were subsidized by the State, he said, 'So the man in the street pays for them, through taxation. And if the man in the street pays, don't you think he should have some say in the matter?' It was during the Vietnam war, and I asked Mr Mondale who was paying for that. Needless to say, the man in the street was paying for it; so I asked Mr Mondale whether the man in the street was consulted as to when the generals should attack and what weapons they should use.

The question of who should decide the moment of death in the case of organ donors is still often raised. But in all these years of transplants this decision has never been made by anyone other than doctors, since they are the only people who can make it, and I am sure that no organs have ever been removed from anyone who was not legally and medically dead.

It is interesting that the same arguments that are used about who should decide when an organ donor is really dead are used about who should make the decision that a patient is a candidate for active euthanasia and that the time has come for it. But there is only one group of people who can make these decisions, and that is the medical profession. I don't think you can let the priest or the lawyer or the patient's family make that decision. And doctors who want to shift the responsibility on to unqualified people are, I think, wrong.

Active euthanasia would be decided on only if the patient had no reasonable quality of life left and there was no possibility of recovery; and in borderline cases, this decision would never be made. Doctors would not terminate a life unless the prognosis was certain—and I can affirm that such decisions are no more difficult to make in medicine than it is to decide that your car will not start again after an accident if the engine is lying in the road. Borderline cases are another matter, of course: just as it would be difficult to tell if your car is going to start again if it has just run into a wall, so there are uncertainties in medicine, but in those circumstances the doctors would not decide to carry out active euthanasia.

It is true that when I was a young doctor—in fact, newly qualified—I almost made a fatal mistake of that kind. I had a hospital patient, Maria, with cervical carcinoma, which had infiltrated the nerves at the back of the pelvis. She was in agony day and night, and often begged me to take her life, to put an end to her suffering, since she believed—and I believed—that the disease was incurable. One night I could not tolerate her crying any longer, and I went to the sister's office and stole ten grains of morphine, which, with shaking fingers, I diluted and drew up into a syringe. Then I walked to Maria's bed with the intention of terminating her suffering. But when I reached the bed, I found Maria was quiet, with a peaceful look in her eyes, so I changed my mind, walked back to the office, and squirted out the contents of the syringe. Three weeks later, Maria walked out of the hospital and was met with great joy by her two children. When I tell people this story, they say, 'You see, mistakes like that will be made if active euthanasia is allowed.' But the mistake that was almost made there was that I was not then sufficiently qualified to take such a decision, which, if active euthanasia were legal, would be for a more experienced doctor to take. In fact, more than one doctor. While I am firmly of the opinion that it should be for the medical profession to make such a decision, I do not believe that it should be left to a single doctor. I think it should be required to be a group decision reached by a special committee of the hospital or institution, including the nurses who look after the patient concerned.

We hear a lot about involving the patient and the patient's family in the decision for active euthanasia, but I don't think it is such a good idea as it may seem. I myself would find it very difficult to decide that my brother, for instance, had reached the stage for active euthanasia. Also, if I were a terminally ill patient, I doubt whether I would want to know exactly when the doctors were going to kill me.

This is not to say, however, that I am against patient involvement altogether. When patients are admitted to hospital, in some instances they sign a declaration that they are willing to have a heart replacement, or any other relevant surgical procedure which the doctor may find necessary, or a declaration allowing the doctors to carry out a post-mortem examination if they should die during this hospitalization. And I think that when the law allows active euthanasia, provision should also be made for the patient to be invited to sign a declaration on admission to hospital saying that if he should be terribly ill and the doctors should have exhausted all means of alleviating his distress or restoring his quality of life, then he gives the doctors the right to bring his life to an end. If he prefers not to sign the paper, that is his choice, and the doctor would have no right, in any circumstances, to carry out active euthanasia. If this procedure were adopted, then, when the time for a decision came, there would be no need to consult either the patient or his relatives, and the decision would be purely that of the medical profession.

Consulting the patient or his relatives when the time has come for this decision seems to me to be to shift the proper responsibility from the medical profession.

So my suggestion is that we ask our legislators to enact a law whereby any patient admitted to hospital may sign a declaration giving the doctors the right to terminate his life if he should become distressingly and incurably ill and all the medical resources available to try to alleviate his condition have been exhausted. If the law allowed us to do this, I think that members of the medical profession should accept this responsibility, and when the time has clearly come and the medical team agrees that the case is an appropriate one for active euthanasia, active euthanasia should be carried out.

Now, how should it be carried out? I am not in favour of giving the patient something by mouth or of leaving an overdose within reach and saying, 'If you drink all that, you will die.' To my mind, that is not really humane. There is, I think, only one acceptable method of active euthanasia, and that is to administer an intravenous injection of barbiturates and a relaxant, so that death will occur within a few minutes, without pain or distress. That, to my mind, is how it should be done.

While I am not totally in agreement with Dr Admiraal and others that the patient should be consulted in the matter immediately before active euthanasia is carried out, I am even more in disagreement with those doctors who, having practised medicine for years, assert that there is no need for active euthanasia. They cannot but have encountered cases in which this was clearly indicated. In general practice it happens from time to time, and in certain specialities (such as cancer) it happens very often. So I cannot believe the doctor who says he has never seen the need for active euthanasia.

Nor do I believe the doctor or clinical psychologist who claims that sufficient comfort can be given to a patient who is incurably ill and in constant pain or distress. There is no way that some pain—for instance, that suffered by a cancer patient with secondaries in the bones—can be totally controlled, except by giving sufficient drugs to render the patient permanently unconscious.

I believe, therefore, that it is our moral duty as doctors to carry out active euthanasia and to persuade our legislators to amend the law accordingly. Otherwise, I think that, like Jesus Christ on the cross, we shall continue having patients who cry out in a loud voice, 'My doctor, my doctor, why hast thou forsaken me?'

NOTE

The above is a summary of a talk given by Professor Barnard at the Fifth Biennial Conference of the World Federation of Right-to-Die Societies, held in Nice in September 1984, to an audience of 700 participants drawn from twenty-six countries. Several of them, speaking in the ensuing discussion—including the Dutch doctor, Dr Pieter Admiraal (see p. 184), who openly carries out active voluntary euthanasia in Delft, Holland—disagreed strongly with Professor Barnard about the need to seek and respect the patient's immediate wishes, right up to the time of carrying out active euthanasia; though all of them were in favour of obtaining an advance declaration, and approved the hospital admission procedure suggested in Professor Barnard's talk. It is always, asserted a Swiss doctor, for the rational individual to take responsibility for his own life and death. Of course, the patient must rely on the doctor for information as to the prognosis and whatever medical alleviation and options are available. However, in the light of that information, the person who has to make the final decision for or against euthanasia must be the patient, and only the patient—if possible, confirming the decision right up to the end. Otherwise, another participant pointed out, every patient who signed an advance declaration would be left wondering whether the time had, in the judgment of the doctor, already come for euthanasia. The only way to avoid such a situation would be to make it a rule for the patient finally to confirm his wish to have his life terminated. Likewise it would be imperative for the patient always to be made aware of his option in the matter.

Pieter V. Admiraal

*Active Voluntary Euthanasia**

Most of the cases of euthanasia at the Delft Reinier de Graaf Gasthui (General Hospital) concern patients suffering from malignant diseases. Therefore I shall discuss these patients first. Subsequently I shall go into euthanasia, which we have learned to accept as a dignified last act in the terminal phase of a patient.

At present some hundreds of thousands will annually die in Europe of cancer, half of them as a result of carcinoma of the lung, the breast or the gastro-intestinal tract. The majority of these patients will be in some form of pain. As a result of his experience at the St Christopher Hospice in London, Twycross[1] stated in 1979 that about 60 per cent of patients with carcinoma will be in pain. Earlier, in 1978, Oster[2] had found that as many as 75 per cent were in forms of pain which required more analgesics than they were getting. This pain can be the direct result of the tumour or its metastases. There is also pain which is an indirect result of the disease or of its therapy. Additionally, there are complications—perhaps less painful but very distressing—such as psychic disturbances (as a result of medicaments or metastases in the brain), respiratory difficulties, vomiting, oedema, gangrene and tumour secretions. The intensity of this pain or distress can vary from mild to agonizing. Nobody, indeed, can quite grasp how severe pain from cancer can and will be. The public's image of this pain is based on

* This is part of a talk (edited by Jim Herrick) given by the author at the fiftieth anniversary celebration of the Voluntary Euthanasia Society held on April 14, 1985. See also Dr Admiraal's *Nederlandse Vereniging voor Vrijwillige Euthanasie* (Justifiable Euthanasia: A Manual for the Medical Profession) (Amsterdam, 1980).

[1] R. G. Twycross, *Incidence and Assessment of Pain in Terminal Cancer*, international seminar on continuing care of terminal cancer patients, Milan, Oct. 1979 (Oxford: Pergamon Press, 1979).

[2] M. W. Oster, 'Pain of Terminal Cancer Patients', *Archives of International Medicine*, 138 (1978), 1801.

accounts from relatives, on hearsay, or even on world literature, such as Tolstoy's *The Death of Ivan Ilyich*—which describes three days of 'unbearable suffering' and 'a torturing pain'. This gives reason enough for the fear of such pain and for the identification of cancer with physical pain: 'cancer pain'.

The patient's reaction to a cancer diagnosis is an expectation of a fatal illness, a death sentence hardly to be survived. In view of this anticipated reaction, doctors in general hesitate to tell patients the truth. Only in cases of carcinoma of the lung or breast, when the patient has to be operated upon, will he have to inform the patient right away. The family, however, most of the time, will hear the diagnosis immediately. And that will create problems. Many a doctor does not realize sufficiently how difficult it will then be to support his hope for a better future. That is where the big lie starts. This big lie, this part of the contact between the patient and his family, causes much sorrow to the relatives, which they can release only in secrecy, unobserved by the patient. Of course, that may be less of a problem when the patient is hospitalized and is met only during visiting hours. But it will be quite difficult when the patient remains at home and in continuous contact with relatives day and night, who then have to find a dodge to leave the patient's room. They can never, however, all leave the house, afraid as they generally are to leave the patient alone. None the less, the patient will have misgivings and will continuously try to find out what the relatives may know about his disease.

All this contributes to the psychological loneliness and isolation of the patient, in addition to his physical isolation. If in hospital he will be put in a separate room in the last phase of his illness. But even at home he will often be left in a room of his own. Generally for two reasons: many people still assume that carcinoma may be contagious from bodily contact; more often, however, it is the fear of sleeping in the same room, only to awaken and discover that the patient has died. Death, indeed, remains terrifying for almost everybody. The consequent isolation intensifies the loneliness of a cancer patient, especially at night. Nights are long, silent and dark. It is normal for a patient, being immobile, not to sleep very well. Even a mild pain is sufficient to keep him awake. But an hour without sleep seems endless. During such nights patients tend to become nervous and depressed. In particular a patient who does not know his diagnosis is anxious about the future. For some, indeed, it is better to know than to suspect! But the patient who knows everything is anxious about the near future, afraid of dying, sorrowful about the family he is to leave behind, and depressed. Most patients with carcinoma are tired or even exhausted, which can also cause a mild pain during the night to become a burden, making the patient long for help.

The word 'pain' in this context stands for real pain, combined with depression, fear, sorrow and fatigue. Does that, however, justify the term 'cancer pain'? Definitely not! 'Cancer pain' is a myth and it would be most desirable if doctors would speak about cancer and about pain as two separate elements. 'Pain' related to depression, fear and sorrow should be recognized as an alarm signal, indicating shortcomings in meeting the patient's needs. One can even say that a lot of this kind of 'pain' is the result of poor interhuman contact and of misunderstanding of the patient's situation. If this kind of patient would ask for euthanasia it would be *medically unjustified* to comply with this request. What this patient really asks for is maximum human and emotional support during the last phase of his life, as was already recognized decades ago in the United Kingdom by Dr Saunders at the St Christopher Hospice.

Nobody can attend a patient just from his own point of view. It is most important today that pastors, nurses and doctors work as a team in close co-operation with the patient's family. In 1980 the English nurse, Tiffany,[3] wrote quite rightly that the most important member of the team is the patient. Today, Tiffany stated, we should treat Mr Smith who accidentally has leukaemia, and not a leukaemia patient whose name accidentally is Mr Smith. Tiffany added that it is worth a lot of time and emotion to approach a patient as a friend and an ally until the very end.

The Medical Team

Let me, in this context, add a few words about the members of a team. Nurses and doctors, of course, are always members of the team. That does not go for pastors. Even in the days when our hospital was still of Roman Catholic denomination only half of the patients wanted any contact with a priest. Behind the curtains, however, he is almost always

[3] R. Tiffany, 'Emotional Support for Cancer Patients in Hospital', *Journal of the Royal Society of Medicine*, 73 (1980), 214.

consulted. The nurses, in my opinion, are the most important members of the hospital team. They observe the patient day and night and he will speak out to them much more freely than to the doctors. Nursing today is recognized as including much more than mere physical care. Marjon Boschman, a Dutch nurse, when writing about the task of the nurse assisting a cancer patient in the terminal phase, viewed the following aspects as the most important:

(a) to take time to sit quietly at the patient's side;

(b) to create the atmosphere in which the patient can give utterance to his feelings;

(c) to substitute for his home as much as possible, since a hospital is not the best place to die;

(d) to protect the patient against unnecessary medical intervention;

(e) to keep the patient interested in normal life as long as possible;

(f) to be an element of calm for the patient and his family;

(g) and last, but not least, to give maximum nursing support as long as possible.

A more satisfactory role of the nurse in the team, therefore, should result from better education and an improved relationship between nurse and physician, requiring each to show a mind independent of the other's opinion. As for the physicians, many of us are still ambivalent. On the one hand medical science gives us more and more possibilities of keeping the patient alive. But on the other, one can well ask whether that is always in the best interests of the patient. Today a growing number of patients request a say in the matter. As a new member of such teams, a doctor will soon realize that a mere white coat does not make a doctor; *profound experience with terminal patients and a very adult attitude are required for adequate functioning in the team.* In my opinion there is place for only one doctor in the team. The more doctors there are, the worse it is!

When the patient is hospitalized, the specialist should consult the family doctor in case of problems. If on the other hand the patient is attended at home, the family doctor would benefit very much from the specialist's advice. The form of help to a patient depends on one important thing: does the patient know the diagnosis or not? The approach of, and contact with, a patient who nurtures a false hope of survival is totally different from that with a patient who is prepared to die.

This brings me to the most important part of our discussion: how to speak with the patient about the fatal character of his disease. Most doctors will agree that this talk has to be done by the specialist whose help was sought by the patient. It is his medical responsibility to tell the patient the truth, for it is he in whom the patient has put his trust. The doctor has to understand that the only basis for such a talk is a very good relationship between patient and doctor, and that such a relationship can never be established during his rounds once or twice a week. You have to meet the patient in private. Today an unfavourable prognosis is not the last and only thing to be told to the patient. Fortunately we can inform him about the means we have for palliative and therapeutic treatment, and the possibilities and results of modern pain treatment with blocks and drugs. We can discuss the side-effects of radiotherapy and chemotherapy and reassure the patient. Some of us will, already in an early phase, speak about death and dying. A lot of patients assume that dying from cancer will always be suffocating, very painful and gruesome. It is my practice to speak with my patients realistically, and for the most part they are relieved to be able to speak about it. The conversation about his illness can be with the patient alone or together with his relatives, depending on individual circumstances. In any case, you have to tell the family what has been said to the patient, and you also will have to tell the other members of the hospital team.

Contrary to the practice of most doctors, who will not discuss euthanasia with a patient before he asks for it, I also discuss the possibility of euthanasia with the patient, for it can be of great value and great comfort to many of them. Not discussing euthanasia with a patient before he asks for it can cause the team to be completely taken by surprise if suddenly he does so. It may even shock the members of the team, who may be disappointed or even angry about the request, which they did not anticipate. But, whatever our approach, how should we respond to such a request? Of course, never just deny it. For a start, ask for the reasons and evaluate whatever opinions you have for your patient. Real pain never can be a reason. Pain can and has to be treated. But the real reason seldom is pain. It is the suffering for a multitude of reasons which you can all imagine, the details of which I shall not elaborate upon here.

Every patient has the right to ask for euthanasia. Every doctor has the right to perform euthanasia. Every doctor has the right to refuse it. One thing, however, is for certain: it is the patient who must make the decision. Neither the family nor the doctor have the right to make that decision for him.

In our hospital at Delft every patient knows that he can always freely discuss with us the option of euthanasia if he wants to. If he opts for it, the decision of the team to perform euthanasia will be discussed in advance with all the nurses in the department involved. We never make a secret of it. Moreover, recent jurisprudence has made clear that a team discussion is one of the prerequisites for avoiding legal prosecution in the Netherlands. Euthanasia as an act of respect to an incurable patient in such a patient's interest and on his request is regarded in our hospital as a dignified last act of medical care for a patient in his terminal phase.

Euthanasia in Practice

Let me now turn to euthanasia itself. Voluntary euthanasia is practised increasingly in the Netherlands. An opinion poll, held in 1980 at the request of the Netherlands Society for Voluntary Euthanasia, indicated that 56 per cent of the population deems euthanasia admissible. According to the most recent poll in 1985, 67 per cent have no objection against active euthanasia and 84 per cent are not against passive euthanasia. It is, therefore, perfectly understandable that the question repeatedly posed is this: in what ways will euthanasia ensure a peaceful death?

In the course of the training for the medical profession and in the literature for physicians, hardly any attention is paid to euthanasia and its application. As a result, patients whose interests are at stake are, at their dying hour, often unable to be sure of expert assistance if they opt for euthanasia. The Netherlands Society for Voluntary Euthanasia, therefore, has invited me to make a contribution towards responsible information aimed at physicians who are going to be confronted with requests for euthanasia in nursing homes, or hospitals, or in their general practices.

In 1980 we published a paper, *Justifiable Euthanasia: A Manual for the Medical Profession*, which was sent to 19,000 doctors and 2,100 pharmacists and was bought by more than 10,000 laymen. In 1982 and 1983 I published papers on this subject in Dutch medical journals. I have expressed the view that euthanasia should be practised only by the attending physician, not by the nursing profession or by relatives, and most certainly not by unqualified third parties. Most doctors in the Netherlands agree with me on this.

The most profound question is: what exactly do I understand by euthanasia? I would proceed from the definition given in the Recommendations of the Dutch Health Council: '. . . a deliberately life-shortening act or the deliberate omission of a life-lengthening act in respect of an incurable patient, in such a patient's interest'. This definition may serve for 'active euthanasia' (a life-shortening act) and 'passive euthanasia' (omission).

I shall say more about these two forms of euthanasia. Up till now, the argument has focused on 'acts' or 'omissions' that will lead to peaceful death. Nowhere, so far, has the question been answered whether such death should be slow or quick, and that, in my opinion is an important starter for any discourse on the techniques of administering euthanasia.

Let me start, therefore, with the administration of so-called 'passive euthanasia', by which I mean 'discontinuation of life-lengthening drugs or acts as a result of which the patient comes to die of his malady sooner or later'. Examples of passive euthanasia are:

(a) discontinuation of artificial ventilation and/or reanimation;

(b) discontinuation of dialysis in case of deficient or absent kidney function;

(c) discontinuation of parenteral feeding or feeding with a stomach-tube;

(d) discontinuation of blood or blood components in cases of malignant disorders of the haemopoetic organs, such as some forms of leukaemia;

(e) discontinuation of the administration of drugs such as:

(i) antibiotics in the case of an intercurrent infection;

(ii) insulin in the case of diabetes.

The above list is of course far from exhaustive.

In the given examples death results from anoxaemia, uraemia, cachexia, anaemia, sepsis and hyperglycaemia, respectively. The lapse of time between discontinuation of therapy and death will be short (minutes) only in the first example of discontinuation (artificial ventilation or re-animation). In all the others it will be long—up to many days, perhaps even weeks! During that time the patient will suffer in different ways. Would anybody dare to assert that this amounts to the peaceful death as desired by the patient and his family? By way of the administration of drugs one could of course advance the last extremity but, strictly speaking, could this still be considered as passive euthanasia? When speaking of passive euthanasia, the 'passive' in my opinion refers only to the physician's attitude. And that may then well be the most important aspect of what I should like to submit here and now: there is no place for passive euthanasia alone. Would practising active euthanasia therefore be a simpler matter? Yes and no!

If I may understand active euthanasia to be 'the deliberate administration of drugs resulting in the patient's death shortly afterwards', two instances can illustrate the problem stated. The administration of a combination barbiturate-curare will always cause an instantaneous deep coma, and, through a respiratory standstill, will lead to death within minutes. After the administration of barbiturates alone, however, it will take at least hours and often days before death supervenes. I know about a case in which the patient did not die for five days. We also know cases of patients who have been for some time in only a superficial coma. What that means for the patient one can only guess. But as each of us knows, the patient in that phase may mutter unintelligibly or make repelling noises, thus giving observers and in particular the family the impression that he is suffering a disagreeable experience. Such a prolonged deathbed is an exhausting experience for the relatives, and quite soon doubts will arise about whether 'it will come off' at all, while the comatose patient's possible reactions may invite anxious questions. This can be a burden and a considerable problem for the family, not just in these very moments, but possibly long afterwards. All this ought to be prevented by its being explained to the family and other attendants, such as a pastor, what actually will or may happen. The guiding consideration, however, should always be the interest of the patient.

After everything has been discussed and commonly agreed upon, the patient, weary of his sufferings, wants only to drop off quietly and quickly. And that is where the consultation between the doctor, the patient and the patient's family should start from. Personally I am of the opinion that the practice of euthanasia should be conditional on the patient's falling quickly into a deep coma and his death not being slow to arrive. My amended definition of euthanasia therefore would be: 'a deliberately life-shortening act in respect of an incurable patient in such a patient's interest, carried out so that quick, peaceful death ensues'.

David H. Clark

The Doctor's Dilemma Today

In the half-century since the Voluntary Euthanasia Society was founded controversy has seldom been still. Lawyers, politicians and moral philosophers, both secular and ecclesiastical, have argued with vigour and conviction. Yet the professional group at the centre of the argument, the doctors, have been curiously muffled and inconsistent. A few doctors have spoken up vigorously, only to be refuted by other doctors. 'Spokesmen for the profession' have made weighty assertions manifestly out of touch with current practice. There seems to be no consistent or definite medical line on euthanasia. What doctors do is apparently often different from what they say they should do. Why is this? I shall attempt to explore these inconsistencies and to throw some light on the changing positions of the compassionate physician challenged by the question 'Doctor, why won't you put me out of pain?'

The practice of medicine is hard work. It usually involves long hours, often physical toil, and hard intellectual work, together with some difficult decisions. The doctor is sustained, however, by the feeling that he is giving a worthwhile service. It is deeply satisfying to be asked for a service and to be able to give it. It is rewarding occasionally to save someone from death, suffering or pain, by the exercise of one's skill. Nevertheless, there are some hard and unpleasant situations in clinical medicine. One of the hardest is when one is asked, or even begged, for a service which one feels one cannot give. This is particularly the case when a doctor is faced with a request from a patient to perform euthanasia—that he kill the patient. It is the pain of this situation which lies behind the reluctance that medical men have shown over the last half-century in allying themselves with the Voluntary Euthanasia Movement.

Along with the respect for their learning, their years of arduous training, and the financial rewards which society gives them, physicians have had much power ascribed to them. The doctor knows of life and birth and death, of deadly diseases and of poisons—frightening mysteries to the ordinary man, particularly when he is suffering—and the doctor has often been seen as very powerful as well as knowledgeable: he has always had power to interfere with vital processes, to speed recovery or to bring about death.

The temptations that these powers cause and the opportunities to misuse them have traditionally led doctors to limit themselves and to accept the limits placed on them by society. Hippocrates made his pupils swear that they would not bring about anyone's death, that they would not procure abortions, and that they would not divulge the secrets that they learnt in the houses they entered, or use their position to abuse the bodies of men or women, even when they offered themselves. Every doctor experiences some of these temptations. It is easier to avoid if they are clearly forbidden and transgressors vigorously punished. All of us welcome externally imposed rules at times. It is easier to say 'I am not allowed to do that' than 'I am not prepared to do that for you'. I remember facing this first as a medical student, when distraught young nurses would beg me to give them something to get rid of unwanted pregnancies. It was much easier to say 'I can't do that, I will be sent to gaol' than 'I am not prepared to take a risk on your behalf'. A number of examples down the centuries where doctors have misused their powers make all of us doctors wary of stepping over the prescribed boundaries. When someone asks us to step over the boundaries, our first instinct, as doctors, is to recoil and refuse.

However, the world changes. Ethical prohibitions are relative and contemporary, not absolute. What is forbidden in one generation may be ordered in the next. I have been involved in the practice of medicine all my life and I practised clinical medicine for some forty years. During that time I saw several of the ancient rules radically altered. The most obvious was the producing of abortions. When I was a medical student and a young doctor this was strictly forbidden and doctors who procured abortions might be sent to prison. One classmate of mine was gaoled. Now that abortion is legal in Britain, women demand that doctors shall rid them of unwanted pregnancies without argument. There are also more subtle changes. The supply of contraceptives was for long illegal in Britain and doctors were wary of supplying them. They are still illegal in some Catholic countries. In

Britain today doctors are expected to prescribe contraceptives without any argument and without consulting the parents of minors (Mrs Gillick notwithstanding).

In my youth the matter of termination of life was clear-cut. Doctors were officially forbidden to bring about the end of a life. Nowadays, after discussion, doctors will decide to switch off life-support machinery. This procedure is fully accepted.

Within my professional lifetime, therefore, a number of the rules have changed markedly. I shall be discussing some of the reasons—technological and other—why these changes have occurred, but I should point out here that this has been a confusing and difficult time for the medical men to whom the requests are made. When they were students they were taught that certain requests must be firmly refused; now they are legally required to grant them. Each individual doctor has had to change his own behaviour and, sometimes, his own beliefs in these important areas. This has been perplexing and difficult. Where we could previously rely on age-old traditions and prohibitions, now we must rethink each situation and be prepared to change our position radically within a few years. This changing climate of public laws, of medical opinion and of personal views is one reason why many individual doctors give equivocal replies to difficult questions and why the publicly held positions of the representatives of the medical profession shift so uneasily.

The central situation we are discussing occurs when an individual doctor is faced by a request from an individual patient that the doctor should do something about which he feels reluctant. This is particularly hard when his compassion is stirred by the suffering of a patient who begs him to be merciful. All of us face these requests during our professional lives. We answer them in different ways and at different times, and gradually learn a way of coping both with the pain of the patient and—more difficult, perhaps—our own inner doubts.

Probably several factors go through one's mind when one is faced with such a request. There is the compassionate desire to help, which may be immensely strong. There is the traditional ethical medical teaching which may indicate that this is an unsuitable form of action. There is the fear of punishment by the law of the land: one could be sent to gaol thirty years ago for helping a woman to terminate an unwanted pregnancy. In recent years we have seen respected doctors being tried in court for ending the lives of malformed infants. Finally, there are the doctor's own personal religious beliefs. Many doctors have no strong religious beliefs, but a minority are committed to Roman Catholicism, or fundamental Protestantism or Hinduism, each of which forbids them to kill or to interfere with the divine process. Many of us envy these committed colleagues: they can give a flat 'No', and say that they are forbidden this act by their faith. For the rest of us it is more difficult, and the decision we take may be influenced by many factors. So most of us follow an uncertain, equivocal course—swaying with the winds of public opinion, moved by greater or less compassion for the suffering patient, and keeping a wary eye on the law and our snooping colleagues.

Fifty Years of Change

Let us look at the changes that there have been in the last fifty years over the issue of voluntary euthanasia in Britain. These changes have been interwoven with one another. There have been changes in medical technology, changes in public attitudes towards the medical profession and its activities, and, finally, changing public attitudes towards interference in both life and death. Each, however, affects the others, and technology in particular has forced ethical debates forward vigorously. This can be seen in other fields, such as contraception and the *in vitro* fertilization of human ova, where scientific advances have forced a hurried rethinking of traditional ethics and produced theological debate as to the moment when the soul is inserted into a foetus.

It is worth going back to the debate in the House of Lords in 1936 on Lord Ponsonby's Bill, which would have made legal the practice that was known to occur occasionally in those days—a doctor easing a suffering patient out of life. One of the main reasons for the rejection of the Bill was a powerful speech by Lord Dawson of Penn, the Royal Physician, who admitted that he practised euthanasia on occasion but said that this matter could not be regulated and should be left to the good sense and judgment of the doctor handling his patient. One can picture that group of elderly English gentlemen in 1936 discussing these issues with peaceful complacency, secure in the knowledge that their doctors were all English gentlemen too and could be relied upon to do the decent thing at the right time. They lived in a world of unquestioned authority where, undoubtedly, some suffering people were helped gently out of their pain. Because such practice was illegal, not many doctors recorded what they had done, though all knew it was being done and most had experience of it.

One of the few published accounts is to be found in *Freud Living and Dying* by Martin Schur. Schur was the personal physician of the great psychoanalyst, Sigmund Freud, for the last twenty years of Freud's life. Freud developed a cancer of his mouth in 1923. It was operated on repeatedly, and a good deal of his face was removed. The cancer recurred over the years and towards his latter days he suffered continual pain. He discussed his suffering with Schur, and said that he did not want to be given any analgesics because they would dull the clarity of his thinking, but he made Schur promise that, when he told him the suffering had become too much, euthanasia would be carried out. The suffering continued through years in Vienna and, after Freud was expelled by the Nazis, through his last years in London. The cancer ulcerated and stank. Freud was now eighty-three, weak, clearly dying of his cancer and in constant pain. On September 21, 1939 Freud told Schur he did not want to go on and reminded him of his promise. Schur gave him an injection of a substantial dose of morphia which put Freud into a coma. Schur repeated the dose twelve hours later, and Freud died peacefully at 3 a.m. on the 22nd. This was the kind of euthanasia which Lord Dawson assured his peers would be readily available for them should they need it; but, alas, this is unlikely to happen nowadays.

I first saw euthanasia practised when I was a senior medical student. A young man was dying of tuberculosis of the stomach in the surgical ward. He had been operated on and it was clear that nothing more could be done for him. It was only a matter of days. The patient suffered continual pain, moaned and begged for release, sedation being relatively ineffective. One night my revered chief came in, and, after a discussion with the ward sister, sent everybody else out and went behind the screens. The young man became peaceful and died some hours later. Some years later in strictest confidence the ward sister told me that the professor had ordered her to draw up a massive overdose of morphia and that he had administered it himself.

Ever since that time, I have been a convinced believer in the propriety of euthanasia and have supported the cause of voluntary euthanasia. I should certainly wish for it for myself if it were necessary.

However, as the years have gone by I have seen the complexities and difficulties of this subject, and realized why many compassionate physicians oppose legislation even though they are not constrained by any doctrinaire faith.

Three years after the 1936 debate came the Second World War, in which human life became cheap. Immense amounts of money were spent to destroy the lives of men, women and children, and we doctors spent our time patching up where we could. Many of us were forced to practise euthanasia in situations where people were dying and in grievous pain. I knew doctors who had had to shoot the battle-wounded before a retreat. The issues seemed clear. Then came the revelations of the extermination camps, followed by the Nuremberg medical trials where it was shown that men with medical degrees had co-operated in mass extermination of the mentally handicapped, in sterilization of the mentally ill, in obscene and indefensible lethal experiments on human beings and, later, in the mass extermination of people simply deemed by the Nazis as unworthy to live. All of us were reminded how necessary restraints were, and there was a widespread tightening up of medical ethical codes. For a time it was almost impossible to mention euthanasia.

Changes in Medical Technology

Medical technology has developed vastly in the last fifty years, and some of the changes have altered the voluntary euthanasia debate radically. With the development of effective anti-bacterial drugs and especially the many antibiotics, it became possible to suppress infection in dying bodies so that people no longer died quickly from pneumonia, as used to happen. Then came the development of resuscitation techniques so that cardiac arrest became a reversible incident. Finally, came the development of life-support machines which are so effective that a body in which the brain is completely dead can be linked with ventilators and pumps and kept going almost indefinitely. Junior medical staff are taught that their duty is enthusiastically to prolong life in all circumstances, and the kind of suffering described so eloquently by Eliot Slater in the present volume became common enough for pressure for voluntary euthanasia to commence again.

Another change is the place of death itself. In the 1930s most people died at home and it was possible for Lord Dawson of Penn and Dr Schur to dispatch their patients without any fuss. In those days the idea of a senior physician, after deep thought, quietly easing the end of the life of a patient whom he knew well and whose family trusted him made good sense. Nowadays most people die in hospital, served by a team of nurses, doctors and other therapists. All of them are knowledgeable about the state of the patient and can watch what is happening. It is very difficult for any one member of the team to take action to end a suffering patient's life without other members suspecting it. All doctors know that there are vigilante groups which encourage members of staff to spy on them and report their behaviour, so that it is extremely unlikely that, say, an insecure, young, recently qualified doctor would feel safe today to take the type of action which Dr Schur took.

Another technological change has been in pain control, markedly effected by a number of new and potent drugs. Fifty years ago the mainstay of pain control was opium, as it had been for centuries. Since then a whole new range of drugs, the tranquillizers, have made it easier to quieten pain sensation while leaving the mind clear. New opiate derivatives and substitutes have been developed. These are powerful, effective new tools in pain control. The painful sufferings of patients with terminal cancer which led some people to the voluntary euthanasia movement in early days also distressed others—among them a Christian social worker, Cicely Saunders, who was appalled in the 1940s by the insensitivity and ineffectiveness of doctors dealing with terminal cancer. She trained herself as a nurse and qualified as a doctor so as to develop the hospice movement, which gives more compassionate and more effective care for those dying of painful disease. Her work has been highly successful and widely imitated, so that severe terminal suffering is less common than it was fifty years ago. This has lessened one of the reasons for pressing for voluntary euthanasia, and Dame Cicely Saunders herself is a sturdy opponent of voluntary euthanasia, speaking against it frequently and with authority.

Medical technology has changed thus the scene for the voluntary euthanasia argument in various ways in the past fifty years. In 1935 pain relief was often ineffective, and suffering could be very great. In 1985 pain relief is much more effective. This has weakened the case for voluntary euthanasia. On the other hand, in 1935 the terminal phase of illness was usually brief; death came quickly, often from pneumonia. In 1985 the end of a life can be obscenely extended. The prospect of extended dying, and particularly of years of degraded senility, threatens all of us, and has strengthened the case for voluntary euthanasia.

Changing Public Attitudes towards Doctors

People have always had mixed attitudes towards doctors. Figures so powerful must arouse ambivalence, respect, awe and affection, when the patient is grievously ill; hostility and cynical contempt when the treatment fails or the bill is presented. Patients honour their doctor's wisdom, compassion and devotion; cynics mock their greed, pomposity and worldliness. However, the reputation of doctors in British society was probably never higher than fifty years ago when the Voluntary Euthanasia Society was founded. In a culture which respected authority figures, the doctor stood alongside the schoolmaster, the clergyman and the policeman. Medical knowledge was part of the great scientific revolution which had transformed the world and promised a bounteous and peaceful future. Medical practitioners, regulated by the General Medical Council and organized into the powerful British Medical Association, were secure pillars of society.

Much has changed in fifty years. All authority figures have been discredited and demoted, the doctors as well as the others. Scientific progress, which has brought us nuclear warfare, pollution and overpopulation, is doubted and discredited. People are better educated, and patients are far better informed on medical matters than they were. Within the National Health Service, doctors now are seen as state employees who are as liable to strike as miners or lavatory cleaners. Many are manifestly foreign, with little English. As a result of all these trends, the public are far more critical of doctors than they used to be. They question and challenge pronouncements, query diagnoses, disagree with plans of treatment, ask for second opinions. There are far more lawsuits against doctors and hospitals and demands for inquiries.

All this has made doctors far more cautious than they were fifty years ago. Then they believed that if they did their best, people would accept and trust them. Many were willing to perform euthanasia quietly.

Today, doctors—especially hospital doctors—know that anything they do may be the subject of inquiry, complaint or lawsuit. They know they are under scrutiny which is always critical, sometimes hostile. They know their judgment is often doubted and their actions questioned, so they are far more cautious. They take too many X-rays, they double check medication, they avoid controversial treatments. They would seldom take the chance of practising euthanasia.

Changing Public Attitudes towards Killing and Self-Killing

Throughout the fifty years there have been shifts in public attitudes towards killing, whether by individuals or by the State. In the 1930s in Britain the rules had not changed for some centuries; it was forbidden to kill other people and, if you were caught doing so, the State killed you. During the war our society entered with zest into the killing of millions of Germans and Japanese and endured the killing of many thousands of our own people. After the war, attitudes changed, and, after much debate, Britain stopped the State killing of murderers. We also changed our collective attitude towards suicide.

When I was a young doctor suicide was a crime. If a person admitted to hospital was believed to have attempted suicide, a policeman sat by his bed until he recovered. Then the patient might be charged with attempted suicide, tried and even sent to gaol. Gradually this practice became repugnant, and since 1961 suicide has no longer been a crime. Suicide is now often discussed, admitted in obituaries, and even admired. Attempted suicide is both more common and more often discussed publicly. It carries little stigma nowadays, whereas fifty years ago a suicide in the family was an occurrence to be treated as a shameful secret.

Every British citizen has felt the changes brought about in the last fifty years, from the horror over killing and self-killing in the thirties, through the enthusiasm for killing in the war years, to the abolition of the death penalty with its official State killing of the present, and the far greater tolerance of suicide. These changing attitudes have also affected every doctor and altered medical practice, especially in the resuscitation of an attempted suicide—formerly a rare and dangerous medical emergency, now commonplace hospital practice. These changes have also affected the voluntary euthanasia debate and are affecting it currently. At present, while it is no crime to kill yourself, it is a crime to assist in the suicide of another. This bizarre position is defended by legal authorities but is largely ignored. There is also an increasing number of cases where people who are known to have been aware that someone had poisoned themselves refrained from taking action, and coroners have even commended such inaction.

Doctors and Voluntary Euthanasia Today

Every time that the matter is publicly debated there is a clamour of different opinions. Elderly doctors, out of touch with current developments, insist that all is well, that Lord Dawson of Penn was right and that there is no need for legislation. 'Pro-life' agitators and Catholic doctors clamour for the rigid application of their moral law, which they wish to impose on others who do not share their faith. I have listed some of the changing facts, attitudes and pressures that have impinged on any concerned English doctor over the last fifty years. I have felt them all myself, and have found my attitudes shifting as the debate has swayed to and fro.

These factors affect both how we doctors behave and what we say publicly—and the two are often different—in a sensitive and controversial area. With any doctor, what he does will depend on the life he has had, his age and experience, the current public debates and his personal religious creed. What he says will also vary. The moral theologians debate and the lawyers argue. But the person in the centre with the painful dilemma is still the doctor, faced by a plea that he end a patient's suffering. Compassion urges him to it, caution urges him not to. The old ethics are in a muddle, and the clamour of public debate is unceasing. What is he to do? Shall he risk exposure, inquiries, trial, publicity, even imprisonment, for the sake of the merciful course? How, either way, will he face his own conscience?

Colin Brewer

The Hospice Movement

Throughout the history of the voluntary euthanasia movement most of the opposition has come from those holding religious views of a more or less doctrinaire kind. Since many of these people are members of churches which once had no qualms about consigning heretics to the flames, or worse, their moral authority in this matter is somewhat questionable. More recently, criticism has come from those who work with hospices for the dying, of whom the best known is Dame Cicely Saunders, a doctor with a strong Christian faith who has devoted much of her professional life not only to expanding the hospice movement but to studying and improving our methods of relieving the various kinds of distress which often accompany terminal illness. Her achievements in this field are not doubted even by those who do not agree with her views on voluntary euthanasia. By teaching and example, she has helped and persuaded doctors to face up to the problems of death and dying, and, while there is still considerable room for improvement, there is undoubtedly much less averting of medical and nursing eyes than there used to be. Although there is naturally more to the management of terminal illness than simply prescribing pain-relieving drugs, Dame Cicely has persuaded many doctors and nurses—though unfortunately not all—that opiates (drugs such as morphine and heroin) can be extremely effective pain relievers provided you give enough of them; and that when dealing with the terminally ill, or even those who are still a few stops short of the terminus, to worry about the development of addiction or the need to give increasing doses is not just absurd but verges on medical malpractice. As if all this were not enough, Dame Cicely is courteous, very approachable and an impressive public speaker. So when she speaks out against voluntary euthanasia, many people are disposed to listen to her.

Nevertheless, there are some aspects of the hospice movement which many people will regard as inappropriate, or even unacceptable, in a pluralist and largely secular society, and which appear to be largely absent from the American hospice movement, despite the seemingly greater importance of religion as an issue in the United States. In an article I wrote for the journal *General Practitioner* in 1983 (April 29, p. 36) I discussed some of these disquieting aspects, and, in the hope of deflecting some of the criticism which seemed likely to follow it, I based the article on a case-study published in the 1982 annual report of St Christopher's Hospice, of which Dame Cicely herself is the Director.

This concerned Mrs N, a sixty-year-old who, eight years after the removal of a cancerous breast, had a recurrence of the cancer in the region of the armpit. The tumour could not be removed by surgery and was resistant to further courses of X-ray therapy and anti-cancer drugs. After a short admission to the hospice, she returned home under the care of the domiciliary nursing team and managed reasonably well for several weeks. However, as the tumour continued to grow and invaded neighbouring tissues, she had to be readmitted for an attempt to destroy the nerves transmitting sensation from the cancerous area, although she had been receiving 120 mg of morphine every four hours. (For comparison, the normal dose of morphine for post-operative pain is in the region of 15 or 20 mg.)

The St Christopher's report continues: 'Unfortunately, the nerve block [was] not successful and she expressed a wish not to try another. The morphine was increased to 150 mg and then to 180 mg four-hourly, with Palfium [another morphine-type drug] being given before dressing the tumour area, which was now not only deeper but also extending down the arm.' So far, one can hardly complain about the treatment, and neither apparently did the patient. But for the last three weeks of her life, the report notes: 'To sit and chat with Mrs N was always tiring, as her mind was so very acute. On several occasions she pleaded with us to end her life. "You wouldn't let this happen to a puppy dog would you?" was a question that was difficult to give a sufficient answer to.'

Her medication was increased further, until towards the very end she was having individual doses of 120 mg of heroin subcutaneously (equivalent to 360 mg of morphine) with additional Palfium between doses. Mrs N, who had trained as a nurse, was a German Jewish refugee whose father had died in a concentration camp. Her mother brought up the children as free-thinkers, though Mrs N's religious belief at the time of her death is not stated. 'Having mentioned on a couple of occasions that she wished she could die from a haemorrhage, that was in fact what happened. Dr V was called to see her after another severe bleed. Having had medication, Mrs N then called out drowsily, "Help, help." "God loves you, Mrs N." "No he doesn't." Silence. "God loves you." "Well, maybe he does."'

This exchange obviously impressed the writer of the report because she quotes Mrs N's last words at the end and adds that they 'will always stick in our minds'.

There are two things about this case history which I found rather disturbing. In spite of the best efforts of the hospice (and no one can accuse them of not pulling out all the stops), this woman suffered severe pain and distress. She requested euthanasia. I do not really blame the hospice for not agreeing to her request, any more than I would blame a Catholic gynaecologist—or anyone else with a conscientious objection—for not doing abortions. However, just as anti-abortion gynaecologists have stopped obstructing or even vilifying those of their colleagues who take a different view of abortion (a majority view as it happens), so I think it is arguable that the hospice movement should now reconsider its attitude to euthanasia.

Dr Saunders has often said that hardly anyone in hospices requests euthanasia once the staff have a chance to treat his or her pain. Yet I find it impossible to believe that the case of Mrs N is unique, or even very unusual. It may well be that hospice patients rarely ask for euthanasia, but then, given the attitude of the staff—well, they wouldn't, would they?

The writer of the report felt that Mrs N's question about puppy dogs was 'difficult to give a sufficient answer to'. I suppose it depends on what is meant by 'sufficient', but a start could have been made by acknowledging that views about euthanasia differ and that those of the hospice staff are actually somewhat out of tune with majority public opinion, as revealed in recent surveys. They might also have answered that, whatever their feelings, euthanasia is technically illegal and that they were law-abiding citizens. Mrs N might well have countered that during her nursing career she had come across many doctors who were not unduly worried by legal niceties in desperate situations of this kind, and could they perhaps refer her to one of them. She might also have decided to try to see whether something good could be achieved in her last wretched days. A letter to *The Times* on hospice notepaper describing her predicament and urging reform of the law would almost certainly have had more effect than all the several hundred similar letters which are received every year by the Voluntary Euthanasia Society.

What do Dame Cicely or any of her like-minded colleagues think the attitude of the law should be to people like the unfortunate Mrs N, for whom no amount of medication, surgery, good nursing and compassion can provide comfort or relief? And what do they have to say to those whose complaint is not so much of physical pain but of unrelievable spiritual anguish? What, in particular, would they have said to a man like James Haig, paralysed in all four limbs following a motor-cycle accident, who burnt himself to death in the flames of his specially constructed bungalow because, not wanting to live, he could not manage to die in any other way? How do they explain the quite remarkable critical and public success of the play and film, *Whose Life Is It Anyway?*

The other thing which concerns me about the case report is the way in which this intelligent and well-informed woman, with her very acute mind, was subjected to some mildly offensive Bible-thumping in her last moments of consciousness. Mrs N was given the gratuitous piece of advice that God loved her. She dissented from this view, as she had every right to do, and as many others might have done. Instead of accepting that everyone has a right to her own religious belief, especially at such times, her medical attendant repeated the assertion that God loved her. Surely this was hardly the occasion for unsolicited theological argument. Perhaps Mrs N thought so too, and perhaps that was why she replied 'Well, maybe he does'—though 'OK, have it your way' might not have been altogether inappropriate.

It seems likely that the religious zeal, which I think this argument illustrates, is responsible for the failure of the hospice movement to come to terms with voluntary euthanasia. The fact of the matter is that in Britain most of the people in the hospice movement are motivated to a considerable extent by a particular religious outlook. They tend to be the sort of people who think there is really only one proper way to live, and therefore it is not surprising that they think there is only one proper way to die. Even in more religious times, this would have indicated a certain amount of theological arrogance, but in a largely secular age it verges, in my view, on the indefensible.

Hospices are fine for people who choose to die the hospice way. I do not know what proportion this might represent, but we can be sure that a large number of people would choose a different way of death if they were given the choice. The American hospice movement is not afflicted by this kind of ethical tunnel vision. Derek Humphry, the former *Sunday Times* journalist, founded an organization in California called Hemlock, after the success of his book *Jean's Way*, which described how he had administered euthanasia with her agreement to his pain-wracked wife for whom, like Mrs N, competent, intensive and sensitive treatment had brought completely inadequate relief.

Like its British counterpart, Hemlock has published what is in effect a suicide guide, but it has excellent links with the American hospice movement. Patients are referred in both directions and Derek Humphry and his colleagues are frequent and respected contributors to medical symposia on death and dying. 'Britain,' I concluded the article, 'is also a pluralist society in which freedom of conscience and belief are fundamental principles. When will Dame Cicely and her movement join with their American colleagues in recognizing this fact?'

The response from Dame Cicely and her supporters followed quickly, though she also had her critics. Dame Cicely herself, in a letter to *General Practitioner*, wrote:

> My own objections to euthanasia are not only based on religious persuasion, nor is that an argument I use, as I do not feel it gives us common ground for discussion. My main objection to any law to give a legally hastened death would be the social dangers which would arise, above all the pressure on many vulnerable people to feel that this was not merely a right but indeed a duty. Certainly there are a few people who wish to choose a quick way out but I do not think a law can establish this as a right without undermining the peace of mind of countless others.

She also quoted Mrs N's husband, who shared his wife's belief in voluntary euthanasia, as saying: 'One cannot expect full agreement in these matters and our different views were unimportant compared with the rest of what happened while she was in the hospice. She was allowed control of all that happened to her *better at St Christopher's than anywhere else.*'

I have italicized the last phrase because, bearing in mind that patients are often reluctant to criticize their doctors, especially when they are as nice as Dame Cicely, this seems a good example of damning with faint praise. This was evidently the view of another correspondent, Dr S. L. Henderson-Smith, who entered general practice after several years as a missionary doctor in Africa.

> A sense of self righteousness [he wrote] is coupled with an arrogance in relation to dying which is patronizing in its implications. The hospice movement obfuscates the real issue of dying. That is: can the sufferer's own wishes be allowed a dominant place or must everyone without exception be willing to settle for unconscious dying [as at] St Christopher's? Is the death wish always, by definition, abnormal, however extreme the agony of continued existence through uselessness, futility and the burden of care laid on others? The only way an intelligent suffering person can die voluntarily today is by that most lonely and awful act, suicide. When will we yield to the requests of our patients to depart at a time of their own choosing in a quick and merciful termination?

One very constructive development which followed my article and the subsequent correspondence was an invitation from Dame Cicely to visit St Christopher's Hospice, which I did a few weeks later. Dame Cicely and her colleague Dr Tom West showed me around and introduced me to several patients, and I was very impressed by the standard of care, as I had expected to be. The whole philosophy of the hospice seems designed to show patients that they are wanted and that, given a certain amount of agreement on fundamental issues, the staff exist for the benefit of the patients and not the other way round.

In our discussions about some of the philosophical and ethical aspects of death and dying, there were naturally major differences of opinion, but our arguments were notably amicable. We discussed the death of Mrs N, and Dr West agreed that if she had been offered euthanasia she would almost certainly have accepted it; and he admitted that this left him 'out on a limb'. Dame Cicely said that although her own religious views did not enable her to see suicide as an acceptable solution to unrelieved and unrelievable distress, she quite accepted that other people had different views and that they were perfectly entitled to them. For this reason she was rather less opposed to the Voluntary Euthanasia Society's *Guide to Self-Deliverance* than she is to attempts to legalize voluntary euthanasia.

I have some sympathy for her view that, if she were more sympathetic to voluntary euthanasia and if the law permitted it, it might be difficult to offer both approaches in the same institution—though no more difficult, in principle, than for gynaecologists to work in a fertility clinic one day and an abortion clinic the next. This is surely an argument for a pluralist approach to hospices rather than an argument for not legalizing voluntary euthanasia.

Dame Cicely introduced me to several terminally ill patients as 'a member of the Voluntary Euthanasia Society'. All of them seemed interested, and none of them seemed in the least shocked or offended. I do not mean by that that these patients would necessarily have been in favour of legislation—though, if repeated public opinion surveys are any guide, they would have been an unrepresentative group if a fair proportion did not agree that the law should be changed. Where there is no choice, sensible people will naturally make the best of what is available, and may even persuade themselves, as with arranged marriages, that it would be presumptuous of them to suggest an alternative.

The democrat and the libertarian are usually, almost by definition, committed to the view that choice is at the very least to be tolerated and generally to be encouraged. For the totalitarian and the prohibitionist, choice is something to be discouraged; and even in death, they do not hesitate to support legal sanctions against those whom they regard as heretics. In this sense, the British hospice movement is still a totalitarian institution. For as long as it continues to be run by people holding religious and philosophical views which, however sincerely held, appear to be at variance with the views held by many of the people who are candidates for terminal care, it cannot claim to offer a truly humane, flexible and comprehensive service.

Raanan Gillon

*Suicide and Voluntary Euthanasia: Historical Perspective**

Hitler's hospitals for incurables, human 'vegetables', heart transplantation, thalidomide babies, mentally deficient children, the old, the senile and the dying—visions of all these may be evoked by the word 'euthanasia'. When it was first recorded, the word simply meant a quick and painless death. Thus, 'as often as Caesar Augustus heard that someone had died quickly and without suffering he prayed for euthanasia for himself and his family', writes Suetonius.[1] The term was simply Greek for 'good', 'easy' or 'happy death' and this is still one of its contemporary meanings. Late in the nineteenth century the word was resuscitated from an elegant obscurity and came to mean the methods of achieving a happy or easy death. As well as drugs and extra comforts and considerations these methods sometimes involved shortening the dying person's life. Today, euthanasia has become widely regarded as synonymous with mercy-killing.

We can differentiate between imposed or compulsory euthanasia and requested or voluntary euthanasia. The former involves killing someone without his desire or request (and often without his knowledge) for reasons which those who do the killing call merciful. This category includes a wide spectrum of euthanasia ranging from Hitler's slaughter of incurables, the killing of deformed babies or incurably sick children, to stopping the special treatment of and drugs for a human being whose heart is beating but whose brain is dead, or increasing the dose of pain-killers to improve, but shorten, the lives of dying patients.

* The author wishes to emphasize that this essay is a slightly amended version (1969) of a paper he first wrote as a medical student (in 1963), and that his approach would be very different were he to write on the subject today (1985). In particular, though basically of the same mind concerning the morality of voluntary euthanasia, he is not sure in which way, if any, he would now wish the law to be changed.

[1] *Lives of the XII Caesars*, Bk II.

The second category of requested or voluntary euthanasia refers, in simple terms, to those cases where an adult of sound mind wishes assistance in dying in order to save himself suffering. Within this category there are different subgroups, but all share one distinguishing feature: the request to die. Thus voluntary euthanasia is essentially a form of suicide, involving the assistance of others.

Suicide has always been a concern of philosophers from ancient times. It is remarkable that, whatever attitude was taken to the concept in general, for the purpose of voluntary euthanasia it was always philosophically acceptable before the Christian era. Pythagoras in the sixth century B.C. rejected suicide on the ground that 'we are the chattels of God . . . and without his command we have no right to make our escape'.[2] Plato rejected it because 'man is a soldier of God and must stay at his post until he calls',[3] and Aristotle rejected it on the civic grounds that man owed a duty to the state. But all three accepted it in cases of incurable disease.

Sophocles was perhaps the first to accept suicide as a more general cure for life's burdens and his lead was enthusiastically followed by most of the Stoics. Zeno, the founder of the school, is said to have committed suicide because he had wrenched a finger. Death was considered morally neutral and sometimes it was preferable to life, sometimes not. Epictetus wrote simply: 'If the room is smoky, if only moderately I will stay; if there is too much smoke I will go. Remember this, keep a firm hold on it, the door is always open'.[4]

On the same theme Seneca wrote:

> Against all the injuries of life I have the refuge of death. If I can choose between a death of torture and one that is simple and easy, why should I not select the latter? As I choose the ship in which I sail and the house which I shall inhabit, so I will choose the death by which I leave life. In no matter more than in death should we act according to our desire . . . why should I endure the agonies of disease . . . when I can emancipate myself from all my torments?[5]

[2] *De Senectute*: 72 Cicero, in Burnett, *Early Greek Philosophy*, p. 108.
[3] *Laws*, IX: 873.
[4] *Dissertations*, I, IX: 16.
[5] Lecky, *History of European Morals*.

Senility was also a reason for voluntary euthanasia, he believed.

> I will not relinquish old age if it leaves my better part intact. But if it begins to shake my mind, if it destroys its faculties one by one, if it leaves me not life but breath, I will depart from the putrid or the tottering edifice. If I know that I must suffer without hope of relief I will depart not through fear of the pain itself but because it prevents all for which I would live.[6]

Not all the Stoics were so restrained about suicide. Hegesias, the Cyreniac, was so convincing an advocate that King Ptolemy forbade him to lecture on suicide any more—too many among his audiences killed themselves after listening to him.

Cicero rejected suicide in most circumstances. However, in cases of extreme suffering, or dishonour, or where 'God himself has given a valid reason', suicide was permissible, he thought.

Epicurus and his school did not recommend suicide, on the ground that death was an evil. But where life became a greater evil than death the Epicureans accepted that suicide was justified.

After the Roman conquest of Greece, Stoic philosophy gradually became accepted throughout the Empire and suicide acquired an exalted status. The Platonic doctrine that it was justified only by a few ineluctable constraints of circumstance was supplanted by the Stoic teaching of *necessitas*—that when a man felt he must leave life, he should do so. The younger Pliny, for instance, believed that the right to die when one pleased was 'God's best gift to men among the sufferings of life'. In the context of voluntary euthanasia he describes one Titus Aristo, afflicted by *longa et pertinax valetudo*:

> He asked me and a few special friends to consult the physicians, his intention being voluntarily to depart from life if the illness was incurable, while if it were merely to be difficult and tedious he would bear up and bide his time . . . for the sake of his wife, daughters and friends. Such conduct I consider eminently high and praiseworthy . . . deliberately to weigh the motives for and against and then, as reason advises, to accept or reject the policy of life or death, that is the conduct of a great soul.[7]

[6] Ibid.
[7] *Epistles* I: 22.

Pliny also discusses a poet who starved himself to death voluntarily:

> Bad health was the cause. He developed an incurable tumour, and wearying of it, he betook himself to death with irrevocable firmness. Up to his last day he had been happy and fortunate except for the death of the younger of his two children.[8]

These, briefly summarized, were the philosophical attitudes of classical Greece and Rome. Popular custom, especially in pre-Stoic times, varied. In Attica, the right hand of a suicide was amputated—a custom supposed to prevent the suicide's ghost from wielding weapons. Yet on Cos, birthplace of Hippocrates, there was a custom for old men, weary of life, to drink hemlock together.[9] Theophrastus, in his book on the history of plants, even writes of improved potions of hemlock for this purpose; and according to the medical historian Sigerist, many instances are recorded where doctors gave poison to patients dying painfully.[10]

For the first two centuries after the death of Christ the Stoic attitude to suicide prevailed. But from its two greatest sources, Judaism and the various strands of Hellenism, Christianity gradually acquired an increasingly intransigent attitude which finally culminated in complete prohibition. This despite the fact that its sources accepted suicide in some circumstances, including incurable and fatal disease. Nor is there evidence that Christ himself rejected suicide.

In the third century after Christ the neo-Platonist school of Plotinus, to which Christian theology also owes a great deal, added a new argument against suicide: that it perturbed the soul and delayed its passage to the after-life. This argument was appropriate against any sort of suicide, irrespective of the circumstances, and before long Christian philosophers had finally prohibited it. Lacantius's declaration that it was wicked to commit suicide unless one was 'expecting all torture and death' at the hands of pagan prosecutors gave way to St Jerome's dictum that it was only justified in defence of virginity—and then even this concession was rejected by St Augustine on the ground that rape could not violate the soul's chastity. Any form of suicide was,

[8] Ibid.
[9] Strabo, *De Uribus.*
[10] *History of Medicine*, II, p. 302.

he declared, contrary to natural law, and this doctrine prevailed almost unquestioned for over a thousand years.

In the fifth century Church Law embodied it, the Council of Arles denouncing suicide as diabolically inspired. Over the next few hundred years various ecclesiastical punishments were prescribed and popular barbarities to the suicide's body became more repulsive. In the thirteenth century St Thomas Aquinas laid down the orthodox Catholic attitude which is still accepted and widely influential today, the misinterpretation of the Sixth Commandment against killing forming the basis of the argument.[11] He also used the other arguments already mentioned, namely: that man is a soldier of God and his own best friend (Plato); that suicide is contrary to man's civic duty (Aristotle); that it perturbs the soul (the neo-Platonists); that it is contrary to natural law; and he added his own argument that it precluded repentance.

The Renaissance brought no changes in orthodox attitudes or popular custom, but it did allow radical opinion to emerge after centuries of suppression. Ironically Sir Thomas More himself advocated voluntary euthanasia in his *Utopia* (1516). There, patients suffering from incurable and painful disease are advised to commit suicide. However, if they refuse they are carefully tended. Almost exactly a hundred years later Francis Bacon, in *New Atlantis* (1626), wrote that it was the physician's duty 'to mitigate pains and dolors, and not onely when such mitigation may conduce to recovery, but when it may serve to make a faire and easy passage'.[12]

Discussion about suicide was shedding its shackles. Indeed, Hamlet's most famous speech debates the problem.

During the seventeenth and eighteenth centuries philosophical consideration of suicide gradually disentangled itself from theological dogma. John Donne, in his posthumously published 'Biathanatos',[13] argued well within the Christian framework to defend suicide in some circumstances, claiming that it was not inherently evil. Montaigne defended it when there was 'very great and just cause', as did Voltaire

[11] See Flew, p. 54 *n.* 7.
[12] Cf. Slater, pp. 32-3.
[13] Written about 1608, this was the second of Donne's prose works and his first essay in controversy. During his lifetime it was circulated in manuscript. A licence for its publication was granted in 1644 and in 1648 sheets of the undated first edition were reissued with a cancel title. See John Donne, *Complete Poetry and Selected Prose*, ed. John Hayward (London: Nonesuch Library, 1955), pp. 420-5, 783-4.

and Rousseau. The rise of the school of French *philosophes*, and of the libertines in England, further eroded the traditional arguments against suicide although, according to Lecky, 'even in 1749, the full blaze of the philosophic movement, we find a suicide named Portier dragged through the streets of Paris with his face to the ground, hung from a gallows by his feet and then thrown into the sewers'.[14]

But intelligent opinion was changing. Montesquieu, supporting man's right to commit suicide, wrote: 'Society is founded upon mutual advantage; when it grows burdensome to me, what should keep me from renouncing it?'[15]

In 1757 Hume in his essay 'On Suicide' refuted the main religious arguments condemning it and asserted that man had a 'native liberty' to determine his death in particular circumstances, including pain and disease. He argued not only, as Donne had done, that suicide was not necessarily sin, but also that it was not 'criminal'. And he pointed out that nowhere in the Scriptures was suicide expressly prohibited. This essay provoked fierce reaction. A certain Caleb Fleming, for instance, condemned suicide as unnatural, depraved, impious and inhuman. He proposed that 'A stop might be put [to it] by having the naked body exposed in some public place: over which the coroner should deliver an oration on the impiety, and then the body like that of the homicide, be given to the surgeons to be anatomized'.[16]

Kant rejected suicide as an insult to humanity; an offence against the categorical imperative which was the fundamental concept of his philosophy. However, as Bertrand Russell points out, his writings can easily be interpreted as permitting suicide. Hegel, a devotee of Kant's philosophy, also rejected suicide, although again his philosophical theories could be used to support or reject it.

Schopenhauer, while he preached the futility of life and claimed that absolute annihilation was the only honest wish man could have, nonetheless rejected suicide as a capitulation to the will. The will, he said, is man's greatest curse and the good man will aim to break his will. Self-torture is one way of achieving this end.

Nietzsche rejected suicide because it was noble to will life in spite of pain and suffering which should be relished. 'I rather entertain the hope', he wrote, 'that life may one day become more evil and more full

[14] Op. cit. (*n.* 5 above).
[15] *Lettres Persanes*, LXXIV.
[16] *Dissertation upon the Unnatural Crime of Self-Murder* (London, 1773).

of suffering than it has ever been'. It is interesting to note that on several occasions Nietzsche, whose health was bad, took overdoses of chloral at night hoping to die. On other nights he would merely think about suicide: 'In that way one gets through many a sad night'. 'Many', he affirmed, 'die too late and some die too soon. Die at the right time'.[17]

Bentham, the leader of the 'philosophical radicals' along with the other Utilitarians, accepted 'happiness as pleasure or absence of pain and unhappiness as pain and the privation of pleasure'. Thus suicide in intolerable circumstances, including those relating to voluntary euthanasia, was acceptable. Indeed, in his dying moments, Bentham demanded euthanasia.

In the latter half of the nineteenth century Durkheim rationalized consideration of suicide by investigating it scientifically. He asserted that the main cause of suicide was social maladaptation. In his monumental work *Le Suicide* he divided suicides into three classes: egoistic, where the individual found difficulty in identifying with his society; altruistic, where he over-identified; and anomic, where social change tended to reduce the influence of society over the behaviour of individuals.

In America, William James rejected suicide on pragmatic grounds —'believe that life is worth living and your belief will help you create the fact'. James himself suffered from suicidal fits of depression. It was he who wrote: 'I take it that no man is educated who has never dallied with the thought of suicide'.[18]

At the beginning of the twentieth century suicide was extensively discussed by Freud and his circle. Freud explained it as the inturning of *thanatos*, the death instinct, in emotionally immature people. This view was later developed by his disciple Menninger in his book *Man against Himself*. However, many Freudian psychoanalysts reject the notion of a death instinct. Interestingly, Freud too asked for a lethal injection to end his sufferings from cancer of the jaw, and received it from his doctor.

Adler believed that the urge to inflict pain and sorrow on relatives as well as the influence of a strong inborn aggressive instinct are important factors in suicide. And one of the important factors

[17] See Bertrand Russell, *History of Western Philosophy*.

[18] *Is Life Worth Living?* Quoted by N. St John Stevas in *Life, Death and the Law* (Eyre & Spottiswoode, 1961), p. 252.

responsible for suicide according to Jung was the 'collective unconscious'.

Suicide is not so avidly discussed by most modern philosophers. The obvious exceptions are the existentialists. Camus, for example, opens his essay 'Le Mythe de Sisyphe' by discussing suicide: 'Here is but one truly serious philosophical problem, and that is suicide'. He bluntly defines as absurd the reasons for living: 'To die voluntarily implies that one has recognized, at least instinctively, the absurd nature of this habit, the absence of any serious reason for living, the senselessness of this daily agitation and the futility of suffering'. To kill oneself means 'simply to recognize that life is not worth the trouble'. However, Camus tempers this pessimistic sense of the absurdity of life in later works. While the world continued to repel him, 'I feel with its suffering inhabitants', he wrote in *L'Homme Révolté*. As Ignazio Silone points out, the premises of modern existentialism present a gloomy picture of the world. Anyone undertaking to explore it 'with absolute intellectual honesty and an uncorrupted heart should sooner or later be able to reach its farthest limit. At that point, one or two things will happen to him: either he will find the abyss of suicide yawning at his feet, or else he will discover some valid meaning in human existance'. Sartre, whose philosophy is based upon the premise that man is abandoned in the world, also rejects suicide as a philosophically valid means of escaping its problems, although he has no moral objection to it; for example, one can always get out of war by committing suicide, he asserts.

The problem of suicide in the context of voluntary euthanasia does not concern the existentialists, and still less most other contemporary philosophers with their prevailing emphasis on logic and linguistic analysis. However, there is a tendency to assert man's right to self-determination, and one tenet of the logical analysts is appropriately mentioned here—namely, that a disinterested search for truth requires that all preconceptions be examined.

Traditional and orthodox Christian teaching about suicide, as exemplified by the Roman Catholic Church, has already been described. Attitudes among Protestants are now less rigid, though there remains deep-rooted prejudice against self-killing. The principle of voluntary euthanasia—or assisted suicide—has been defended by such varied Christian thinkers and theologians as: Hastings Rashdall (*The Theory of Good and Evil*, 1907); T. H. Green (1836–82) (*The Problem of Right Conduct*); W. R. Inge (1860–1954) (*Christian Ethics and Modern Problems* and *Problems of Life and Death*); and more recently by the American theologian and writer on social ethics, Dr Joseph Fletcher (*Morals and Medicine* and *Situation Ethics*). In 1962, among those giving public support to 'A Plan for Voluntary Euthanasia'[19] were the Bishop of Birmingham (Dr J. L. Wilson), a distinguished Methodist preacher (the Rev Dr Leslie D. Wetherhead) and six other Nonconformist ministers. Supporters of the Euthanasia Society have also included a President of the Free Church Council and a Chairman of the (then) Congregational Union.

Judaism is permissive about suicide in some circumstances, including, according to some interpretations, incurable fatal disease. Suicide has never been definitively a sin for Jews and there are several suicides mentioned, with neither approval nor disapproval, in the Old Testament (for instance Abimelech, Samson, Saul, Ahithophel, Razis). An historically famous occurrence of mass-suicide of which Judaism positively approves was at Massada (A.D. 73), when Eleazar exhorted all but four of 960 people to suicide rather than submit to Roman conquest.

The Islamic attitude is as uncompromising as the Roman Catholic: 'Whosoever shall kill himself shall suffer in the fire of hell . . . and shall be excluded from heaven for ever'.[20]

Confucian ethics accept suicide in some circumstances, including hopeless disease, and in China voluntary suicide in cases of incurable disease was acceptable, at any rate before the Communist régime. It is difficult to know what the attitude is today. Shintoism accepts suicide in a wider variety of circumstances, including pain and incurable disease. Buddhism condemns suicide in general, but accepts it in cases of painful and incurable disease. Two examples in *The Dialogues of Buddha* described holy men racked by incurable disease who commit suicide and nonetheless achieve 'nirvana', the Buddhist conception of ultimate fulfilment. In Japan, where Buddhism and Shintoism are the predominant religions, suicide has an honoured role as a solution to various problems, not least of which are physical pain and disease.

Even Hinduism and its various sects, with their intense reverence for life, accept a voluntary euthanasia type of suicide. Thus one who

[19] Euthanasia Society pamphlet.

[20] Quoted from the Koran by W. Patton in 'Suicide', *Hastings Dictionary of Religion and Ethics*.

suffers from disease or great misfortune is permitted to 'walk straight on in a north-easterly direction subsisting on water and air until his body sinks to rest'. In old age, indeed, it is the 'duty and privilege' of a man to adopt a hermit's life unless he prefers to terminate his existence.[21]

The attitudes of primitive societies to suicide and voluntary euthanasia vary greatly. Often suicide is acceptable, and even when it is not, it may be tolerated, or indeed expected, when incurable disease or old age become a burden upon both individual and society. Icelandic sagas depict a society in which it is accepted that when life has no more to offer it is right to commit suicide. The same social acceptance seems to have prevailed in Greenland and Siberia. The ancient Celts often committed suicide rather than let old age or disease kill them; they believed that those who died of disease or senility went to hell, while those who committed suicide before they had been 'spoilt' went to heaven.

The social anthropologist Westermark, writing of the Karens, a Burmese tribe, tells us that 'if a man has some incurable or painful disease, he says in a matter of fact way that he will kill himself and he does as he says'.[22] Simmons[23] described various Polynesian, Siberian, Eskimo, African and other communities in which suicide and voluntary euthanasia were accepted. On the Isle of Vao, in Melanesia, when an invalid entreats his family to kill him, a last meal is taken and the family reluctantly follows the afflicted's desire and strangles or buries him.

More recent work by the American anthropologist Bohannan,[24] on six primitive African tribes in Nigeria, Uganda and Kenya, shows that all of them considered suicide evil and indeed took various measures to propitiate the spirits and protect the tribe after suicides had occurred. However, incurable illness was one situation in which the tribes could tolerate, and indeed encourage suicide. Firth,[25] in another recent anthropological study, on the Western Pacific island of Tikopia, found disapproval of certain methods of suicide—for instance hanging, when the gods would reject the soul of the dead person. But the gods do not

[21] *Panchatantra* (trans. T. Bentley).
[22] Quoted by A. Rose in 'Euthanasia', *Hastings Dictionary of Religion and Ethics.*
[23] *The Role of the Aged in Primitive Society.*
[24] *African Homicide and Suicide* (Princeton Univ. Pr., 1960).
[25] 'Suicide and Risk-taking in Tikopia Society', in *Psychiatry*, 24 (1961), I.

object if someone, suffering from an incurable disease for instance, commits suicide by swimming out to sea. However, the few Christian converts in this community of two thousand people believe that the soul of any suicide goes to hell.

An interesting custom in seventeenth-century Brittany was based upon the right of an incurable to appeal to the priest for the holy stone. The family gathered, the last rites were administered and the oldest living relative raised the heavy stone above the patient's head and let it fall.

Until this century medical attitudes to voluntary euthanasia were governed, ostensibly at least, by the ecclesiastical and legal prohibition of both suicide and murder. Actual behaviour may have been secretly different. For example Greville, in his diaries, writes that the President of the Board of Trade, Huskisson, when he was dying 'begged that they would open a vein and release him from his pain'.[26] Greville, however, does not tell us whether or not the request was met.

Euthanasia, in the sense of an improved but not accelerated death, exercised a few medical minds in the nineteenth century. One German doctor, for example, wrote a professorial thesis about it, advocating special institutions for the dying, intense care, both physical and spiritual, with emphasis in the former upon symptomatic and palliative treatment using 'soothing, soporific, sedative, analgesic, anti-spasmodic, and narcotic drugs'.[27] Another German elevated euthanasia to an independent discipline equivalent to medicine or surgery and called it 'obstetrics of the soul'.[28]

The first medical advocacy of voluntary euthanasia was probably in 1907 when Goddard proposed a scheme to the Willesden Medical Society. In 1931 Millard, in his presidential address to the Society of Medical Officers of Health, brought voluntary euthanasia proposals to public attention; and in 1935 the Voluntary Euthanasia Society was created with the eminent surgeon Lord Moynihan as its President and many figures from the medical establishment as sponsors. However, the Bill sponsored by the society to legalize voluntary euthanasia was defeated in the House of Lords in 1936 with two medical peers, Horder and Dawson, opposing it mainly because in their opinion it involved too many formalities and because euthanasia was a matter best left to

[26] *Leaves from the Greville Diary* (Eveleigh Nash & Grayson, 1930), p. 112.
[27] See W. Cane, *Journal of the History of Medicine and Allied Sciences*, 7 (1952), 401.
[28] Ibid.

the discretion of doctors. Nevertheless, Lord Dawson affirmed that euthanasia was carried out by many doctors. When the 'gap between life burdened by incurable disease and death' was wide, there was a great variety in practice between individual doctors and patients; 'nonetheless there is in the aggregate an unexpressed growth of feeling that the shortening of the gap should not be denied when the real need is there', he told the Lords.[29]

In general, medical opinion on euthanasia may be divided into three broad categories. First there are the opponents of any sort of deliberate shortening of life. This group includes most Roman Catholic doctors. They are prepared, however, on the advice of Pope Pius XII, among others, to give enough pain-killing drugs to kill pain, even if they know that such quantities of drugs will also kill the patient. According to Pope Pius XII if 'the actual administration of drugs brings about two distinct effects, the one the relief of pain, the other the shortening of life, the action is lawful'.[30]

A second group supports the Dawson/Horder views that euthanasia, whether or not it is requested by the patient, should be left to each doctor's discretion. Many doctors, probably a majority, come into this category. Indeed in one of the few medical textbooks discussing the subject, Davidson's *Medical Ethics* (1962), an article actually advocates killing the dying patient in certain circumstances, and suggests two suitable potions for doing so.[31] It does not state whether or not the patient's consent is required.

A third group within the medical profession would like the law to be changed to allow voluntary euthanasia. Dr Charlotte Gilman perhaps summarized the belief of this group when she wrote, just before her death:

> When all usefulness is over, when one is assured of an imminent and unavoidable death, it is the simplest of human rights to choose a quick and easy death in place of a slow and horrible one. . . . Believing this choice to be of social service in promoting wider views on the subject, I have preferred chloroform to cancer.[32]

[29] *House of Lords Debates*, 103, 5th series (1936), cols 488-9.
[30] Quoted by N. St John Stevas, op. cit., p. 276.
[31] C. Hoyle, 'Care of the Dying'.
[32] Her valediction to the world is quoted in part by several writers: Wolbarst in the *Medical Record* (May 17, 1939) quotes it in full.

British law explicitly forbids deliberate shortening of another's life. Thus according to M. Hale, an early writer on the criminal law:

> If a man is sick of some disease which, by the course of nature might possibly end his life in half a year, and another gives him a wound or hurt which hastens his death by irritating or provoking the disease to operate more violently and speedily, this is murder or other homicide according to the circumstances in the party by whom such wound or hurt was given. For the person wounded does not simply die *ex visitatione Dei*, but his death is hastened by the hurt which he received and the offender is not allowed to apportion his own wrong.[33]

This opinion was later reiterated by Mr Justice Byles who stated that to hasten death 'constitutes murder or at least manslaughter'.

However, the administration of the law is less severe. The charge against a doctor is difficult to establish, more difficult to prove; and there is reluctance to prosecute. In practice the charges brought are against parents who kill their suffering children. The verdict is one of manslaughter, and the judge will usually impose a lenient sentence.

An important change in the law occurred in 1961, legalizing suicide and attempted suicide. However, the offence of aiding and abetting, counselling or procuring the suicide of another person came in, with a maximum penalty of fourteen years' imprisonment. Nonetheless, unintentional acceleration of death, as a result of administering pain-killing drugs, seems to be legally acceptable following the judgment at the murder trial of Dr Bodkin Adams in 1957.

Many lawyers are dissatisfied with the law and various changes have been proposed, several going considerably further than the advocacy of voluntary euthanasia. For instance, in 1927, Mr Justice Branson, in a case where a man drowned his incurable and miserably suffering child after nursing her for six weeks, said: '. . . it gives one food for thought . . . that had this poor child been an animal instead of a human being, so far from there being anything blameworthy in the man's action in putting an end to its suffering, he would actually have been liable to punishment if he had not done so'. And in 1957 Lord Goddard said that it might be wise to alter the existing law 'so that the passing of a person afflicted with an incurable disease, either in mind or

[33] *Pleas of the Crown*, p. 428.

body, might be expedited'.

Those lawyers who limit themselves to advocating voluntary euthanasia have made several alternative proposals. The simplest involves a change to Clause 2 of the 1961 Suicide Act so that aiding and abetting would not be illegal unless it was shown that it was done with malice or for selfish motives. This would be comparable to a provision in the Swiss penal code.

A similar proposal by Professor Glanville Williams contains more safeguards in providing that 'no medical practitioner shall be guilty of an offence in respect of an act done intentionally to accelerate the death of a patient who is seriously ill, unless it is proved that the act was not done in good faith with the consent of the patient and for the purpose of saving him severe pain in an illness believed to be of an incurable and fatal character'. An amendment would also be necessary to Clause 2 of the Suicide Act.

The earlier proposals of the Euthanasia Society involved even more safeguards. A patient of sound mind over the age of twenty-one suffering from an incurable and fatal disease, would be entitled to euthanasia. An application approved by his doctor would be submitted to a euthanasia referee, who would be a doctor appointed by the Ministry of Health. If the conditions of the Act were fulfilled, the referee would authorize euthanasia which would be carried out either by the patient under the doctor's guidance or by the doctor or, if the doctor is not prepared to do it, by the referee. Suggestions for a bill to this effect were put forward in 1961 by the Euthanasia Society in 'A Plan for Voluntary Euthanasia'.[34] Now, however, the Society has put forward new proposals which would legalize euthanasia where a statutory declaration has been made *in advance* requesting its administration in certain specified circumstances and in anticipation of certain possible medical eventualities. These proposals, in the form of a draft Voluntary Euthanasia Bill (see Appendix), will undergo further modification in the light of expert and interested opinion.

Some Current Arguments Against Euthanasia

Various arguments, not based on the orthodox Christian prohibition

[34] This pamphlet was later revised to take into account the new situation created by the Suicide Act 1961.

of suicide, are frequently used against voluntary euthanasia. Many of these are presented in detail by Professor Yale Kamisar in this volume, and they should be studied in conjunction with the rejoinder by Professor Glanville Williams. Several of them are used by medical opponents in particular.

One of the strongest is that modern pain-killing drugs obviate the need for euthanasia. This is very nearly true in the case of some specialized terminal-care hospitals. In these, usually run by devotees of some religious order who are often trained nurses and provide the continual care necessary for adequate pain control, there is frequently a surprisingly cheerful atmosphere of faith and hope. Cicely Saunders, who is both a nurse and doctor, is medical director of such a hospital and also one of the firmest opponents of voluntary euthanasia. In such hospitals, she declares, none of the patients would accept voluntary euthanasia even if it were available. Enough praise for her admirable work, and for this sort of medical care for the dying, can hardly be given; but even in such institutions, as Cicely Saunders herself has admitted in the columns of *The Lancet*, very occasionally pain can only be controlled by putting the patient 'continually asleep'.[35] As Judge Earengay has pointed out, there is little practical difference between this sort of pain-killing and actually killing the patient.

More crucial is the fact that terminal-care hospitals are exceptional and most people die either at home or in general and geriatric wards of ordinary hospitals. In a study of 220 patients dying in a London geriatric hospital, Dr Exton-Smith found that eleven 'continually expressed a wish to die'. While his sample is small, few doctors would deny his conclusions that 'dying is still very often an ugly business'.[36] For it is not only pain which can make the end of life miserable; as Exton-Smith's study clearly demonstrates, breathlessness, with its attendant sense of suffocation, nausea and vomiting, the inability to swallow or talk, urinary and faecal incontinence, are all symptoms which medicine cannot properly control.

Clearly voluntary euthanasia is not the only answer to these problems: improved teaching on the care of the dying, more hospitals for terminal care, continued research into the prevention, therapy and cure of disease, improved analgesia and more medical staff are all long-term objectives which will eventually minimize the need for euthanasia.

[35] *The Lancet* (Sept. 2, 1961), p. 548.

[36] Exton-Smith, 'Terminal Illness in the Aged', *The Lancet* (Aug. 5, 1961).

And the pioneering research into these problems, prosecuted by Dr Saunders and her colleagues and followers, is fully supported by advocates of voluntary euthanasia. But today and in the foreseeable future patients will be dying painfully from incurable diseases. While Exton-Smith's 5 per cent of patients who 'continually expressed a wish to die' were not necessarily a typical sample, it seems highly probable that some of the people dying in pain each year would accept voluntary euthanasia if it were available. A comparatively simple change in the law would allow them an easy death instead of a hard one.

Another medical argument, not often discussed except within the profession, is that voluntary euthanasia presupposes a patient who knows that he has a fatal and incurable disease. Many doctors do not believe in disclosing such information. Conversely, others are discouraged from telling patients the truth by the realization that, if they do so, some are likely to ask for euthanasia which in the present state of the law involves the doctor in committing murder.

While medical opinion is divided about the effects on terminal patients of knowing their diagnoses, some revealing research has been done. For instance a study written by Aitken Swan and Esson[37] indicates that most people would prefer to know if they have a disease with a poor outlook, while Gierle, Lundun and Sandblom[38] found that patients with probably fatal cancer who are told the diagnosis make at least as satisfactory an adjustment to their disease as those who are not told.

There are further arguments against medical lies. They tend to undermine the confidence and trust upon which the relationship between patient and doctor should be based, and indeed they may also undermine the trust between relatives, especially patient and spouse. Often, for example, the latter is told the diagnosis and urged to withhold it from the patient. Furthermore, lying may destroy any reassurance for the patient's relatives if they ever come under the same doctor's care and he tells them, this time truthfully, that there is no evidence of serious disease. On a more mundane but still important level, lying may prevent a dying patient from settling his will and other affairs. Finally, many argue that the doctor simply has no right to withhold information from a patient about his health if the patient has

[37] See *British Medical Journal* (1959), pp. 779–83.
[38] See *Cancer*, 13 (1960), 1206–17.

specifically requested it. Clearly, if patients who ask to be told the truth about their condition are answered truthfully, several advantages can arise in the management of terminal illness in addition to facilitation of voluntary cuthanasia.

Some doctors, while they may accept the morality of voluntary euthanasia, argue that it is wrong for doctors to have any part in it. A doctor's job, they say, is to save life not to take it. But although part of a doctor's duty is to preserve life and cure disease he also has an important obligation to allay suffering. Voluntary euthanasia concerns a situation in which life cannot be saved nor the disease cured: there is no reason to ignore the third obligation.

It is true that the Hippocratic Oath (which very few medical schools require their graduates to accept) prohibits the administration of any poison, even if requested. It also prohibits the use of 'a knife on sufferers from the stone' and the imparting of 'precept, oral instruction and all other learning' to any person except 'my sons, the sons of my teacher and to pupils who have signed the indenture and sworn obedience to the physicians' law'. Moreover, it begins: 'I swear by Apollo, by Æsculapius, by Health, by Panacea and by all the gods and goddesses'. These parts have, of course, been rejected. Similarly, while it is remarkable how much of an oath formulated in the sixth or fifth century B.C. remains relevant to contemporary medical ethics, we must always remain free to reject any part that is not.

Perhaps it should be reiterated that the proposed legislation would not impose a duty to kill on doctors who refused to do so. It would give a patient the right to find a doctor who accepted euthanasia, and it would give such a doctor the legal right to accede to his patient's wishes. Many doctors today would already be prepared to do this. A glance at the list of those supporting the legislation proposed by the Euthanasia Society is enough to show that many eminent medical authorities are among them; and if it were realized that society and the profession have accepted the principle of voluntary euthanasia, doubtless more would join their ranks. Among them may be confidently expected a proportion of the doctors who at present secretly administer compulsory euthanasia when they consider it appropriate, but paradoxically reject the concept that the patient should have any legal right to ask for it.

Such doctors often use another argument against any change in the law. It is based on a piece of medical folklore which tells the doctor:

'Thou need'st not strive officiously to keep alive.' This dictum, originating in a satirical poem,[39] is often claimed to solve the whole problem of euthanasia for the doctor and to render any change in the law superfluous. But what exactly does it mean? Does the negative refer to 'need'st' (in which case 'thou need'st not' means 'please yourself') or to 'strive' or to 'officiously'? Does 'officiously' refer to 'strive' or to 'keep alive'? Finally, what is meant by 'officiously'? A number of different meanings are offered by the *Oxford Dictionary* to define 'officious'. The two most appropriate in this context are probably 'unduly forward in offering one's services' and 'meddlesome'. Both are imprecise and depend largely on a subjective interpretation of what is 'unduly forward' or 'meddlesome'. An analysis of its possible interpretations reveals this phrase to be meaningless, which is possibly the reason for its popularity: every doctor may use it to justify his own actions and beliefs. But even if some arbitrary meaning is extracted, in what circumstances may it be applied? Clearly not in general, for there are countless situations where it would be proper for the doctor to strive his utmost to keep his patient alive, 'officiously' or otherwise.

The injunction is nonetheless uttered in a wide variety of situations. Perhaps the most common is when a patient is being kept alive but unconscious by a dialysing machine, blood transfusion, mechanical respirator or a pacemaker for maintaining the heartbeat. At some stage it is recognized that there is no prospect of recovery and the apparatus is disconnected. Heart transplantations have afforded the most publicized examples of this. However, such behaviour, whether or not the dictum is uttered, is no different either morally (as Joseph Fletcher makes clear) or legally (as Earengey emphasizes) from deliberately injecting a fatal dose of morphine. All such procedures are deliberate and premeditated acts of shortening another's life and are therefore condemned as murder at English law.

In important ways this injunction may be interpreted to go much further than voluntary euthanasia, for it may imply not only that the law is inadequate, but also that it may reasonably be broken by doctors, that there is no need to try to change it and, above all, that a doctor may justifiably kill his patient without his knowledge, desire, consent or request. Because of the widespread acceptance of this

[39] 'The Latest Decalogue' by Arthur Hugh Clough (1819–61).

meaningless dictum in the medical profession, it deserves a thorough and rigorous rebuttal.

A further set of arguments against voluntary euthanasia rests on the fallibility of medicine, doctor and patient. Incurable diseases occasionally regress spontaneously, cures can be discovered, maldiagnoses are sometimes made, and the patient may make a wrong decision. These arguments are closely examined by other contributors to this volume.

It is important, however, to point out that any proposal simply to legalize the aiding and abetting of suicide, as distinct from the proposals of the Euthanasia Society, suffers from the great disadvantage that it does not specify in which conditions a request for assistance in suicide can be granted. It is indisputable that the great majority of people who demand to die or attempt suicide are suffering from some sort of social maladaptation or psychiatric condition which is usually curable. Various studies, in which the lives of people attempting suicide were followed for a period of years, show that only about 5 to 10 per cent of these people actually do kill themselves later. As Stengel points out in his book *Suicide*, the 'large majority of people who make suicidal attempts are likely to survive'. Every doctor would reject a law which allowed him to assist such people to die, for his primary duties, namely to save life and to cure disease, are both of them potentially possible of fulfilment and they will take precedence over his duty to alleviate suffering.

Occasionally the argument is heard that euthanasia should not be permitted because it is an unpleasant obligation for doctors to have to assume. This may well be true: nevertheless, it need hardly be said that a doctor's first duty is to his patient, who for his part may prefer euthanasia to prolonging his fatal disease.

Another argument, not infrequently heard from doctors, is that euthanasia is an admission of defeat and that, as one correspondent wrote, 'only by keeping our failures before our eyes can solutions be found'.[40] While medical experimentation to find better methods of looking after the dying patient is necessary, like all medical experimentation it should be based on the knowledge and consent of the patient. It may reasonably be assumed that patients requesting euthanasia do not desire to go on living for experimental purposes. Those brave persons who are prepared to help in such experimentation

[40] See *The Lancet* (Sept. 2, 1961).

will presumably not ask for euthanasia. Ultimately a person must be free to choose for himself. For although, as Paulsen once wrote,[41] heroism is not a duty, neither should it be prohibited. The legalization of voluntary euthanasia would help to strike a balance.

[41] Paulsen, *Ethik*, II, 101.

Mary Rose Barrington

The Case for Rational Suicide

Of the many disagreeable features inherent in the human condition, none is more unpalatable than mortality. Many people declare that they find the concept of survival and immortal life both inconceivable and preposterous; but they will usually admit to a minimal pang at the thought of being snuffed out in due course and playing no further part in the aeons to come. That aeons have already passed before they were born is a matter that few people take to heart, and they tend on the whole to be rather glad not to have experienced the hardships of life before the era of the Public Health Acts and pain-killing drugs. To cease from being after having once existed seems altogether different and altogether terrible. This is an odd conclusion, bearing in mind that whereas before birth one must be reckoned to have had no effect on the course of events at all, the very act of birth and the shortest of lives may produce incalculable and possibly cataclysmic effects by indirect causation. Viewed in this light we might all be filled with satisfaction to think that our every move will send ripples of effects cascading down time. In fact, speculations of this kind do little if anything to satisfy the immortal longings, and even though being remembered kindly by others is generally felt to be something of a comfort, absolute death remains absolutely appalling. Many people who have no religious convictions save themselves from despair by filing away in their minds some small outside chance that they might, after all, survive, perhaps as some semi-anonymous cog in a universal system; many others resolutely refuse to give any thought to death at all.

If human convictions and behaviour were a direct function of logical thinking, one would expect that the more firmly a person believed in the survival of his soul in an existence unhampered by the frequently ailing body, the more ready he would be to leave this world and pass on to the next. Nothing of the sort appears to be the case, at least for those whose religion is based on the Old Testament. Self-preservation is presented in such religions as a duty, though one that is limited by some inconsistent provisos. Thus a person may sacrifice his life to save others in war, or he may die a martyr's death in a just cause; but if he were to reason that there was not enough food in the family to go round, and therefore killed himself to save the others from starvation (a fate, like many others, considerably worse than death), this would be regarded as the sin, and erstwhile crime, of suicide. Whether performed for his own benefit or to benefit others, the act of suicide would be condemned as equivalent to breaking out from prison before the expiry of the term fixed, a term for which there can be no remission.

The old notions about suicide, with an influence still lingering on, are well summarized by Sir William Blackstone in his famous *Commentaries on the Laws of England* (1765–9): 'The suicide is guilty of a double offence: one spiritual, in invading the prerogative of the Almighty and rushing into his immediate presence uncalled for; the other temporal, against the King, who hath an interest in the preservation of all his subjects.'[1]

Religious opposition to suicide is of decreasing importance as people become ever more detached from dogmas and revelationary teachings about right and wrong. The important matter to be considered is that while the humanist, the agnostic or the adherent of liberal religion seldom condemns suicide as a moral obliquity, he appears on the whole to find it as depressing and horrifying as the religious believer for whom it is sinful. There are many reasons for this, some good, and some regrettable.

Indoctrination against suicide is regrettably to be found at all levels. In itself the tendentious expression 'to commit suicide' is calculated to poison the unsuspecting mind with its false semantic overtones, for, apart from the dangerous practice of committing oneself to an opinion, most other things committed are, as suicide once was, criminal offences.[2] People are further influenced by the unhappy shadow cast over the image of suicide by the wide press coverage given to reports of suicide by students who are worried about their examinations, or girls who are upset over a love affair, or middle-aged people living in bed-

[1] *Commentaries*, IV, 189.

[2] Professor Flew points out (see p. 56 *n*. 13) the greater virtues of the French '*se suicider*'. We should perhaps be grateful not to be burdened with an expression like the German '*Selbstmord*', i.e. 'self-murder'.

sitting-rooms who kill themselves out of depression—troubles that might all have been surmounted, given time. In pathetic cases such as these, it is not, as it seems to me, the act of suicide that is horrifying, but the extreme unhappiness that must be presumed to have induced it. Death from despair is the thing that ought to make us shudder, but the shudder is often extended to revulsion against the act of suicide that terminates the despair, an act that may be undertaken in very different circumstances.

The root cause of the widespread aversion to suicide is almost certainly death itself rather than dislike of the means by which death is brought about. The leaf turns a mindless face to the sun for one summer before falling for ever into the mud; death, however it comes to pass, rubs our clever faces in the same mud, where we too join the leaves. The inconceivability of this transformation in status is partly shot through with an indirect illumination, due to the death of others. Yet bereavement is not death. Here to mourn, we are still here, and the imagination boggles at the notion that things could ever be otherwise. Not only does the imagination boggle, as to some extent it must, but the mind unfortunately averts. The averted mind acknowledges, in a theoretical way, that death does indeed happen to people here and there and now and then, but to some extent the attitude to death resembles the attitude of the heavy smoker to lung cancer; he reckons that if he is lucky it will not happen to *him*, at least not yet, and perhaps not ever. This confused sort of faith in the immortality of the body must underlie many a triumphal call from the hospital ward or theatre, that the patient's life has been saved—and he will therefore die next week instead of this week, and in rather greater discomfort. People who insist that life must always be better than death often sound as if they are choosing eternal life in contrast to eternal death, when the fact is that they have no choice in the matter; it is death now, or death later. Once this fact is fully grasped it is possible for the question to arise as to whether death now would not be preferable.

Opponents of suicide will sometimes throw dust in the eyes of the uncommitted by asking at some point why one should ever choose to go on living if one once questions the value of life; for as we all know, adversity is usually round the corner, if not at our heels. Here, it seems to me, a special case must be made out for people suffering from the sort of adversity with which the proponents of euthanasia are concerned: namely, an apparently irremediable state of physical debility that makes life unbearable to the sufferer. Some adversities come and go; in the words of the Anglo-Saxon poet reviewing all the disasters known to Norse mythology, 'That passed away, so may this'. Some things that do not pass away include inoperable cancers in the region of the throat that choke their victims slowly to death. Not only do they not pass away, but like many extremely unpleasant conditions they cannot be alleviated by pain-killing drugs. Pain itself can be controlled, provided the doctor in charge is prepared to put the relief of pain before the prolongation of life; but analgesics will not help a patient to live with total incontinence, reduced to the status of a helpless baby after a life of independent adulthood. And for the person who manages to avoid these grave afflictions there remains the spectre of senile decay, a physical and mental crumbling into a travesty of the normal person. Could anything be more reasonable than for a person faced with these living deaths to weigh up the pros and cons of living out his life until his heart finally fails, and going instead to meet death half-way?

It is true, of course, that, all things being equal, people do want to go on living. If we are enjoying life, there seems no obvious reason to stop doing so and be mourned by our families and forgotten by our friends. If we are not enjoying it, then it seems a miserable end to die in a trough of depression, and better to wait for things to become more favourable. Most people, moreover, have a moral obligation to continue living, owed to their parents while they are still alive, their children while they are dependent, and their spouses all the time. Trained professional workers may even feel that they have a duty to society to continue giving their services. Whatever the grounds, it is both natural and reasonable that without some special cause nobody ever wants to die *yet*. But must these truisms be taken to embody the whole truth about the attitude of thinking people to life and death? A psychiatrist has been quoted as saying: 'I don't think you can consider anyone normal who tries to take his own life'.[3] The abnormality of the suicide is taken for granted, and the possibility that he might have been doing something sensible (for him) is not presented to the mind for even momentary consideration. It might as well be argued that no one can be considered normal who does not want to procreate as many children as possible, and this was no doubt urged by the wise men of yesterday; today the tune is very different, and in this essay we are

[3] Reported in *The Observer* (June 26, 1967).

concerned with what they may be singing tomorrow.

There is an obvious connection between attitudes to birth and to death, since both are the fundamentals of life. The experience of this century has shown that what may have appeared to be ineradicably basic instincts can in fact be modified in an advanced society, and modified not merely by external pressures, but by a corresponding feedback movement from within. Primitive people in general take pride in generating large families, apparently feeling in some deep-seated way that motherhood proves the femaleness of the female, and that fatherhood proves the maleness of the male, and that the position in either case is worth proving very amply. This simple pride is not unknown in advanced countries, although public applause for feats of childbearing is at last beginning to freeze on the fingertips, and a faint rumble of social disapproval may be heard by an ear kept close to the ground. The interesting thing is that it is not purely financial considerations that have forced people into limiting their progeny, and least of all is it the public weal; people have actually come to prefer it. Women want to lead lives otherwise than as mothers; men no longer feel themselves obliged to assert their virility by pointing to numerous living tokens around them; and most parents prefer to concentrate attention and affection upon a couple rather than a pack. The modification in this apparently basic drive to large-scale procreation is now embraced not with reluctance, but with enthusiasm. My thesis is that humane and advanced societies are ripe for a similar and in many ways equivalent swing-away from the ideal of longevity to the concept of a planned death.

It may be worth pausing here to consider whether the words 'natural end', in the sense usually ascribed to the term, have much bearing on reality. Very little is 'natural' about our present-day existence, and least natural of all is the prolonged period of dying that is suffered by so many incurable patients solicitously kept alive to be killed by their disease. The sufferings of animals (other than man) are heart-rending enough, but a dying process spread over weeks, months or years seems to be one form of suffering that animals are normally spared. When severe illness strikes them they tend to stop eating, sleep and die. The whole weight of Western society forces attention on the natural right to live, but throws a blanket of silence over the natural right to die. If I seem to be suggesting that in a civilized society suicide ought to be considered a quite proper way for a well-brought-up person to end his life (unless he has the good luck to die suddenly and without warning), that is indeed the tenor of my argument; if it is received with astonishment and incredulity, the reader is referred to the reception of recommendations made earlier in the century that birth control should be practised and encouraged. The idea is no more extraordinary, and would be equally calculated to diminish the sum total of suffering among humankind.

This will probably be taken as, or distorted into, a demand for the infliction of the death penalty on retirement. And yet the bell tolls for me no less than for others. Apart from the possibility that he may actually have some sympathy for the aged, no one casting a fearful eye forward into the future is likely to advocate treatment of the old that he would not care to see applied to himself, lest he be hoist with his own petard. It cannot be said too many times that so long as people are blessed with reasonable health, reasonable independence and reasonable enjoyment of life, they have no more reason to contemplate suicide than people who are half their age, and frequently half as sprightly as many in their seventies and eighties today. Attention is here being drawn to people who unfortunately have good reason to question whether or not they want to exercise their right to live; the minor infirmities of age, and relative weakness, and a slight degree of dependence on younger people who regard the giving of a helping hand as a natural part of the life-cycle, do not give rise to any such question. The question arises when life becomes a burden rather than a pleasure.

Many middle-aged people are heard to express the fervent wish that they will not live to be pain-ridden cripples, deaf, dim-sighted or feeble-minded solitaries, such that they may become little else than a burden to themselves and to others. They say they *hope* they will die before any of these fates descend upon them, but they seldom affirm that they *intend* to die before that time; and when the time comes, it may barely cross their minds that they could, had they then the determination, take the matter into their own hands. The facile retort will often be that this merely goes to show that people do not really mean what they say and that like all normal, sensible folk, they really want to live on for as long as is physically possible. But this, I would suggest, is a false conclusion. They mean exactly what they say, but the conditions and conditioning of society make it impossible for them to act in accordance with their wishes. To face the dark reality that the future holds nothing further in the way of joy or meaningful experience, and to face the fact without making some desperate and false reservation, to take the ultimate decision and act upon it knowing that it is a gesture that can never be repeated, such clear-sightedness and resolution demand a high degree of moral strength that cannot but be undermined by the knowledge that this final act of self-discipline would be the subject of head-shakings, moralizings and general tut-tutting.

How different it would be if a person could talk over the future with his family, friends and doctors, make arrangements, say farewells, take stock of his life, and know that his decision about when and how to end his life was a matter that could be the subject of constructive and sympathetic conference, and even that he could have his chosen ones around him at the last. As things are at present, he would always be met with well-meant cries of 'No, no, you mustn't talk like that', and indeed anyone taking a different line might feel willy-nilly that his complicity must appear unnatural and lacking in affection. We feel that we *ought* to become irrational at the idea that someone we care for is contemplating ending his own life, and only the immediate spectacle of intense suffering can shock us out of a conditioned response to this situation. The melancholy result is that a decision that cries out for moral support has to be taken in cheerless isolation, and if taken at all is usually deferred until the victim is in an advanced state of misery.

But supposing the person contemplating suicide is not in fact undergoing or expecting to undergo severe suffering, but is merely an elderly relation, probably a mother, in fragile health, or partially disabled, and though not acutely ill is in need of constant care and attention. It would be unrealistic to deny the oppressive burden that is very often cast on the shoulders of a young to middle-aged person, probably a daughter, by the existence of an ailing parent, who may take her from her career when she is a young woman in her thirties or forties, and leave her, perhaps a quarter of a century later, an elderly, exhausted woman, demoralized over the years by frequently having had to choke back the wish that her mother would release her by dying. Even in a case such as this, human feeling does demand, I would think, that the younger person must still respond to intimations of suicide with a genuinely felt 'No, no'.

But what of the older person's own attitude? Here we arrive at the kernel of the violent and almost panic-stricken reaction of many people to the idea of questioning whether it is better, in any given situation, to be or not to be. For if there is no alternative to continued living, then no choice arises, and hence there can be no possibility of an older person, who is a burden to a younger person, feeling a sense of obligation to release the captive attendant from willing or unwilling bondage, no questioning of the inevitability of the older person's living out her full term. But what if there were a real choice? What if a time came when, no longer able to look after oneself, the decision to live on for the maximum number of years were considered a mark of heedless egoism? What if it were to be thought that *dulce et decorum est pro familia mori*? This is a possibility that makes many people shrink from the subject, because they find the prospect too frightful to contemplate. Is it (to be charitable) because they always think themselves into the position of the younger person, so that 'No, no' rises naturally to their lips, or is it (to be uncharitable) because they cannot imagine themselves making a free sacrifice of this sort?

This very controversial issue is, it may be remarked, outside the scope of voluntary euthanasia, which is concerned exclusively with cases where a patient is a burden to *himself*, and whether or not he is a burden to others plays no part whatever. The essence of voluntary euthanasia is the co-operation of the doctor in making crucial decisions; the 'burden to others', on the contrary, must make all decisions and take all responsibility himself for any actions he might take. The issue cannot, however, be ignored, because the preoccupation of many opponents of voluntary euthanasia with its supposed implications, suggests that few people have any serious objection to the voluntary termination of a gravely afflicted life. This principal theme is usually brushed aside with surprising haste, and opponents pass swiftly on to the supposed evils that would flow from making twilight existence optional rather than obligatory. It is frequently said that hard-hearted people would be encouraged to make their elderly relatives feel that they had outlived their welcome and ought to remove themselves, even if they happened to be enjoying life. No one can say categorically that nothing of the sort would happen, but the sensibility of even hard-hearted people to the possible consequences of their own unkindness seems just as likely. A relation who had stood down from life in a spirit of magnanimity and family affection would, after an inevitable period of heart-searching and self-recrimination, leave behind a pleasant memory; a victim of callous treatment hanging like an accusing albatross around the neck of the living would suggest another and rather ugly story. Needless to say, whoever was responsible would not in any event be the sort of person to show consideration to an aged person in decline.

Whether or not some undesirable fringe results would stem from a free acceptance of suicide in our society, the problem of three or four contemporaneous generations peopling a world that hitherto has had to support only two or three is with us here and now, and will be neither generated nor exacerbated by a fresh attitude to life and death. The disabled, aged parent, loved or unloved, abnegating or demanding, is placed in one of the tragic dilemmas inherent in human existence, and one that becomes more acute as standards of living rise. One more in the mud-hut is not a problem in the same way as one more in a small, overcrowded urban dwelling; and the British temperament demands a privacy incompatible with the more sociable Mediterranean custom of packing a grandmother and an aunt or two in the attic. Mere existence presents a mild problem; disabled existence presents a chronic problem. The old person may have no talent for being a patient, and the young one may find it intolerable to be a nurse. A physical decline threatens to be accompanied by an inevitable decline in the quality of important human relationships—human relationships, it is worth repeating, not superhuman ones. Given superhuman love, patience, fortitude and all other sweet-natured qualities in a plentitude not normally present in ordinary people, there would be no problem. But the problem is there, and voluntary termination of life offers a possible solution that may be better than none at all. The young have been urged from time immemorial to have valiant hearts, to lay down their lives for their loved ones when their lives have hardly started; it may be that in time to come the disabled aged will be glad to live in a society that approves an honourable death met willingly, perhaps in the company of another 'old soldier' of the same generation, and with justifiable pride. Death taken in one's own time, and with a sense of purpose, may in fact be far more bearable than the process of waiting to be arbitrarily extinguished.[4] A patient near the end of his life who arranged his death so as, for example, to permit an immediate

[4] It will be noted that reference is made here in all cases to the aged. In a longer exposition I would argue that very different considerations apply to the young disabled who have not yet enjoyed a full lifespan, and who should be given far greater public assistance to enable them to enjoy life as best they can.

transfer of a vital organ to a younger person, might well feel that he was converting his death into a creative act instead of waiting passively to be suppressed.

A lot of kindly people may feel that this is lacking in respect for the honourable estate of old age; but to insist on the obligation of old people to live through a period of decline and helplessness seems to me to be lacking in a feeling for the demands of human *self*-respect. They may reply that this shows a false notion of what constitutes self-respect, and that great spiritual qualities may be brought out by dependence and infirmity, and the response to such a state. It is tempting in a world dominated by suffering to find all misery purposeful, and indeed in some situations the 'cross-to-bear' and the willing bearer may feel that they are contributing a poignant note to some cosmic symphony that is richer for their patience and self-sacrifice. Since we are talking of options and not of compulsions, people who felt like this would no doubt continue to play their chosen parts; but what a truly ruthless thing to impose those parts on people who feel that they are meaningless and discordant, and better written out.

What should be clear is that with so many men and so many opinions there is no room here for rules of life, or ready-made solutions by formula, least of all by the blanket injunction that, rather than allow any of these questions to be faced, life must be lived out to the bitter end, in sickness and in health, for better or for worse, until death brings release. It is true that the embargo on suicide relieves the ailing dependant of a choice, and some would no doubt be glad of the relief, having no mind for self-sacrifice. But in order to protect the mildly disabled from the burden of choice, the severely sick and suffering patient who urgently wants to die is subjected to the same compulsion to live. The willingness of many people to accept this sheltering of the stronger at the expense of the crying needs of the incomparably weaker may be because the slightly ailing are more visible and therefore make a more immediate claim on sympathy. Everyone knows aged and dependent people who might find themselves morally bound to consider the advisability of continuing to live if an option were truly available; the seriously afflicted lie hidden behind hospital windows, or secluded from sight on the upper floors of private houses. *They* are threatened not with delicate moral considerations, but with the harder realities of pain, disease and degeneration. Not only are they largely invisible, but their guardians are much given to the issuing of soothing reports about, for example, the hundred thousand or more patients who die of cancer every year, reports in which words like 'happiness' and 'dignity' are used liberally, and words like 'pain' and 'humiliation' tactfully suppressed. Let us not be misled by the reassuring face so often assumed by doctors who would have us believe that terminal suffering is just a bad fairy-tale put out by alarmist bogey-men. One can only hope that the pathetic human wrecks who lie vomiting and gasping their lives out are as sanguine and cheerful about their lamentable condition as the smiling doctor who on their behalf assures us that no one (including the members of the Euthanasia Society) really wants euthanasia.

That voluntary euthanasia is in fact assisted suicide is no doubt clear to most people, but curiously enough many who would support the moral right of an incurably sick person to commit suicide will oppose his having the right to seek assistance from doctors if he is to effect his wish. The argument has so far been concentrated upon the person who clearly sees the writing on the wall (perhaps because he has a doctor who is prepared to decipher it) and has the moral courage, whether or not encouraged by a sympathetic society, to anticipate the dying period. Further, this hypothetical person has access to the means of suicide and knows how to make use of those means. How he has acquired the means and the knowledge is obscure, but a determined person will make sure that he is equipped with both as a standby for the future. Yet the average patient desperately in need of help to cut short his suffering could well be a person unaccustomed to holding his own against authority, enfeebled by illness, dependent on pain-killing drugs, having no access to the means of suicide and not knowing how to make use of the means even if they were available; an entirely helpless person, in no way in a position to compass his own death. To acknowledge the right of a person to end his own life to avoid a period of suffering is a mere sham unless the right for him to call on expert assistance is also acknowledged. The law in its characteristically sledgehammer form makes it an offence for a doctor to assist the suicide of a patient, lumping a compassionate and disinterested professional man together with quasi-murderers who have to be restrained from aiding, abetting, counselling or procuring impressionable victims into suicide so that they can derive financial advantage or some other personal benefit from it. What is needed is an amendment to section 2 of the Suicide Act 1961, excluding from its provisions a doctor who in good faith accedes to a request made by a patient suffering from incurable physical illness to be given assistance in terminating his life in order to be spared from severe distress. Some doctors would no doubt feel that this was a request that they could not bring themselves to grant, just as some patients would feel that it was a request they could never bring themselves to make; this presents no problem so long as it is borne in mind that the proposal is merely that those who are prepared to make or grant such a request should be allowed to do as they wish.

Hostile sections of the medical profession will continue to assert that it is their business to cure and not to kill, and that in any case a patient who is in a miserable state from having his body invaded with cancers (or whatever) is in no state to make a decision about life and death. A patient who is in so pitiable a condition that he says he wishes to die is *ipso facto* not in a fit condition to make a reliable statement about his wishes. Arguments of this ilk seem at times to pass from black comedy to black farce. With the same sort of metaphysical reasoning it will be maintained that a patient who requested, and was given, euthanasia on Monday evening might, had he lived until Tuesday morning, have changed his mind. It has even been suggested that patients would, if voluntary euthanasia were available for incurable patients, feel themselves reluctantly obliged to ask for it to spare the nursing staff. And, as was remarked earlier, although laying down one's life in battle is generally considered praiseworthy, to lay down your life to spare yourself pointless suffering, to release medical staff so that they can tend people who would have some chance of living enjoyable lives given greater attention and assistance, to release your family and friends from anxiety and anguish, *these* motives are considered shocking. More accurately, a mere contemplation of these motives shocks the conditioned mind so severely that no rational comment can fight its way through to the surface; it is forced back by the death taboo.[5]

Here again it must be made clear that what is needed is the fostering of a new attitude to death that should ultimately grow from within, and not be imposed from without upon people psychologically unable to rethink their ingrained views. The suffering and dying patients of today have been brought up to feel that it is natural and inevitable,

[5] On this subject see Dr Slater's essay.

and even some sort of a duty, to live out their terminal period, and it would do them no service to try to persuade them into adopting an attitude that to most of them would seem oppressive, as aimed against them rather than for their benefit. If people have an ineradicable instinct, or fundamental conviction, that binds them to cling to life when their body is anticipating death by falling into a state of irrevocable decay, they clearly must be given treatment and encouragement consistent with their emotional and spiritual needs, and kindness *for them* will consist of assurances that not only is their suffering a matter of the greatest concern, but that so also is their continued existence. It is future generations, faced perhaps with a lifespan of eighty or ninety years, of which nearly half will have to be dependent on the earning power of the other half, who will have to decide how much of their useful, active life is to be devoted to supporting themselves through a terminal period '*sans* everything', prolonged into a dreaded ordeal by ever-increasing medical skill directed to the preservation of life. It may well be that, as in the case of family planning, economic reality will open up a spring, the waters of which will filter down to deeper levels, and that then the new way of death will take root. The opponents of euthanasia conjure up a favourite vision of a nightmare future in which anxious patients will be obsessed with the fear that their relatives and doctors may make surreptitious plans to kill them; the anxiety of the twenty-first-century patient may, on the contrary, be that they are neglecting to make such plans.

Prophets of the enlightenment to come usually have to content themselves with denouncing things as they are without going so far as to make practical propositions for inaugurating the new dawn. It is possible at this present time to be more constructive. For although planned death will be a minority ideal for this generation, it has enough adherents to warrant an attempt being made to ensure that those who wish to be assisted to end their lives should be entitled to receive the help they seek. With this end in view, members of the Euthanasia Society have considered a possible code to form the basis of a proposed draft Bill (see Appendix 1).[6] The Bill would authorize the giving of euthanasia to an incurable sufferer who had made a declaration subscribing to the code; and to meet some of the less

[6] After this essay was written, the Bill was presented, unsuccessfully, in the House of Lords. A new, simpler draft Bill has since been prepared (see Appendix 2).

fanciful objections usually urged against the execution of documents of this sort, it is proposed that the effect of the declaration should be deferred for a period of thirty days, so that the declarant would have to subscribe to the idea of a planned death before he was actually *in extremis*—and hence, as we have seen, pronounced incapable of knowing whether or not he wanted the state to be prolonged.

It may justifiably be felt that the enactment of a statute authorizing euthanasia smacks not of the present, but of the infinitely remote future. A good alternative case can be made out for the contention that under existing law a doctor is entitled, at least in some of the circumstances envisaged, to accede to a request made by a patient who wishes his life to be brought to an end as soon as possible, much as a doctor was entitled, if he thought fit, to perform an abortion before the enactment of the Abortion Act 1967. It is well known that he is allowed to give analgesic drugs in doses that will shorten life and even cause death; less widely accepted is the view that a patient whose terminal suffering would not be remedied by such drugs could ask to be sedated into unconsciousness, so that he need not be aware of being choked or suffocated. It is further recognized that a patient must never be given treatment that he has declined to receive, so that a subscriber to the code who feared, for example, that he might one day be hopelessly mangled in a motor accident and then carefully brought back to a hideously maimed or half-witted existence, could make a declaration stating that in these circumstances he declined to receive any treatment designed to prolong his life. He could go further and state that if actually reduced to the horrifying status of a semi-vegetable he would decline to receive any nourishment. These non-statutory declarations (the form of which is set out in Appendix 1) would, of course, have to be brought to the notice of the medical profession, and this might be done by subscribers wearing a bracelet inscribed with words making it clear that the wearer has made a declaration, or in some other effective way.

Are these matters within the scope of an apologia for suicide? One of the purposes of this detour into possible euthanasia legislation is to contend that this is indeed the case. It is true that the code is not confined to matters involving an immediate request made by a patient for the administration of euthanasia, but also vests in the doctor a wide discretion, in some cases asking him to choose the moment when death will be given, or even asking him to judge that the circumstances have occurred in which euthanasia has been requested in advance, his decision to be contingent upon the occurrence of those circumstances. It is only these aspects of voluntary euthanasia that make it distinguishable from assisted suicide, and it will now be my contention that this is a distinction without a difference.

I know here and now that I never want to be what is sometimes genially described as a 'lame-brain', for whatever cause, and let us assume I make a declaration to this effect. As every day goes by, and I do not revoke the declaration, I confirm my request. I do not forget that I have made it, because every time I miss hitting another vehicle by a carefully estimated second or two (an everyday experience that one accepts with phlegmatic calm) I murmur a few thankful words to myself for the security of my declaration, which ranks with my small hoard of sodium amytal capsules as a bulwark against intolerable fate. One day I do indeed, by reason of disease, decay or injury, become incapable of leading a rational existence, and, at the same time, of understanding the situation or making a contemporary request for euthanasia. But bearing in mind my lifelong wish expressed in the declaration not to be allowed to live such a degraded existence, distressing as it must be to my family and friends (and even possibly to myself, if I am capable of some dim understanding of my plight), can it then be said that the doctor, in acceding to my advance request for euthanasia, is any more than the instrument of my will?

It is true that he takes the responsibility of ascertaining that my state is apparently permanent; but if he is willing to play this part, surely he is acting as my representative in much the same way as a trustee who is dealing with trust funds carries out the will of the person who declared the trust. So that despite the degree of discretion vested in the doctor (a discretion that is not dissimilar from that sometimes vested in a trustee), it is still suicide that is in question, or at least an extended concept of suicide, not mercy-killing undertaken, albeit from compassionate motives, without reference to the wishes of the patient. The will of the declarant is the factor persistently ignored by those who utter cries of 'Hitler' whenever voluntary [*sic*] euthanasia is under discussion, and who take us on excursions into a world of fantasy in which gipsies are to be exterminated to ease the caravan-site problems of local planning authorities.

Legislation or no legislation, the co-operation of a substantial section of the medical profession in these express or implied forms of assisted suicide is *sine qua non*, especially as human frailty requires that it should be open to a patient to ask the doctor to choose a time for the giving of euthanasia that is not known to the patient. The views of doctors whose religion would prevent them from assisting suicide is well known, and generally voiced as if they represented the views of the majority. The volume of protest is in no way muted when it is pointed out that no doctor would be required, under the proposed Bill, to take part in the practice of euthanasia if it was against his conscience. The purpose of the Bill would be to enable doctors who favoured the giving of euthanasia on request to act in accordance with *their* conscience. In this connection we may note the selectivity of conscience among those convinced that they are the repositories of absolute truth. The Catholic doctor will usually argue that out of a ward of twenty terminal patients, one patient may have an unpredictable recovery, and live a few years more; so that if he permitted the twenty patients to die before their time, he would have the one statistically probable case of spontaneous remission on his conscience. But in a world where death was seen in a proper perspective, and in which the patients had agreed that they did not want their lives prolonged so that one of them might live to die another day, it would surely be the nineteen sacrificial victims who would lie heavy on the conscience of a humane person.

There are many more doctors who are not at all opposed in principle to suicide, but who feel, whatever the logic of the matter, that they could not personally give a patient a lethal dose. This might be regarded as the same sort of squeamishness (for lack of a better word) that would prevent another sort of person from hitting a hopelessly injured bird over the head to put it out of its suffering. He would have to waste time filling a biscuit-tin with household gas, or taking the wounded creature to a clinic, or just looking for someone less squeamish. If really cowardly he may consider putting it back in the bushes in the delusive hope that it will make a recovery. But an honest person would have to admit that it was wrong in principle to let the animal suffer because of his 'sensitive' inaction.

Euthanasia is necessarily the product of medical sophistication, with its hypodermics and quick-acting drugs; for if the only way to give a suffering patient a swift and painless death were to creep in with a knife and stab him to the heart, then the persons humane enough to want the right to curtail the suffering would be too squeamish to take advantage of it. Feelings of this sort must obviously be respected. Fortunately we can afford to respect them, because one man's squeamishness is not another's. There are doctors who find the spectacle of prolonged and useless suffering more terrible than the giving of a lethal dose, and there must be many more who would be prepared to provide a patient with the means of cutting short his own life. The numbers would no doubt increase if planned death became incorporated into the normal scheme of life.

Again focusing attention on practical steps, how is this to be brought about? Should schoolchildren be asked to write essays on 'How I Would Feel if I Had to Die at Midnight' or compositions envisaging why and in what circumstances they propose to end their lives? The answer may well be that they should. An annual visit to a geriatric ward might also be in order. The usual argument against facing up to such reality is that life is long and death is short, and that dwelling on an unfortunate aspect is morbid and best shunned. These arguments would be maintainable to some extent if we were constituted in the same enviable way as Olaf Stapledon's[7] race of pre-last men who died instantly if they became subjected to undue stress. If death were in fact short, there would be no need for euthanasia. But instant death is granted to few, and the others would be well advised to expect to be an unconscionable time a-dying, and partly a-dying, and be prepared to meet the challenge not only of death, but of the unconscionable time preceding it. I would contend that the true end of education should be to prepare the pupil to learn in the course of life to orientate all knowledge and experience within the framework of a life bounded by decline and death, and to regard a timely and possibly useful death as the summation of the art of living. Pending the comfort of a death-conditioned society, a recommended exercise for the individual who is minded to reconcile himself to dying is a constant making and remaking of wills. An evening spent distributing largesse, followed by the clearing of the desk, the answering of letters and the paying of accounts, has the effect of a direct invitation to the Almighty to take you while you are in the mood to add your final touch to the day's work.

It is, of course, all too easy to make light of death when it seems far from imminent, and all too easy for someone who has had a satisfying life to say that other people, who may have had very little happiness,

[7] *Last and First Men.*

must learn to accept that their one and (ostensibly) only life must now cease. It may well turn out that we who insist on the right to come to terms with death before life becomes a burden may, when the time comes, be found to fail in our resolute purpose, and may end our lives by way of punishment in one of the appalling institutions provided by the state for the care of the aged. The failure may be due to physical helplessness coupled with the refusal of others to give the necessary help, or it may be due to a moral failure ascribable to personal weakness and the pressures of society, pressures that sometimes take a form too oblique to be recognized as twisters of the mind. Ending with a further complaint about linguistic misdirection, my final objection to tainted words is that a patient ending his own life, or a doctor assisting him to end it, is said to 'take life', just as a thief 'takes' property with the intention of depriving the owner of something he values. Whatever it is that is taken from a dying patient, it is nothing he wants to keep, and the act is one of giving rather than taking. The gift is death, a gift we shall all have to receive in due course, and if we can bring ourselves to choose our time for acceptance, so much the better for us, for our family, for our friends and for society.

A Suggested Non-Statutory Declaration

THIS DECLARATION is made

by

of

I DECLARE AS FOLLOWS:

If I should at any time suffer from a serious physical illness or impairment thought in my case to be incurable and expected to cause me severe distress or render me incapable of rational existence, then, unless I revoke this declaration or express a wish contrary to its terms, I REQUEST the administration of whatever quantity of drugs may be required to prevent my feeling pain or distress and, if my suffering cannot be otherwise relieved, to be kept continuously unconscious at a level where dreaming does not take place, AND I DECLINE to receive any treatment or sustenance designed to prolong my life.
I ASK sympathetically disposed doctors to acknowledge the right of a patient to request certain kinds of treatment and to decline others, and I assure them that if in any situation they think it better for me to die than to survive, I am content to endorse their judgment in advance and in full confidence that they will be acting in my interests to spare me from suffering and ignominy, and also to save my family and friends from anguish I would not want them to endure on my behalf.

SIGNED

WE TESTIFY that the above-named declarant signed this declaration in our presence, and appeared to appreciate its significance. We do not know of any pressure being brought upon him/her to make a declaration, and we believe it is made by his/her own wish. So far as we are aware, we do not stand to benefit by the death of the declarant.

Signed by

of

Signed by

of

Notes on Contributors

Dr PIETER V. ADMIRAAL, M.D., Ph.D., F.R.S.M., is Chief Anaesthetist at the Reinier de Graaf Gasthui, Delft, Holland, and author of *Justifiable Euthanasia: A Manual for the Medical Profession* (1980).

CHRISTIAAN BARNARD, M.D., M.Med., Ph.D., F.A.C.S.(1963), F.A.C.C. (1967), was Professor of Surgical Science, Cape Town University, 1968–83. He holds many honorary doctorates, foreign orders and awards, having performed the world's first human heart transplant (Dec. 3, 1967) and first double-heart transplant (Nov. 25, 1974). He has written a number of medical books, including *Good Life Good Death* (U.S. edn, 1980; U.K. edn, 1985), and has contributed numerous articles to medical and other journals.

MARY ROSE BARRINGTON, a professional lawyer, originally intended to read medicine. She took her degree in English at Oxford University in 1947 and was called to the Bar in 1957. Now Legal Assistant to a firm of property developers, she was Chairman of the Executive Committee of the Euthanasia Society in 1974–76 and made a leading contribution in drawing up proposals for the Voluntary Euthanasia Bill 1969, which appears as Appendix 1.

Dr COLIN BREWER, M.B., B.S., D.P.M., M.R.C.Psych., is a Research Fellow at the University of Birmingham and Director of the Community Alcoholism Treatment Service at the Westminster and All Saints' Hospitals, London. His published work includes articles in *The Times, The Guardian, The Sunday Times* and *Spectator* on medico-ethical topics, as well as scientific papers on alcoholism, brain damage, abortion, and psychiatric aspects of crime.

Dr DAVID H. CLARK, M.D., Ph.D., F.R.C.Psych., F.R.C.P.E., was until his recent retirement senior Consultant Psychiatrist to Fulbourn and Addenbrooke's Hospitals, Cambridge. He was formerly Vice-Chairman of the National Association for Mental Health (MIND), is a Vice-President of the Voluntary Euthanasia Society, and author of *Social Therapy in Psychiatry* (1971 and 1984).

The Reverend A. B. DOWNING, M.A., B.D., who was Chairman of the Euthanasia Society (later the Voluntary Euthanasia Society) from 1965 to 1970 and Editor of *The Inquirer* from 1962 to 1967, died in 1980.

JOSEPH FLETCHER was Professor of Social Ethics and Moral Theology at the Episcopal Theological School, Cambridge, Massachusetts, 1944–70, and visiting Professor of Medical Ethics at the University of Virginia (Charlottesville), 1970–75. He is Professor Emeritus of the Society for the Right to Die (New York) and the author of *Morals and Medicine* (1954), *Situation Ethics* (1966) and *Moral Responsibility: Situation Ethics at Work* (1967). His article originally appeared in *Harper's Magazine*, New York (Oct. 1960).

ANTONY FLEW, Emeritus Professor of Philosophy in the University of Reading, is the author of fourteen books and many articles. He was Chairman of the Executive Committee of the Voluntary Euthanasia Society from 1976 to 1979.

Dr RAANAN GILLON, B.A.(Phil.), M.B., B.S., M.R.C.P., is Director of the Imperial College Health Centre and Editor of the *Journal of Medical Ethics*. He was formerly Editor of *Medical Tribune*, and has written a number of papers on the philosophical aspects of medical ethics.

LUKE GORMALLY, Lic.Phil., was (1977–81) Research Officer and since 1981 has been Director of the Linacre Centre, London, a research and study centre in the field of health care and ethics, working in the Roman Catholic tradition. He was a contributor to *Euthanasia and Clinical Practice: Trends, Principles and Alternatives. The Report of a Working Party* (Linacre Centre, 1982).

Dr G. A. GRESHAM, T.D., M.A., Sc.D. (Cantab.), F.R.C.Path., is the Morbid Anatomist and Histologist in the University of Cambridge and Honorary Consultant to Addenbrooke's Hospital, Cambridge. His publications include *General Pathology* (1971) and *Forensic Pathology* (1975).

YALE KAMISAR is Professor of Law in the University of Michigan Law School. He is co-author of the following works: *Criminal Justice in Our Time* (1965), *Modern Criminal Procedure: Cases, Comments and Questions* (4th edn, 1974), *Constitutional Law: Cases, Comments and Questions* (4th edn, 1975) and *Sum and Substance of Criminal Procedure* (1977). His essay is an abridged version of an article which originally appeared in the *Minnesota Law Review*, 42 (1958), 969.

The Right Honourable the EARL OF LISTOWEL, P.C., G.C.M.G., Ph.D., Chairman of Committees in the House of Lords from 1965 to 1976 and now Deputy Speaker, is President of the Voluntary

Euthanasia Society, London. His publications include *The Values of Life* (1931) and *Modern Aesthetics: An Historical Introduction* (1967).

The Very Reverend W. R. MATTHEWS, K.C.V.O., C.H., D.D., D.Lit. (London), who was Dean of St Paul's, London, from 1934 to 1967, died in 1973. His article is based on an address he gave to the Euthanasia Society in London in 1950.

Dr ELIOT SLATER, C.B.E., M.A., M.D., F.R.C.P., who died in 1983, was one of Britain's leading specialists in the study and treatment of mental illness, and was Editor-in-Chief of the *British Journal of Psychiatry* and Director of the Medical Research Council's Psychiatric Genetics Research Unit at the Maudsley Hospital, London. His article was originally given as an address to the Euthanasia Society in London.

BARBARA SMOKER is a polemical writer and broadcaster. Having been a Roman Catholic for the first twenty-six years of her life, she rejected religion and became active in the secular humanist movement, writing a booklet on it for secondary schools, entitled *Humanism* (1973; 5th edn, 1984). She was Chairman of the Executive Committee of the Voluntary Euthanasia Society from 1981 to 1985, and has been President of the National Secular Society since 1971.

GLANVILLE WILLIAMS, Q.C., F.B.A., Ph.D., LL.D. (Cantab.), was a Fellow of Jesus College (1955–78), Hon. Fellow (1978) and Rouse Ball Professor of the Laws of England in the University of Cambridge (1968–78). A former Professor of Public Law and Quain Professor of Jurisprudence in the University of London, he has been a member of the Standing Committee on Criminal Law Revision since 1959. His many publications include: *Learning the Law* (1945; 7th edn, 1963), *Criminal Law: The General Part* (1953; 2nd edn, 1961), *The Proof of Guilt* (1955; 3rd edn, 1963), *The Sanctity of Life and the Criminal Law* (U.S. edn, 1957; U.K. edn, 1958), *The Mental Element in Crime* (1965), *Foundations of the Law of Tort* (1976) and *Textbook of Criminal Law* (1978).

PART TWO

THE VOLUNTARY EUTHANASIA MOVEMENT

1

The Voluntary Euthanasia Society

The seeds of the Voluntary Euthanasia Society (Britain) and of the subsequent world-wide movement[1] were planted, and took root, in the 1931 presidential address of Dr C. Killick Millard to the Society of Medical Officers of Health. His speech, entitled 'A Plea for the Legalisation of Voluntary Euthanasia under Certain Conditions', was then published as a pamphlet, with an introduction by the eminent surgeon, Sir William Arbuthnot Lane, and with a draft Bill appended; and the revolutionary proposal received widespread publicity.

Four years of correspondence on the subject ensued between Dr Millard and interested members of the medical and other professions. They met in Leicester in January 1935, and set up a small steering committee, comprising three doctors, three clergymen and a solicitor. Within a few months Millard had brought in more supporters, including three distinguished churchmen, Dean Inge, W. R. Matthews and Dick Sheppard, and a consultative medical committee was formed, comprising eight eminent doctors. (So far, the total financial turnover of the movement amounted to £24. 12*s*. 5*d*.)

In October 1935 the Voluntary Euthanasia Legalisation Society was formally founded, with Lord Moynihan as President, C. J. Bond as Chairman, the Revd A. S. Hurn as Treasurer, and Dr C. Killick Millard as Honorary Secretary. The following became Vice-Presidents: the Revd. Professor Creed, Lord and Lady Denman, Havelock Ellis, Lord Henley, Julian Huxley, Sir William Arbuthnot Lane, Harold Laski, Lord Listowel (its President today, fifty years later), the Revd. H.D.A. Major, Sir Roderick Meiklejohn, Lord Ponsonby, Eleanor Rathbone, Sir Humphrey Rolleston and Sir Arnold Wilson. Two months later, on December 10 (now, coinci-

[1]See pp. 269–71.

dentally, Human Rights Day), the inaugural public meeting was held at BMA House, London. On February 4, 1936, a consultative legal council was established under the chairmanship of Professor Winfield, and in November 1936 Lord Ponsonby introduced the Voluntary Euthanasia (Legalisation) Bill in the House of Lords.

Though it fell at its second reading, this Bill generated considerable public discussion, gaining for the Voluntary Euthanasia Legalisation Society new members and supporters, including again many who were distinguished in the arts, sciences and professions. But it was to be another three decades (1969) before the next Voluntary Euthanasia Bill would be introduced—and again unsuccessfully. Meanwhile, however, the Suicide Act was passed in 1961, removing suicide from the criminal law, though making it a criminal offence to assist in the suicide of another. In 1976 the Society tried a very moderate Bill, concerned mainly with passive euthanasia—the Incurable Patients Bill, introduced into the House of Lords by Baroness Wootton. But this too was unsuccessful.

At one time the Society dropped the words 'Voluntary' and 'Legalisation' from its name, but in 1969 reinstated 'Voluntary'. Then, at the 1979 annual meeting, the name was again changed—for the sake of modernity, to Exit. Three years later, however, it was decided by a large majority of the membership (in a postal referendum) to revert to the former name, the Voluntary Euthanasia Society. This was at least partly due to the adverse publicity the Society had sustained when, in 1981, the Society's then secretary was convicted of conspiring to assist a number of suicides. Although the Society dissociated itself from his abuse of his position in thus pre-empting euthanasia legislation, its public image was certainly tarnished by it. The Society has since found it an uphill struggle to regain its reputation as a respectable pressure group rather than, as one newspaper[2] dubbed it, a 'suicide club'.

In 1979 a proposal had been mooted that the Society publish a practical guide to rational suicide ('self-deliverance')—a sort of do-it-yourself manual, as a stopgap expedient, pending the legalization of active voluntary euthanasia that would be medically induced. Legal opinions on the proposed publication were obtained, only to cancel one another out. While Society members were overwhelmingly in

[2] *The Times* (Oct. 31, 1981).

favour of publishing the guide—indeed, its pre-publication publicity brought a sudden surge in membership, from about 2,000 to 11,000—the executive was divided. Even after the election (in October 1980) of a new executive that was largely committed to publication, this was further delayed by a member of the Society applying for a civil injunction. An amendment was then made to the Society's constitution, so as to bring a publication of this kind within its purview.

Meanwhile, the fact that the specific law against assisting the suicide of another does not apply in Scotland persuaded the newly formed Scottish Exit to bring out its own similar guide (entitled *How to Die with Dignity*), which thus, in September 1980, became the first such publication in the world. The more comprehensive English *Guide to Self-Deliverance* finally appeared in June 1981, soon to be followed by similar publications in France, Germany, Switzerland and the United States. However, the English booklet was almost immediately threatened with criminal prosecution by the Director of Public Prosecutions. This threat, however, was then modified: first to one of a civil injunction, to be sought by the Attorney-General, and then to a mere application by him to the High Court for a 'declaration' of illegality under section 2 of the Suicide Act 1961. In the event, on April 28, 1983, Mr Justice Woolf turned down the Attorney-General's declaration of the law, finding in favour of the Voluntary Euthanasia Society, with costs.

The press reports, which this time were mainly friendly to the Society, again led to an increased spurt in membership applications—a spurt which had already begun as a result of the widely, and most sympathetically, reported 'self-deliverance' (on March 3, 1983) of Arthur Koestler, who was incurably ill with Parkinson's disease and leukaemia. Koestler was a Vice-President of the Society and author of (alongside his better known writings) the Preface to the Society's *Guide to Self-Deliverance* (see p. 260).

However, in spite of the technical victory in its favour, the guide was not given total clearance by Mr Justice Woolf. Although he held that publishing such factual information was not unlawful, he also said that the legality of distributing it would depend on there being no intent (either individually or in general) 'to assist those who are contemplating suicide'. Stocks of the booklet, of which almost 9,000 copies had been sold to members, happened to run out at about this time; and the Society's executive had to decide whether to reprint it as it was, or take the opportunity to revise it, or not to reissue it at all. Finally, on a majority vote, it was decided that the guide should not be reissued. The two main reasons for this were: first, the guide was felt, increasingly, to be of limited usefulness to those who were ill or disabled enough to need physical aid to suicide, or who were unable to obtain the required drugs—its chief importance, perhaps, being seen in the context of freedom of information rather than that of functional do-it-yourself euthanasia; and second, the Woolf judgment appeared to prevent the Society from distributing the guide in any useful way within the law—and to keep within the law was imperative as long as the Society wished to continue, as its primary aim, to press for legislation.

A random sample postal survey of members of Exit (as it then was) living in England and Wales was carried out in 1981 by Rosalind Lam for the Institute for Social Studies in Medical Care. A summary of the results, analysed with particular reference to statistical suicide 'risk', took up a full page of *The Times Health Supplement*.[3] It shows that two-thirds of the members replying were aged sixty or over, and only 6 per cent were under the age of forty. Women outnumbered men by three to two. Nearly half the women and more than a quarter of the men were living alone (a significantly higher proportion than for the general population of the same ages). Asked to describe their health for their age as excellent, good, fair or poor, almost three-quarters of the respondents answered 'excellent' or 'good'. Witnessing the slow death of a relative or friend was given by one in four as their reason for joining the Society. Three-quarters came from non-manual occupations—the majority from the professions—and 7 per cent were, or had been, nurses. Only 43 per cent had a religious affiliation, though almost all had had an ordinary religious upbringing.

A public opinion survey conducted by Mass Observation throughout Britain in 1969 showed 51 per cent of the population in favour of active voluntary euthanasia. A similar poll conducted by National Opinion Polls in 1976 showed an increase in favour to 69 per cent. A repetition of the same question, in a survey again conducted by National Opinion Polls, for the Voluntary Euthanasia Society, in February 1985 (as a run-up to the Society's Golden Jubilee celebrations), shows a further increase to 72 per cent in favour.

Similar statistical surveys are carried out every four years in the

[3] *TES* (Oct. 30, 1981).

United States (conducted by Harris). These showed only 37 per cent in favour of active voluntary euthanasia in that country in 1973, but a steady increase since then, culminating in 61 per cent in favour in January 1985.

Regional analysis of the 1985 British (N.O.P.) survey shows that the highest percentage of the population in favour of voluntary euthanasia is (as in 1976) found in Wales and the West (77 per cent), while the lowest is in Scotland (64 per cent). There is little statistical difference in terms of sex or economic class, but there is a certain age divergence—the younger respondents now tending to be more in favour of voluntary euthanasia than the older age groups.

All the main religious denominations (including Roman Catholic) in Britain show a majority in favour of active voluntary euthanasia. Roman Catholics (self-declared) show 54 per cent, and members of the Church of England 75 per cent in favour. Interestingly (in view of the Nazi misuse of the word 'euthanasia'), the poll shows the religious group with the highest percentage in favour of voluntary euthanasia as the Jewish community, with 84 per cent—though the small size of the sample in this group makes that figure statistically uncertain. Not surprisingly, atheists come out highest of all, with 89 per cent in favour.

Yet, in spite of all this public support for voluntary euthanasia, Parliament still drags its feet. In the Netherlands, where a pressure group (Nederlandse Vereniging voor Vrijwillige Euthanasie), similar to the Voluntary Euthanasia Society, has existed only since 1980, they have already overtaken Britain, with juridical acceptance of even active voluntary euthanasia, provided that it is carried out by the medical profession and that particular conditions are observed. Other countries, including Britain, must surely follow suit within the next few years.

B.S.

2

*Arthur Koestler and Suicide**

Arthur Koestler, the world-famous writer and philosopher, joined the Voluntary Euthanasia Society in 1969. He became a Vice-President in 1981, and wrote the Preface to the *Guide to Self-Deliverance*, which is reproduced below.

*

When people talk of 'the fear of death', they often fail to distinguish between two types of fear which may be combined in experience but are separate in origin. One is the fear of the *state* of death (or non-existence); the other the fear of the *process* of dying, the agony of the transition to that state. The aim of this booklet—and of the Society which, after much soul-searching, decided to publish it—is to overcome the second of these fears. For the first, we must obviously rely on whatever consolations religion, philosophy or parapsychology have to offer.

However, the division is not as clear-cut as that, because the two fears are interwoven. Mystics of all denominations have always claimed that a strong faith in after-life deprives not only the grave of its victory, but also death of its sting. Listen to Pope's 'Dying Christian to his Soul':

> Vital spark of heav'nly flame!
> Quit, oh quit this mortal frame:
> Trembling, hoping, ling'ring, flying,
> Oh the pain, the bliss of dying.

In other words, the mystic's faith can produce a form of euthanasia—a peaceful death of the body. The sceptic may call it a

* Abstracted from the *Voluntary Euthanasia Society Newsletter*, No. 18 (June 1983).

placebo-effect: it makes no difference. But now we come to the crucial point: this connection is reversible. If the agnostics among us could be assured of a gentle and easy way of dying, they would be much less afraid of *being* dead. This is not a logical attitude, but fear is not governed by logic. We tend to be guided by first impressions—of persons, landscapes, countries. An unknown country to which the only access leads through a torture chamber is frightening. And vice versa, the prospect of falling peacefully, blissfully asleep, is not only soothing but can make it positively desirable to quit this pain-racked mortal frame and become un-born again. For after all, reason tells us—when not choked by panic—that before we were born we were all dead, and that our post-mortem condition is no more frightening than the pre-natal twilight. Only the process of transition, of *getting* un-born makes cowards of us all. The whole concept of death as a condition would be more acceptable if dying would be less horrendous and squalid. Thus euthanasia is more than the administration of a lethal analgesic. It is a means of reconciling individuals with their destiny.

We are in dire need of such reconciliation and acceptance, for (apart from other obvious shortcomings) our species suffers from two severe biological handicaps imposed at the entry and exit gates of existence. Animals appear to give birth painlessly or with a minimum of discomfort. But owing to some quirk of evolution, the human foetus is too large for the birth-canal and its hazardous passage can entail protracted agony for the mother and—presumably—a traumatic experience for the new-born child. Hence we need midwives to aid us to be born. A similar situation prevails at the exit-gate. Animals in the wild, unless killed by a predator, seem to die peacefully and without fuss, from old age—I cannot remember a single description to the contrary by a naturalist, ethologist or explorer. The conclusion is inescapable: we need midwives to aid us to be un-born—or at least the assurance that such aid is available. Euthanasia, like obstetrics, is the natural corrective to a biological handicap.

If active euthanasia were legal in this country (as it is for certain cases in the Netherlands), the justification—or need—for this booklet would be debatable. But as the progress toward legislation will be slow, a matter of years or even decades, the publication of a practical guide to 'auto-euthanasia' will, we hope, bring peace of mind to many who would otherwise despair. There is only one prospect worse than being chained to an intolerable existence: the nightmare of a botched attempt to end it. I know that I am speaking in the name of many (some of them personal friends) who tried and failed—or who don't dare to try for fear of failure.

As matters stand, assisted suicide, in whatever form, places a heavy burden of responsibility on doctors, relatives, and other 'accomplices' in the eyes of the law. If this booklet succeeds in lifting some of this burden, it will have fulfilled its purpose.

*

Koestler died on March 3, 1983. At the inquest held at the Westminster Coroner's Court on March 30 the verdict was that Arthur Koestler and his wife Cynthia killed themselves by taking an overdose of barbiturates. Mr Koestler was found seated in front of a window. Mrs Koestler was sitting on the settee. A half-full glass of whisky and empty wine glasses containing the residue of a white powder were in the room. A jar of honey and an empty bottle of tuinal tablets were on the table. In the words of the police spokesman 'It was a scene of calmness'.

The following note, addressed 'To whom it may concern', was written and signed by Arthur Koestler in June 1982, and is reproduced by kind permission of his literary executor:[1]

> The purpose of this note is to make it unmistakeably clear that I intend to commit suicide by taking an overdose of drugs without the knowledge or aid of any other person. The drugs have been legally obtained and hoarded over a considerable period.
>
> Trying to commit suicide is a gamble the outcome of which will be known to the gambler only if the attempt fails, but not if it succeeds. Should this attempt fail and I survive it in a physically or mentally impaired state, in which I can no longer control what is done to me, or communicate my wishes, I hereby request that I be allowed to die in my own home and not be resuscitated or kept alive by artificial means. I further request that my wife, or physician, or any friend present, should invoke *habeas corpus* against any attempt to remove me forcibly from my house to hospital.
>
> My reasons for deciding to put an end to my life are simple and compelling: Parkinson's Disease and the slow-killing variety of

[1] This note was written by Arthur Koestler nine months before he gave effect to his decision.

leukemia (CCL). I kept the latter a secret even from intimate friends to save them distress. After a more or less steady physical decline over the last years, the process has now reached an acute state with added complications which make it advisable to seek self-deliverance now, before I become incapable of making the necessary arrangements.

I wish my friends to know that I am leaving their company in a peaceful frame of mind, with some timid hopes for a depersonalised after-life beyond due confines of space, time and matter and beyond the limits of our comprehension. This 'oceanic feeling' has often sustained me at difficult moments, and does so now, while I am writing this.

What makes it nevertheless hard to take this final step is the reflection of the pain it is bound to inflict on my few surviving friends, and above all my wife Cynthia. It is to her that I owe the relative peace and happiness that I enjoyed in the last period of my life—and never before.[2]

Memorial Meeting

A meeting to honour the memory of Arthur and Cynthia Koestler was held on Thursday April 7, 1983 in Burlington House, in a room which was bare except for a wall-to-wall backcloth of a fifteenth-century 'Last Supper' behind the platform. Sir Hugh Casson, President of the Royal Academy and a personal friend of the Koestlers, chaired the meeting, and the speakers included David Astor, Mary Benson, Professor Maurice Cranston, Professor Holger Hyden, Brian Inglis and George Mikes. Barbara Smoker, speaking on behalf of the Voluntary Euthanasia Society, said:

In the unique pattern of his life, Arthur Koestler manifested the Art of Living—living intensely, whole-heartedly, exuberantly, with intellectual wonder and excitement, and with manifold interests,

[2] The last paragraph explains the references in the press to 'a late decision' on the part of Cynthia Koestler. In a note written on the last day of her life, she said: 'I should have liked to finish my account of working for Arthur—a story which began when our paths happened to cross in 1949. However, I cannot live without Arthur, despite certain inner resources.'

purposes and satisfactions. When life of an acceptable quality was no longer possible, he manifested the Art of Dying—bringing his life-span to a serene and dignified close, in his own home and at the time of his own choosing. Having partaken fully of the feast of life, he made ready for a brisk departure, with the quiet contentment of a satisfied guest.

The following comment on Arthur Koestler's death appeared in *The Times* of March 6, 1983, under the headline 'Suicide: The Right and the Dilemma'. It was written by Jonathan Glover.

Moral views about suicide have changed in our century at least as radically as about sex. In the Notebooks that Ludwig Wittgenstein kept during the First World War, he wrote, 'If suicide is allowed then everything is allowed. If anything is not allowed then suicide is not allowed. This throws a light on the nature of ethics, for suicide is, so to speak, the elementary sin.' But here, the outlook of our grandparents seems very remote. The 1961 Suicide Act, removing the legal prohibition, did not arouse the opposition run into by other liberalizing laws of the Sixties. And few now think that suicide calls for moral condemnation.

Even now, news of a suicide can give us a greater sense of shock than when we hear of a natural death, but we no longer rationalize this as an awareness of moral wrongdoing. Our responses vary according to cases. Where the suicide is of someone suffering from severe depression or other mental disturbance, we see it as a product of the illness, and so we are reluctant to hold the person responsible. When we hear that Arthur Koestler has decided to end his life rather than face further illness and decline in old age, and that his wife has chosen to go with him, we have no difficulty in seeing how this decision could be perfectly rational. Who, in such a case, is in a position to say they made the wrong choice?

It may seem there is nothing to say about the morality of suicide. In the case of the disturbed person not responsible for his acts, moral criticism does not arise. And, in other cases, surely people have a right to decide for themselves whether to go on living? In general, the change in attitudes is surely an improvement. In the past, the victims of moral disapproval were either those whose suicide attempts had failed, or the families of successful attempts, who were made to feel that the death was somehow disgraceful. It is obvious that the last way to help either of these groups is by moralizing after the event. The decline in this is an unqualified good.

But it does not follow that there are no problems about whether an act of suicide is right. Where someone thinking of suicide is sufficiently in control to deliberate about it, there are questions to consider about the rationality of the act and about its morality.

The question about rationality is easier to state than sometimes to answer. Would the person's future life be worth living? In the case of a progressively worsening illness, a stable view may sometimes not be hard to arrive at. But, where you are being driven to suicide by losing your job, or your husband's desertion, or by mounting debts, the matter may be less clear. Most of us are bad at predicting how likely things are to improve. And suicide cannot be justified without comparing it with less drastic steps. Someone who would not usually even consider leaving his family, changing his job, emigrating or seeking psychiatric help is unwise to rule out such steps when he enters the region where he does not rule out suicide. It is worth talking to others, whether friends or the Samaritans, who may provide a different perspective. And because moods are so fluctuating, it is hard to be sure that any suicide decision is rational unless it is adhered to for a fairly long time.

The moral question is about the effect of suicide on others. Some people may have lives (perhaps with severe and incurable mental disorders, or involving great pain) where their interests should come before any loss to others. But sometimes an act of suicide, particularly at the vulnerable student stage of life, can shatter the lives of parents and family to a degree the person would not have guessed. And someone who is old or ill, and fears being a burden, should not assume that suicide will help others. Our psychology is not so simple. Shock, grief and guilt can be a far greater burden.

We are halfway towards the right climate of opinion on suicide. We have moved away from legal penalties and from insensitive condemnation. We no longer think suicide a blasphemous interference with a divine plan, and prefer to think that people have a right to dispose of their own lives. But cases vary, and some rights need to be exercised with gentleness and consideration for others.

3

The Legal Position (England and Wales)

There are no specific laws in Britain relating directly either to 'mercy-killing' or to voluntary euthanasia, but the ordinary homicide laws dealing with murder, attempted murder, or (when there are extenuating circumstances or the act was carried out as part of a suicide pact) manslaughter, are applicable. Assisted suicide, however, is subject to a specific law in England and Wales (not applicable to Scotland): section 2 (1) of the Suicide Act 1961. This reads: 'A person who aids, abets, counsels or procures the suicide of another, or an attempt by another to commit suicide, shall be liable on conviction on indictment to imprisonment for a term not exceeding fourteen years.' Case law arising out of this section includes the case against Yolande McShane (1977), which established that an attempt to assist a suicide constitutes an offence even though no suicide takes place.

Before 1961, suicide (or attempted suicide) was a criminal offence, and during the early years of the nineteenth century it carried very heavy penalties. There are horrific stories of unsuccessful suicides being nursed back to health in order to be hanged. Gradually, as the nineteenth century progressed, less serious penalties were imposed, and often none at all. Eventually, the criminal law against suicide was felt to be anachronistic. However, when Parliament finally debated the 1961 Bill to remove suicide from the criminal law altogether, it was decided to incorporate a proviso making it a criminal offence to assist in the suicide of another person.

Parliamentary Bills (drafted by the Voluntary Euthanasia Society) to legalize voluntary euthanasia were presented unsuccessfully in the House of Lords in 1936 (for terminal cases only, and with cumbersome safeguards) and in 1969* (introducing the advance declaration), with

* See House of Lords Official Report, *Parliamentary Debates* (Hansard), Vol. 300, No. (March 25, 1969), cols 1143–1254.

a similar proposal in the House of Commons in 1970. There was also a Bill—the Incurable Patients Bill, dealing mainly with passive euthanasia and the rights of patients, and introducing the term 'self-deliverance'—presented by Baroness Wootton, in the House of Lords in 1976, but this too was unsuccessful. Also in 1976, in a 'Working Paper on Offences against the Person', the Criminal Law Revision Committee proposed the creation of a new offence with a maximum penalty of two years' imprisonment for 'mercy-killing' (i.e. unlawfully killing an incurable patient out of compassion, not necessarily at the patient's request). The idea was obviously to avoid a conviction of either murder (which carries the mandatory sentence of life imprisonment) or of manslaughter (to which the charge of murder is generally reduced in compassion cases 'by reason of diminished responsibility', with medical evidence for this often spurious, and insulting, plea). However, the Committee's final report in 1980 concluded that it was not possible to distinguish in law between 'mercy-killing' and other kinds of homicide, a conclusion which echoed that of the Royal Commission on Capital Punishment in 1953. And the statutory recognition of a separate offence of 'mercy-killing' has never been incorporated in a Parliamentary Bill.

The 1980 report was mentioned in the House of Lords on January 23, 1985, by Lord Elton (Minister of State, Home Office), dismissing a request by Lord Broxbourne for a review of the law relating to euthanasia. However, a mini-debate on the subject ensued, and this received considerable public attention owing to the fact that that afternoon happened to be the first time a debate in either House was televised.

The term 'mercy-killing' can refer to any category of active euthanasia that is non-voluntary or that physically goes beyond merely assisting a suicide; but the Voluntary Euthanasia Society prefers to limit its application to *non-voluntary* euthanasia (the patient being an infant, or permanently comatose, or otherwise incapable of making any such decision). With this restricted connotation, it is outside the province of the Society.

The Society has now prepared a new draft Voluntary Euthanasia Bill (not yet introduced into Parliament, but published in this volume—see Appendix 2). This is both simpler and more comprehensive than any of its predecessors, and includes a modification of the present law against assisting a suicide—making it a good defence against such a charge that the grounds for the suicide were sufficiently serious and incurable and that the primary motive of the defendant was compassion (this being determined, in the last resort, by a jury). However, there would be less need for such a modification if the law allowed the medical profession to administer voluntary euthanasia.

As discussed earlier (pp. 257–8), the booklet published in 1980 by the Voluntary Euthanasia Society (then known as Exit) under the title *A Guide to Self-Deliverance*, was the subject of a High Court hearing in April 1983.

4

Societies for Voluntary Euthanasia

AUSTRALIA	The Voluntary Euthanasia Society of New South Wales, PO Box 25, Broadway 2007, N.S.W., Australia.
	The Voluntary Euthanasia Society of Victoria, PO Box 71, Mooroolbark 3138, Victoria, Australia.
	West Australian Voluntary Euthanasia Society, PO Box 7243, Cloisters Square, Perth 6000, Australia.
	South Australian Voluntary Euthanasia Society, 18 Seaforth Avenue, Hazlewood Park, Adelaide, South Australia 5066.
AUSTRIA	Dr Ilse Dorfler, 1050 Wien, Margaretengurtel 24/3/6, Austria.
BELGIUM	Association Belge pour le Droit de Mourir dans la Dignité, 84 rue de la Pastorale, B-1080 Brussels, Belgium.
CANADA	Dying with Dignity, PO Box 232, Station Z, Toronto, Canada M5N 2Z3.
	Dying with Dignity, PO Box 46408, Station G, Vancouver, Canada V6R 4G7.
COLOMBIA	Fundación Pro-Derecho a Morir Dignamente, Apartado Aéreo 89314, Bogotá, Colombia.
DENMARK	Landsforeningen Mit Livstestamente, Jaegersborgvej 68 st., 2800 Lyngby, Denmark.
ENGLAND and WALES	The Voluntary Euthanasia Society, 13 Prince of Wales Terrace, London W8 5PG.

FRANCE	Association pour le Droit de Mourir dans la Dignité, 103 rue La Fayette, 75010 Paris, France.
GERMANY	Deutsche Gesellschaft für Humanes Sterben, Postfach 110 529, 8900 Augsburg, West Germany.
HOLLAND	Nederlandse VVVE, Postbus 5331, 1007 AH-Amsterdam, Holland. Informatie Centrum Vrijwillige Euthanasie, Zuiderweg 42, 8393 KT, Vinkega, Holland.
INDIA	The Society for the Right to Die with Dignity, 4th Floor, Maneckjee Wadia Building, 127 Mahatma Gandhi Road, Fort, Bombay 400-001, India. The Indian Society for the Right to Die, J-13 Prasad Nagar, New Delhi 110005, India.
JAPAN	Japan Society for Dying with Dignity, Hamaso Building, 7th Floor, 1-11 Ogawa-Machi, Kanda, Chiyoda-ku, Tokyo, Japan 101.
NEW ZEALAND	The Voluntary Euthanasia Society, 95 Melrose Road, Island Bay, Wellington 2, New Zealand. The Voluntary Euthanasia Society of Auckland, PO Box 77-029, Mount Albert 3, Auckland, New Zealand.
NORWAY	Landsforeningen Mitt Livstestament, P.T. Mallings vei 24, 0286 Oslo 2, Norway.
SCOTLAND	The Voluntary Euthanasia Society of Scotland, 17 Hart Street, Edinburgh EH1 3RO, Scotland.
SOUTH AFRICA	South African Voluntary Euthanasia Society, PO Box 37141, Overport 4067, Durban, South Africa.
SPAIN	Asociación Derecho a Morir Dignamente, Apartado 9.094, Madrid, Spain.
SWEDEN	Ratten Till Var Dod, Linnegatan 7, 114.47 Stockholm, Sweden.

SWITZERLAND	German-speaking: EXIT, Zwinglistr. 14, 2540 Grenchen, Switzerland.
	French-speaking: EXIT, Box 100, 1222 Vésenaz, Geneva, Switzerland.
U.S.A.	Hemlock, PO Box 66218, Los Angeles, California 90066, U.S.A.
	Concern for Dying, 250 West 57th Street, New York, N.Y. 10107, U.S.A.
	The Society for the Right to Die, 250 West 57th Street, New York, N.Y. 10107, U.S.A.

APPENDICES

Appendix 1

Voluntary Euthanasia Bill 1969

EXPLANATORY MEMORANDUM

General

The main purpose of the Bill is to authorize physicians to give euthanasia to a patient who is thought on reasonable grounds to be suffering from an irremediable physical condition of a distressing character, and who has, not less than 30 days previously, made a declaration requesting the administration of euthanasia in certain specified circumstances one or more of which has eventuated.

Clause 1 provides that a physician may administer euthanasia to a 'qualified patient' who has made a declaration in the form set out in the schedule. A qualified patient is defined as a patient over the age of majority who has been certified by two physicians, one being of consultant status, to be apparently suffering from an irremediable condition. Subsection (2) defines the expressions used in the Bill.

Clause 2 provides that a declaration shall come into force 30 days after being made, and shall remain in force for 3 years. A declaration re-executed within the 12 months preceding its expiry date shall remain in force for life, unless revoked.

Clause 3 provides that a declaration may be revoked at any time.

Clause 4 provides that before euthanasia may be given to a mentally responsible patient the physician in charge must ascertain to the best of his ability that the declaration and steps proposed to be taken under it accord with the patient's wishes. Subsection (2) provides that a nurse, acting on the directions of a physician, may cause euthanasia to be administered to a patient, and subsection (3) provides that no physician or nurse who is opposed on principle to euthanasia shall be required to take any steps in its administration.

Clause 5 protects physicians and nurses who act in good faith in the belief that their actions are in accordance with a patient's declaration or further requests made under the Act and provides that they shall not be in breach of any professional oath by administering euthanasia.

Clause 6 provides that a person who conceals, destroys, falsifies or forges a declaration commits an offence punishable by life imprisonment, and that an attesting witness who wilfully makes a false statement commits an offence punishable by up to 7 years' imprisonment.

Clause 7 provides that euthanasia shall not, except in limited circumstances, invalidate any insurance policy.

Clause 8 declares that all terminal patients are entitled to receive whatever quantity of drugs may be required to keep them entirely free from pain; and that in a case where severe distress cannot be alleviated by pain-killing drugs, the patient is entitled, if he so desires, to be made and kept entirely unconscious. The section applies to patients whether or not they have made any declaration, and is expressed to be for the removal of doubt as to the existing state of the law.

Clause 9 provides for the Secretary of State for Social Services to make regulations specifying classes of persons entitled or not entitled to witness a declaration, defining the duties of hospital physicians having responsibility for patients in relation to euthanasia, regulating the custody of declarations, and for any other purpose.

Clause 10 contains the short title and extent of the Act.

Voluntary Euthanasia Bill

ARRANGEMENT OF CLAUSES

Clause

Voluntary Euthanasia

A
BILL
INTITULED

A.D. 1969

An Act to provide in certain circumstances for the administration of euthanasia to persons who request it and who are suffering from an irremediable condition, and to enable persons to request in advance the administration of euthanasia in the event of their suffering from such a condition at a future date.

Be it enacted by the Queen's most Excellent Majesty, by and with the consent of the Lords Spiritual and Temporal, and Commons, in this present Parliament assembled, and by the authority of the same, as follows:—

Authorization of euthanasia

1.—(1) Subject to the provisions of this Act, it shall be lawful for a physician to administer euthanasia to a qualified patient who has made a declaration that is for the time being in force.

(2) For the purposes of this Act:

'physician' means a registered medical practitioner;

'euthanasia' means the painless inducement of death;

'qualified patient' means a patient over the age of majority in respect of whom two physicians (one being of consultant status) have certified in writing that the patient appears to them to be suffering from an irremediable condition;

'irremediable condition' means a serious physical illness or impairment reasonably thought in the patient's case to be incurable and expected to cause him severe distress or render him incapable of rational existence:

'declaration' means a witnessed declaration in writing made substantially in the form set out in the schedule to this Act.

Declaration made in advance

2.—(1) Subject to the provisions of this section, a declaration shall come into force 30 days after being made and shall remain in force (unless revoked) for 3 years.

(2) A declaration re-executed within the 12 months preceding its expiry date shall remain in force (unless revoked) during the lifetime of the declarant.

Mode of revocation

3. A declaration may be revoked at any time by destruction or by notice of cancellation shown on its face, effected (in either case) by the declarant or to his order.

Duties and rights of physicians and nurses

4.—(1) Before causing euthanasia to be administered to a mentally responsible patient the physician in charge shall ascertain to his reasonable satisfaction that the declaration and all steps proposed to be taken under it accord with the patient's wishes.

(2) Euthanasia shall be deemed to be administered by a physician if treatment prescribed by a physician is given to the patient by a state registered or state enrolled nurse.

(3) No person shall be under any duty, whether by contract or by any statutory or other legal

requirement, to participate in any treatment authorized by this Act to which he has a conscientious objection.

Protection for physicians and nurses

5.—(1) A physician or nurse who, acting in good faith, causes euthanasia to be administered to a qualified patient in accordance with what the person so acting believes to be the patient's declaration and wishes shall not be guilty of any offence.

(2) Physicians and nurses who have taken part in the administration of euthanasia shall be deemed not to be in breach of any professional oath or affirmation.

Offences

6.—(1) It shall be an offence punishable on indictment by a sentence of life imprisonment wilfully to conceal, destroy, falsify or forge a declaration with intent to create a false impression of another person's wishes with regard to euthanasia.

(2) A person signing a declaration by way of attestation who wilfully puts his signature to a statement he knows to be false shall be deemed to have committed an offence under section 2 of the Perjury Act 1911.

1911 c. 6

Insurance policies

7. No policy of insurance that has been in force for 12 months shall be vitiated by the administration of euthanasia to the insured.

Administration of drugs to patients suffering severe distress

8. For the removal of doubt it is declared that a patient suffering from an irremediable condition reasonably thought in his case to be terminal shall be entitled to the administration of whatever quantity of drugs may be required to keep him free from pain, and such a patient in whose case severe distress cannot be otherwise relieved shall, if he so requests, be entitled to drugs rendering him continuously unconscious.

Power to make regulations

9.—(1) The Secretary of State for Social Services shall make regulations under this Act by statutory instrument for determining classes of persons who may or may not sign a declaration by way of attestation, for regulating the custody of declarations, for appointing (with their consent) hospital physicians having responsibility in relation to patients who have made or wish to make a declaration, and for the prescribing of any matters he may think fit to prescribe for the purposes of this Act.

(2) Any statutory instrument made under this Act shall be subject to annulment in pursuance of a resolution of either House of Parliament.

Short title and extent

10.—(1) This Act may be cited as the Voluntary Euthanasia Act 1969.

(2) This Act does not extend to Northern Ireland.

SCHEDULE

Section 1.

FORM OF DECLARATION UNDER THE VOLUNTARY EUTHANASIA ACT 1969

Declaration made 19 [and re-executed 19]

by

of

I DECLARE that I subscribe to the code set out under the following articles:—

A. If I should at any time suffer from a serious physical illness or impairment reasonably thought in my case to be incurable and expected to cause me severe distress or render me incapable of rational existence, I request the administration of euthanasia at a time or in circumstances to be indicated or specified by me or, if it is apparent that I have become incapable of giving directions, at the discretion of the physician in charge of my case.

B. In the event of my suffering from any of the conditions specified above, I request that no active steps should be taken, and in particular that no resuscitatory techniques should be used, to prolong my life or restore me to consciousness.

C. This declaration is to remain in force unless I revoke it, which I may do at any time, and any request I may make concerning action to be taken or withheld in connection with this declaration will be made without further formalities.

I WISH it to be understood that I have confidence in the good faith of my relatives and physicians, and fear degeneration and indignity far more than I fear premature death. I ask and authorize the physician in charge of my case to bear these statements in mind when considering what my wishes would be in any uncertain situation.

SIGNED

[SIGNED ON RE-EXECUTION]

WE TESTIFY that the above-named declarant *[signed] *[was unable to write but assented to] this declaration in our presence, and appeared to appreciate its significance. We do not know of any pressure being brought on him to make a declaration, and we believe it is made by his own wish. So far as we are aware, we are entitled to attest this declaration and do not stand to benefit by the death of the declarant.

Signed by

of

[Signed by

of

on re-execution]

Signed by

of

[Signed by

of

on re-execution]

* Strike out whichever words do not apply.

Appendix 2

Voluntary Euthanasia Bill
Provisional Draft 1983

EXPLANATORY MEMORANDUM

Clause 1 provides that a doctor may give euthanasia to a severely incapacitated patient at his request if the patient has made an advance declaration stating that he might one day wish to make such a request, and any such patient who becomes incapable of rational existence by reason of brain damage or degeneration is deemed to have made such a request.

Clause 2 provides that a doctor may assist an act of self-deliverance by a severely incapacitated patient; s.2(1) of the Suicide Act 1961, which makes it an offence to aid, abet, counsel or procure the suicide of another, would apply to any other person rendering such assistance unless that person could show that he acted reasonably and was motivated primarily by compassion.

Clause 3 provides an effective machinery whereby a patient may appoint another person to speak for him and make decisions regarding his medical care and treatment.

Clause 4 provides that patients may be relieved of terminal suffering by the administration of drugs leading to total unconsciousness.

Clause 5 deals with definitions.

Clause 6 contains the short title and commencement date.

Voluntary Euthanasia

A BILL INTITULED

An Act to enlarge the authority of physicians to comply with the wishes of severely incapacitated patients who ask for euthanasia, and for related purposes.

Patient's request for euthanasia

1.—(1) It shall be lawful for a physician to give euthanasia to a patient whose condition has been diagnosed as irremediable if the patient has, not less than 30 days earlier, when of sound mind, made (and not subsequently revoked) a written and witnessed statement declaring that in the event of his suffering from such a condition he might wish to be given euthanasia.

(2) A physician acting under this section shall give euthanasia only at the patient's immediate request and then only if the physician is satisfied that the request is firm, settled and reasonable.

(3) A patient who when of sound mind has made (and not subsequently revoked) a written and witnessed statement declaring that in the event of his suffering from a condition diagnosed as irremediable he might wish to be given euthanasia, and who subsequently is diagnosed to be suffering from brain damage or degeneration rendering him permanently incapable of giving directions, shall be deemed to have made an immediate request for euthanasia that is firm, settled and reasonable and also to have declined all life-sustaining treatment (including

involuntary feeding) except for care and treatment designed primarily to relieve pain or discomfort.

Deliverance

2.—(1) It shall be lawful for a physician to give advice and assistance facilitating the self-deliverance of a patient whose condition has been diagnosed as irremediable if the patient has, not less than 30 days earlier, when of sound mind, made (and not subsequently revoked) a written and witnessed statement declaring that in the event of his suffering from such a condition he might wish to bring about his own death by self-deliverance.

(2) A physician acting under this section shall facilitate self-deliverance only at the patient's immediate request and then only if the physician is satisfied that the request is firm, settled and reasonable.

(3) It shall be a defence to any charge under the Suicide Act 1961 that the physician was acting in good faith under this Act.

(4) It shall be a defence to any charge under the Suicide Act 1961 that the deceased was a patient within the terms of subsection (1) of this section and that the defendant was motivated primarily by compassion and acted reasonably.

Attorney under a special power

3. A patient may by deed appoint another person (or more than one) to act as his attorney under a special power to speak on the patient's behalf and make known any wishes the patient may have expressed regarding his future care and treatment, and such an appointment shall remain in force notwithstanding any subsequent incapacity on the part of the patient.

Protection from suffering

4. For the removal of doubt it is declared that a patient may with his consent be kept free from

terminal suffering by the administration of sedative and analgesic drugs even if his death is accelerated by continuous unconsciousness.

5. In this Act: *Interpretation*

'diagnosed' means diagnosed by two physicians, one or both being a consultant in a speciality relevant to the patient's condition;

'irremediable' means a serious and distressing physical illness or impairment from which the patient is suffering without reasonable prospect of cure;

'of sound mind' means of testamentary capacity;

'patient' means a person over the age of majority;

'physician' means a registered medical practitioner;

'self-deliverance' means suicide undertaken by a patient in circumstances justifying euthanasia;

'witnessed' means attested by a solicitor empowered to administer oaths.

6. This Act may be cited as the Voluntary Euthanasia Act 198 , and it shall come into force on 1st January 198 . *Short title and commencement*

Appendix 3

The Advance Declaration

The purpose of the Advance Declaration is to indicate to the doctor your wishes in the event of there being no reasonable prospect of your recovery from serious illness expected to cause you severe distress or to render you incapable of rational existence.

It does not ask the doctor to do anything contrary to existing law, but should he be faced with a difficult decision regarding the prolongation of life in the circumstances specified, it would be helpful to him to know the considered opinion of his patient, expressed when in full possession of his faculties, and not when in great pain or distress.

The law fully upholds the right of a patient to decline life-sustaining (or any other) treatment, and to receive analgesic drugs in quantities sufficient to relieve intolerable distress.

The form should be signed and witnessed at the same time by two persons who are not your relatives, and have no knowledge of any expectation of material gain from your estate. One form should be given to your doctor with a request that it be placed with your medical records; you should retain a second copy. The green card is to be signed and carried on your person.

It is possible to place a third Declaration form with the person you judge best able to protect your interests in an emergency. You may wish to confer some legal authority on that person by appointing him your 'special attorney'. He would then have the right to see that your wishes are carried out as stated in your Declaration. The Society can provide a model for a special form of attorney.

TO MY FAMILY AND MY PHYSICIAN:

This Declaration is made by me ....
(full name and address)

....

....

at a time when I am of sound mind and after careful consideration.

If the time comes when I can no longer take part in decisions for my own future, let this Declaration stand as the testament to my wishes:

If there is no reasonable prospect of my recovery from physical illness or impairment expected to cause me severe distress or to render me incapable of rational existence, I request that I be allowed to die and not be kept alive by artificial means and that I receive whatever quantity of drugs may be required to keep me *free* from pain or distress even if the moment of death is hastened.

This Declaration is signed and dated by me in the presence of the two undermentioned witnesses present at the same time who at my request in my presence and in the presence of each other have hereunto subscribed their names as witnesses.

Signed ....

Dated ....

Witnessed by:

Name ....

Address ....

....

....

Occupation ....

Name ....

Address ....

....

....

Occupation ....

Signed ....

Signed ....

NOTE: Witnesses should not be members of the family.

TO WHOM IT MAY CONCERN **URGENT—please read**

Should I be unable to communicate, please note that I have signed, in the presence of two witnesses, the following Declaration:

If the time comes when I can no longer take part in decisions for my own future, let this Declaration stand as the testament to my wishes:

If there is no reasonable prospect of my recovery from physical illness or impairment expected to cause me severe distress or to render me incapable of rational existence, I request that I be allowed to die and not be kept alive by artificial means and that I receive whatever quantity of drugs may be required to keep me **free** from pain or distress even if the moment of death is hastened.

Date................ *Signed*.............................

P.T.O.

Name ....

Address ....

....

Phone No. ....

Please contact; *Name* ....

Address ....

....

Phone No. ....

My Doctor is: Name..............................

Address ....

....

Phone No. ....

P.T.O.

PROTECTION BY A SPECIAL POWER OF ATTORNEY

It is desirable to appoint your friends or relations to be your 'attorney' under a special power, and vest in them the legal right to see that your Advance Declaration is respected. This may be done by executing a deed on the form attached.

If possible, it may be better to act through a solicitor, since a document engrossed on impressive paper and attested by a solicitor is more likely to carry weight.

The form has provision for appointing two attorneys, partly because two can speak louder than one (and either louder than a mere document), and partly to ensure that if one attorney dies or cannot act, the other can carry on. A copy of the form, together with a copy of your Advance Declaration, should be held by each attorney.

It is important to have the power of attorney officially stamped and dated to enable it to be used in evidence in a court of law. If you are not acting through a solicitor, you should send the power of attorney (within 30 days of signing), together with a 50p cheque or postal-order, or 50p in postage stamps, to: The Controller of Stamps, Inland Revenue, Bush House, South West Wing, Strand, London WC2 (Tel: 01-438 6622). The document will be returned to you within about a fortnight.

An Advance Declaration, reinforced by a power of attorney, should bring our more determined members quite close to obtaining the benefits of passive euthanasia.

A POWER OF ATTORNEY given this 19 by me

of

WHEREAS

(1) I have signed a declaration dated 19 stating that in circumstances there set out I decline to receive life-sustaining medical treatment and ask to be kept free from pain and distress

(2) I seek to ensure that the wishes expressed in my declaration will be fully respected

NOW THIS DEED WITNESSES that I appoint

of

and

of

jointly and severally to be my attorneys for the purpose of securing compliance with the terms of my said declaration and I vest in my attorneys jointly and severally power to interpret make decisions and take action on my behalf with regard to my said declaration (notwithstanding any contrary views held by any other person) including power to deal on my behalf with medical practitioners hospital staff and other persons concerned with my care and treatment

I declare that this Power of Attorney shall remain in force during my lifetime until notice of its revocation is received by my attorneys

AS WITNESS my hand this day

SIGNED SEALED AND DELIVERED

by me

in the presence of

of

Appendix 4

*The Vatican's Declaration on Euthanasia, 1980**

INTRODUCTION

The rights and values pertaining to the human person occupy an important place among the questions discussed today. In this regard, the Second Vatican Ecumenical Council solemnly reaffirmed the lofty dignity of the human person, and in a special way his or her right to life. The Council therefore condemned crimes against life "such as any type of murder, genocide, abortion, euthanasia, or wilful suicide" (Pastoral Constitution *Gaudium et Spes*, 27).

More recently, the Sacred Congregation for the Doctrine of the Faith has reminded all the faithful of Catholic teaching on procured abortion.[1] The Congregation now considers it opportune to set forth the Church's teaching on euthanasia.

It is indeed true that, in this sphere of teaching, the recent Popes have explained the principles, and these retain their full force;[2] but the progress of medical science in recent years has brought to the fore new aspects of the question of euthanasia, and these aspects call for further elucidation on the ethical level.

In modern society, in which even the fundamental values of human life are often called into question, cultural change exercises an influence upon the way of looking at suffering and death; moreover, medicine has increased its capacity to cure and to prolong life in particular circumstances, which sometimes give rise to moral problems. Thus people living in this situation experience no little anxiety about the meaning of advanced old age and death. They also begin to wonder whether they have the right to obtain for themselves or their

* The notes for this document, which is reproduced here in unedited form, appear on p. 301.

fellowmen as "easy death", which would shorten suffering and which seems to them more in harmony with human dignity.

A number of Episcopal Conferences have raised questions on this subject with the Sacred Congregation for the Doctrine of the Faith. The Congregation, having sought the opinion of experts on the various aspects of euthanasia, now wishes to respond to the Bishops' questions with the present Declaration, in order to help them to give correct teaching to the faithful entrusted to their care, and to offer them elements for reflection that they can present to the civil authorities with regard to this very serious matter.

The considerations set forth in the present document concern in the first place all those who place their faith and hope in Christ, who, through his life, death and Resurrection, has given a new meaning to existence and especially to the death of the Christian, as Saint Paul says: "If we live, we live to the Lord, and if we die, we die to the Lord" (*Rom* 14:8; cf. *Phil* 1:20).

As for those who profess other religions, many will agree with us that faith in God the Creator, Provider and Lord of life—if they share this belief—confers a lofty dignity upon every human person and guarantees respect for him or her.

It is hoped that this Declaration will meet with the approval of many people of good will, who, philosophical or ideological differences notwithstanding, have nevertheless a lively awareness of the rights of the human person. These rights have often in fact been proclaimed in recent years through declarations issued by International Congresses;[3] and since it is a question here of fundamental rights inherent in every human person, it is obviously wrong to have recourse to arguments from political pluralism or religious freedom in order to deny the universal value of those rights.

I
THE VALUE OF HUMAN LIFE

Human life is the basis of all goods, and is the necessary source and condition of every human activity and of all society. Most people regard life as something sacred and hold that no one may dispose of it at will, but believers see in life something greater, namely a gift of God's love, which they are called upon to preserve and make fruitful.

And it is this latter consideration that gives rise to the following consequences:

1. No one can make an attempt on the life of an innocent person without opposing God's love for that person, without violating a fundamental right, and therefore without committing a crime of the utmost gravity.[4]

2. Everyone has the duty to lead his or her life in accordance with God's plan. That life is entrusted to the individual as a good that must bear fruit already here on earth, but that finds its full perfection only in eternal life.

3. Intentionally causing one's own death, or suicide, is therefore equally as wrong as murder; such an action on the part of a person is to be considered as a rejection of God's sovereignty and loving plan. Furthermore, suicide is also often a refusal of love for self, the denial of the natural instinct to live, a flight from the duties of justice and charity owed to one's neighbour, to various communities or to the whole of society—although, as is generally recognized, at times there are psychological factors present that can diminish responsibility or even completely remove it.

However, one must clearly distinguish suicide from that sacrifice of one's life whereby for a higher cause, such as God's glory, the salvation of souls or the service of one's brethren, a person offers his or her own life or puts it in danger (cf. *Jn* 15:13).

II
EUTHANASIA

In order that the question of euthanasia can be properly dealt with, it is first necessary to define the words used.

Etymologically speaking, in ancient times *euthanasia* meant an *easy death* without severe suffering. Today one no longer thinks of this original meaning of the word, but rather of some intervention of medicine whereby the sufferings of sickness or of the final agony are reduced, sometimes also with the danger of suppressing life prematurely. Ultimately, the word *euthanasia* is used in a more particular sense to mean "mercy killing", for the purpose of putting an end to extreme suffering, or saving abnormal babies, the mentally ill or the incurably sick from the prolongation, perhaps for many years, of a miserable life, which could impose too heavy a burden on their families or on society.

It is therefore necessary to state clearly in what sense the word is used in the present document.

By euthanasia is understood an action or an omission which of itself or by intention causes death, in order that all suffering may in this way be eliminated. Euthanasia's terms of reference, therefore, are to be found in the intention of the will and in the methods used.

It is necessary to state firmly once more that nothing and no one can in any way permit the killing of an innocent human being, whether a foetus or an embryo, an infant or an adult, an old person, or one suffering from an incurable disease, or a person who is dying. Furthermore, no one is permitted to ask for this act of killing, either for himself or herself or for another person entrusted to his or her care, nor can he or she consent to it, either explicitly or implicitly. Nor can any authority legitimately recommend or permit such an action. For it is a question of the violation of the divine law, an offence against the dignity of the human person, a crime against life, and an attack on humanity.

It may happen that, by reason of prolonged and barely tolerable pain, for deeply personal or other reasons, people may be led to believe that they can legitimately ask for death or obtain it for others. Although in these cases the guilt of the individual may be reduced or completely absent, nevertheless the error of judgment into which the conscience falls, perhaps in good faith, does not change the nature of this act of killing, which will always be in itself something to be rejected. The pleas of gravely ill people who sometimes ask for death are not to be understood as implying a true desire for euthanasia; in fact it is almost always a case of an anguished plea for help and love. What a sick person needs, besides medical care, is love, the human and supernatural warmth with which the sick person can and ought to be surrounded by all those close to him or her, parents and children, doctors and nurses.

III

THE MEANING OF SUFFERING FOR CHRISTIANS AND THE USE OF PAINKILLERS

Death does not always come in dramatic circumstances after barely tolerable sufferings. Nor do we have to think only of extreme cases. Numerous testimonies which confirm one another lead one to the conclusion that nature itself has made provision to render more bearable at the moment of death separations that would be terribly painful to a person in full health. Hence it is that a prolonged illness, advanced old age, or a state of loneliness or neglect can bring about psychological conditions that facilitate the acceptance of death.

Nevertheless the fact remains that death, often preceded or accompanied by severe and prolonged suffering, is something which naturally causes people anguish.

Physical suffering is certainly an unavoidable element of the human condition; on the biological level, it constitutes a warning of which no one denies the usefulness; but, since it affects the human psychological makeup, it often exceeds its own biological usefulness and so can become so severe as to cause the desire to remove it at any cost.

According to Christian teaching, however, suffering, especially suffering during the last moments of life, has a special place in God's saving plan; it is in fact a sharing in Christ's Passion and a union with the redeeming sacrifice which he offered in obedience to the Father's will. Therefore one must not be surprised if some Christians prefer to moderate their use of painkillers, in order to accept voluntarily at least a part of their sufferings and thus associate themselves in a conscious way with the sufferings of Christ crucified (cf. *Mt* 27:34). Nevertheless it would be imprudent to impose a heroic way of acting as a general rule. On the contrary, human and Christian prudence suggest for the majority of sick people the use of medicines capable of alleviating or suppressing pain, even though these may cause as a secondary effect semiconsciousness and reduced lucidity. As for those who are not in a state to express themselves, one can reasonably presume that they wish to take these painkillers, and have them administered according to the doctor's advice.

But the intensive use of painkillers is not without difficulties, because the phenomenon of habituation generally makes it necessary to increase their dosage in order to maintain their efficacy. At this point it is fitting to recall a declaration by Pius XII, which retains its full force; in answer to a group of doctors who had put the question: "Is the suppression of pain and consciousness by the use of narcotics . . . permitted by religion and morality to the doctor and the patient (even at the approach of death and if one foresees that the use of narcotics will shorten life)?", the Pope said: "If no other means exist, and if, in the given circumstances, this does not prevent the carrying out of other religious and moral duties: Yes".[5] In this case, of course, death is in no way intended or sought, even if the risk of it is reasonably taken; the intention is simply to relieve pain effectively, using for this purpose painkillers available to medicine.

However, painkillers that cause unconsciousness need special consideration. For a person not only has to be able to satisfy his or her moral duties and family obligations; he or she also has to prepare himself or herself with full consciousness for meeting Christ. Thus Pius XII warns: "It is not right to deprive the dying person of consciousness without a serious reason".[6]

IV

DUE PROPORTION IN THE USE OF REMEDIES

Today it is very important to protect, at the moment of death, both the dignity of the human person and the Christian concept of life, against a technological attitude that threatens to become an abuse. Thus, some people speak of a "right to die", which is an expression that does not mean the right to procure death either by one's own hand or by means of someone else, as one pleases, but rather the right to die peacefully with human and Christian dignity. From this point of view, the use of therapeutic means can sometimes pose problems.

In numerous cases, the complexity of the situation can be such as to cause doubts about the way ethical principles should be applied. In the final analysis, it pertains to the conscience either of the sick person, or of those qualified to speak in the sick person's name, or of the doctors, to decide, in the light of moral obligations and of the various aspects of the case.

Everyone has the duty to care for his or her own health or to seek such care from others. Those whose task it is to care for the sick must do so conscientiously and administer the remedies that seem necessary or useful.

However, is it necessary in all circumstances to have recourse to all possible remedies?

In the past, moralists replied that one is never obliged to use "extraordinary" means. This reply, which as a principle still holds good, is perhaps less clear today, by reason of the imprecision of the term and the rapid progress made in the treatment of sickness. Thus some people prefer to speak of "proportionate" and "disproportionate" means. In any case, it will be possible to make a correct judgment as to the means by studying the type of treatment to be used, its degree of complexity or risk, its cost and the possibilities of using it, and comparing these elements with the result that can be expected, taking into account the state of the sick person and his or her physical and moral resources.

In order to facilitate the application of these general principles, the following clarifications can be added:

> If there are no other sufficient remedies, it is permitted, with the patient's consent, to have recourse to the means provided by the most advanced medical techniques, even if these means are still at the experimental stage and are not without a certain risk. By accepting them, the patient can even show generosity in the service of humanity.
>
> It is also permitted, with the patient's consent, to interrupt these means, where the results fall short of expectations. But for such a decision to be made, account will have to be taken of the reasonable wishes of the patient and the patient's family, as also of the advice of the doctors who are specially competent in the matter. The latter may in particular judge that the investment in instruments and personnel is disproportionate to the results foreseen; they may also judge that the techniques applied impose on the patient strain or suffering out of proportion with the benefits which he or she may gain from such techniques.
>
> It is also permissible to make do with the normal means that medicine can offer. Therefore one cannot impose on anyone the obligation to have recourse to a technique which is already in use but which carries a risk or is burdensome. Such a refusal is not the equivalent of suicide; on the contrary, it should be considered as an

acceptance of the human condition, or a wish to avoid the application of a medical procedure disproportionate to the results that can be expected, or a desire not to impose excessive expense on the family or the community.

When inevitable death is imminent in spite of the means used, it is permitted in conscience to take the decision to refuse forms of treatment that would only secure a precarious and burdensome prolongation of life, so long as the normal care due to the sick person in similar cases is not interrupted. In such circumstances the doctor has no reason to reproach himself with failing to help the person in danger.

CONCLUSION

The norms contained in the present Declaration are inspired by a profound desire to serve people in accordance with the plan of the Creator. Life is a gift of God, and on the other hand death is unavoidable; it is necessary therefore that we, without in any way hastening the hour of death, should be able to accept it with full responsibility and dignity. It is true that death marks the end of our earthly existence, but at the same time it opens the door to immortal life. Therefore all must prepare themselves for this event in the light of human values, and Christians even more so in the light of faith.

As for those who work in the medical profession, they ought to neglect no means of making all their skill available to the sick and the dying; but they should also remember how much more necessary it is to provide them with the comfort of boundless kindness and heartfelt charity. Such service to people is also service to Christ the Lord, who said: "As you did it to one of the least of these my brethren, you did it to me." (*Mt* 25: 40).

At the audience granted to the undersigned Prefect, His Holiness Pope John Paul II approved this Declaration, adopted at the ordinary meeting of the Sacred Congregation for the Doctrine of the Faith, and ordered its publication.

Rome, the Sacred Congregation for the Doctrine of the Faith, 5 May 1980.

FRANJO Card. ŠEPER
Prefect

† Jérôme Hamer, O. P.
Tit. Archbishop of Lorium
Secretary

NOTES

[1] *Declaration on Procured Abortion*, 18 November 1974: *AAS* 66 (1974), pp. 730–747.
[2] PIUS XII, *Address to those attending the Congress of the International Union of Catholic Women's Leagues, 11 September* 1947: *AAS* 39 (1947), p. 483; *Address to the Italian Catholic Union of Midwives*, 29 October 1951: *AAS* 43 (1951), pp. 835–854; *Speech to the members of the International Office of military medicine documentation*, 19 October 1953, pp. 744–754; *Address to those taking part in the IXth Congress of the Italian Anaesthesiological Society*, 24 February 1957: *AAS* 49 (1957), p. 146; cf. also *Address on "reanimation"* 24 November 1957: *AAS* 49 (1957), pp. 1027–1033; PAUL VI, *Address to the members of the United Nations Special Committee on Apartheid*, 22 May 1974: *AAS* 66 (1974), p. 346; JOHN PAUL II, *Address to the Bishops of the United States of America*, 5 October 1979: *AAS* 71 (1979), p. 1225.
[3] One thinks especially of Recommendation 779 (1976) on the rights of the sick and dying, of the Parliamentary Assembly of the Council of Europe at its XXVIIth Ordinary Session; cf. SIPECA, No. 1, March 1977, pp. 14–15.
[4] We leave aside completely the problems of the death penalty and of war, which involve specific considerations that do not concern the present subject.
[5] PIUS XII, *Address* of 24 February 1957: *AAS* 49 (1957), p. 147.
[6] PIUS XII, *ibid.*, p. 145; cf. *Address* of 9 September 1958: *AAS* 50 (1958), p. 694.

Selected Bibliography

Voluntary Euthanasia

Barnard, Christiaan. *Good Life Good Death.* Englewood Cliffs, N.J.: Prentice-Hall, 1980; London: Peter Owen, 1985.

Clark, Brian. *Whose Life Is It Anyway?* London: Samuel French, 1978.

Glover, Jonathan. *Causing Death and Saving Lives.* Harmondsworth, Middx: Penguin, 1977.

Gould, Jonathan (ed.). *Your Death Warrant: The Implications of Euthanasia.* London: Geoffrey Chapman, 1971.

Humphry, Derek. *Jean's Way.* London: Fontana, 1978.

Kohl, Marvin (ed.). *Beneficent Euthanasia.* New York: Prometheus Books, 1975.

Rachel, James. *The End of Life: The Morality of Euthanasia.* London and New York: Oxford University Press, 1986.

Russell, Dr O. Ruth. *Freedom to Die.* New York: Human Sciences Press, 1977.

Steinbock, Bonnie (ed.). *Killing and Letting Die.* Englewood Cliffs, N.J.: Prentice-Hall, 1980.

Wilshaw, Charles. *The Right to Die.* London: British Humanist Association, 1974/1983.

Suicide

Alvarez, A. *The Savage God: A Study of Suicide.* Harmondsworth, Middx: Penguin, 1974.

Portwood, Doris. *Common Sense Suicide.* New York: Dodd, Mead, 1978.

Suicide and Deliberate Self-Harm. The Office of Health Economics, 12 Whitehall, London SW1.

Death and Dying

Hinton, John. *Dying.* Harmondsworth, Middx: Penguin, 1972.

Kübler-Ross, Elisabeth. *On Death and Dying.* London: Tavistock Publications, 1973.

Pincus, Lily. *Death and the Family: The Importance of Mourning.* London: Faber & Faber, 1976.

Toynbee, Arnold, *et al. Man's Concern with Death.* London: Hodder & Stoughton, 1968.

The Hospice Movement

Lack, Dr Sylvia, and Lamerton, Dr Richard (eds). *The Hour of Our Death.* London: Geoffrey Chapman, 1974.

Lamerton, Dr Richard. *Care of the Dying.* Harmondsworth, Middx: Pelican, 1980.

Stoddard, Sandol. *The Hospice Movement: A Better Way of Caring for the Dying.* London: Jonathan Cape, 1979.

Ageing

Carver, Vida, and Liddiard, Penny (eds). *An Ageing Population.* London: Hodder & Stoughton (in association with the Open University Press), 1978.

Skeet, Muriel. *The Third Age: A Guide for Elderly People, Their Families and Friends.* London: Darton, Longman & Todd, 1982.

Stott, Mary. *Ageing for Beginners.* Oxford: Basil Blackwell, 1981.

Euthanasia and Religion

Larue, Gerald A. *Euthanasia and Religion: A Survey of the Attitudes of World Religions to the Right to Die.* Los Angeles, Calif.: Hemlock Society, 1985.

Linacre Centre. *Euthanasia and Clinical Practice: Trends, Principles and Alternatives. The Report of a Working Party.* London, 1982.

Pohier, J., and Mieth, D. (eds). *Suicide and the Right to Die.* Concilium Religion in the Eighties series no. 179. Edinburgh: T. & T. Clark, 1985.